Historic Catholic Churches of Northwestern New Mexico

Historic Catholic Churches of Northwestern New Mexico

David Policansky

Santa Fe

Sunstone books may be purchased for educational, business, or sales promotional use.
For information please write: Special Markets Department, Sunstone Press,
P.O. Box 2321, Santa Fe, New Mexico 87504-2321.
Printed on acid-free paper

Library of Congress Cataloging-in-Publication Data

Names: Policansky, David, 1944- author, photographer.
Title: Historic Catholic churches of northwestern New Mexico / David Policansky.
Description: Santa Fe : Sunstone Press, [2025] | Includes bibliographical references and index. | Summary: "A photographic collection of historic Catholic churches of northwestern New Mexico"-- Provided by publisher.
Identifiers: LCCN 2024058114 | ISBN 9781632937414 (paperback) | ISBN 9781632937421 (hardcover)
Subjects: LCSH: Catholic church buildings--New Mexico--Pictorial works. | Catholic church buildings--New Mexico--History.
Classification: LCC NA5230.N62 N677 2025 | DDC 726.509789/8--dc23/eng/20250122
LC record available at https://lccn.loc.gov/2024058114

WWW.SUNSTONEPRESS.COM
SUNSTONE PRESS / POST OFFICE BOX 2321 / SANTA FE, NM 87504-2321 /USA
(505) 988-4418

Dedication

I dedicate this book to all the individuals and communities that care for and cherish their historic churches.
Long may they and their churches endure.

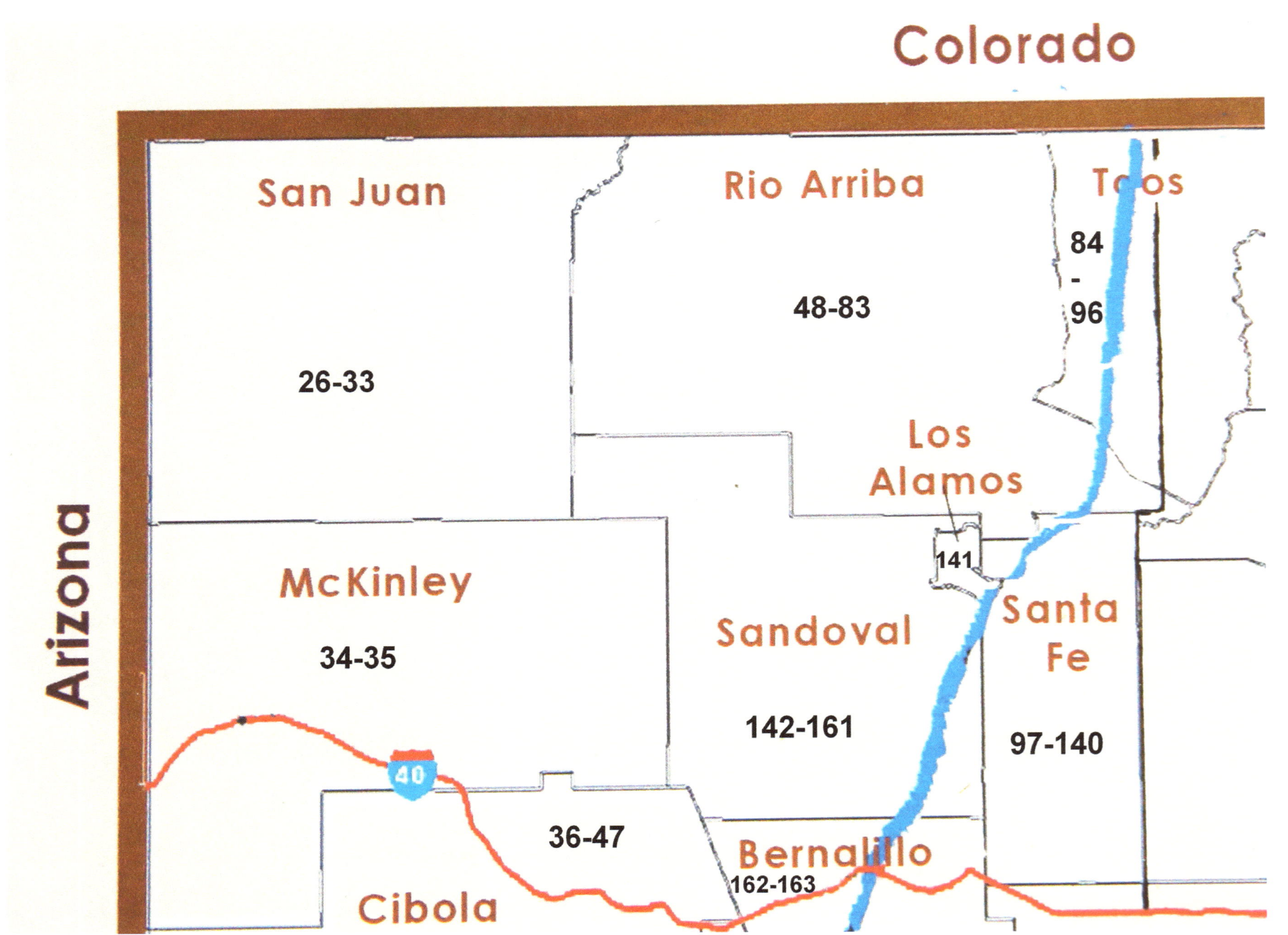

Map of approximate locations of churches in this book. The numbers in each county are the pages where each church is illustrated and briefly described, and location information is given. The arrangement of churches in the book is intended to facilitate planning road trips to see groups of them.

Contents

Introduction

Catholic churches, more than other denominations of organized religion, are an enormous part of New Mexico's history, culture, and landscapes. When European settlement of New Mexico, led by Don Juan de Oñate, began in 1598—earlier than in any other U.S. state except Florida—the Spanish Franciscans introduced the indigenous inhabitants to Catholicism, and New Mexico was changed forever. These Hispanic people were Catholics themselves, and until 1853, when a Baptist church was established in Santa Fe, Catholicism remained the only Christian religion in the state. The history of the interactions between Catholicism and the religions of New Mexico's indigenous inhabitants, as well as with the Spanish and Mexican and later U.S. rulers of New Mexico, has been long, complicated, and sometimes ugly. But it is quintessentially New Mexican. It explains why other Christian denominations weren't established here until after New Mexico became a U.S. territory in 1848, and it influenced the types of Catholic churches that are in New Mexico and where they are today. The role of Catholicism in New Mexico's history is dealt with more extensively in several of the books in the Selected Further Readings toward the end of this book.

Old Catholic churches are all over New Mexico, and each of them has a story. Like the churches, each story is unique, but most of them involve communities, families, individual memories, and a sense of place. The stories include weddings, births, baptisms, confirmations, communions, deaths and funerals, parents and grandparents, aunts and uncles, hard times and good times, feast days, deterioration of the building, repair, restoration, and rebuilding; all the things that give the churches character and make them so important to their communities. It is these stories that explain, at least in part, why so many small, rural churches in New Mexico continue to survive against all odds.

There are more than four hundred historic Catholic churches in New Mexico, and I have tried to find and photograph all of them. That might be a never-ending mission, but I have photographed at least a large majority of them. I wish I could tell the story of each of them, too. However, that is not this book, which presents photographs and brief descriptions of each church and directions to find them. Nonetheless, I hope readers will remember that each of these churches has a story, and how important the stories are.

This is my fourth book on historic Catholic churches in New Mexico. My first book, *Historic Catholic Churches Along the Rio Grande in New Mexico*, focused on the churches along and near the Rio Grande; the second, *Historic Catholic Churches of Central and Southern New Mexico*, covered Catholic churches in the rest of central and southern New Mexico; the third, *Historic Catholic Churches of Northeastern New Mexico*, covered the churches north of Interstate 40 and in the eastern half of northern New Mexico. This book covers northwestern New Mexico, as described below, again with a cut-off date for church construction of 1955. Also included are a few others of relevance or design or historic value, even though they are more recent. This book follows the general format of the first three, but each book is different from the others. Each time I do one of these books, I learn more: more about Catholic churches, more about the artwork in them, more about New Mexico, more about the communities and individuals that care for their churches, more about photography, and more about the churches' importance in New Mexico's natural, social, and cultural landscapes. This learning is reflected in the books' contents. Also, each book covers a distinct set of landscapes, cultures, and architecture. Northern New Mexico has more old Catholic churches than the rest of the state, and to keep the books' sizes manageable I divided it into two parts: the northeast and the northwest (this book).

Once again, I have used Interstate Highway 40 as the divider between central and southern New Mexico and northern New Mexico. Because that highway isn't straight, some unavoidable arbitrariness results in the division, but it works pretty well. The east-west divide was a little harder. The divider I chose was the Santa Fe-San Miguel county line from Interstate 40 to Mora County, and from there to the Colorado border, the divider is slightly to the east: the line of 105° 39' West (105.65° West); this line is marked in the *DeLorme Atlas & Gazetteer: New Mexico* (see reading list). The result is the churches around Santa Fe and much of the High Road to Taos are in this book, while the churches in and around Taos are in the previous book.

As in my previous books, the churches are arranged by county. The counties are not in alphabetical order (except, of course, in the index), but instead begin with San Juan County in the far northwest, then heading south to the northern parts of McKinley and Cibola counties. Then to the east are Rio Arriba County and the western part of Taos County. Moving south leads to Santa Fe, Sandoval, and Los Alamos counties, then the northern part of Bernalillo County. I hope this arrangement, although it is somewhat arbitrary, facilitates road trips to see some of the churches in this book by putting adjacent churches close to each other. The most difficult part is arranging the churches along and near the High Road to Taos (New Mexico highways 68, 518, 75, and 76), because that route passes through church-rich Santa Fe, Rio Arriba, and Taos counties. I have provided directions to most of the churches that should be detailed enough to make finding them fairly easy. Santa Fe County is the winner with 36 churches. It is followed by Rio Arriba County with 33 churches (but two of Santa Fe County's churches are shared with Rio Arriba County), followed by Sandoval County with 19, then Taos and Cibola counties, each with 11. Of course, some of the above counties have churches covered in my other books. Adding the rest brings the total in this book to 123 churches (including a few Penitente Brotherhood moradas). A few of the churches in this book would have been in my first book covering churches along the Rio Grande, but COVID-19 and some other obstacles to access at that time led me to put them in this book. They are indeed in northwestern New Mexico.

Some churches are easy to find; San Francisco Cathedral in Santa Fe is a notable example. It is just off the plaza on paved San Francisco Street. Others, such as San José Catholic Church in Cabezon, require traveling many miles on remote, unpaved roads and are not easy to find. While finding such remote churches gives me a great feeling of achievement, and satisfaction in knowing that through these photographs people who never would see them otherwise can appreciate these treasures, I expect that most of my readers will content themselves with visiting churches that are easier to reach.

The people I've met as I've traveled New Mexico searching out historic Catholic churches have been kind, interesting, and eager to show me their churches, many of which have been cared for by members of their family for generations. It is hard to overemphasize the degree to which many rural churches depend for their survival on dedicated individuals and communities, and it is hard not to wonder what will happen to them as rural depopulation continues in New Mexico and church membership continues to decline. The kindness of these people and others, and the pride they have in their churches have been an inspiration to me, and a motivation to document these churches as well as I can.

The more time I spend finding and photographing old Catholic churches and meeting the people who love and care for them, the clearer it becomes that New Mexico's current blend of Indigenous, Hispanic, Anglo, and Catholic traditions is uniquely fascinating, and that the buildings in these photographs reflect that blend. Furthermore, as I see many rural churches that once served dozens of people but now serve maybe only a handful or fewer, it also is clear that these buildings, which reflect so much cultural history, are disappearing. Most of the larger, iconic churches will likely survive, but many of the smaller and more-remote ones might not. Indeed, many of them already have disappeared, and too many are in disrepair. I hope that drawing attention to them will broaden the constituency of people who value them and contribute to their continued survival. At a minimum, I hope that these books will inspire readers to explore, cherish, and enjoy New Mexico's glorious landscapes.

—Mountainair, New Mexico, 2024.

Finding and Photographing New Mexico's Old Churches

New Mexico has great richness and diversity in its Catholic churches, although none has the opulence of those in Europe and in Latin America. Many of New Mexico's older Catholic churches are along and near waterways. In addition to the Rio Grande, the Chama, Mimbres, Mora, Pecos, Santa Fe, and other rivers and their tributaries have many wonderful churches along and near them. Even some churches that are reached by dirt roads through rugged terrain turn out to be near streams. Most New Mexico streams do not have roads along much of their distance, and so other than the Rio Grande and parts of the Chama, Mimbres, Mora, and Pecos rivers, planning to drive along them is not an effective way to find churches. But there are other methods, including using this and my previous books, which provide detailed directions to almost all of the churches in them. Some other books cited here also are quite helpful in finding churches, as are websites, pamphlets, friends, and acquaintances. If you know someone who has lived in an area for a while, ask about nearby churches. Then there is old-fashioned exploration. Do you see a place name on a map at the end of a road, or a road that passes through interesting areas? Go there. Be careful that you and your vehicle can handle the roads and the conditions, but much of the time you will be rewarded, if not by a gem of a church, then by wonderful scenery. And there still will be detective work after you find a church; sometimes its name and often its construction date are not easy to find.

Two rules are important. The first is that you should please be respectful of private property and of local communities and their inhabitants, including pueblos. In my experience, people in small communities are proud of their churches and will gladly show them to you and tell you what they know about them. Be careful before photographing churches. Most of the time, photographs of the outside of a church are fine, especially if you are on public property or on a public right-of-way (even if the church is not). However, if someone unlocks a church for you, ask before photographing the interior. Be particularly careful in pueblos. Some allow photography of buildings; some require permits for any photography, and others prohibit photography within the pueblo entirely. Please obey all posted signs in pueblos. When you visit them, you are their guest.

The second rule concerns navigation. All U.S. and state highways in New Mexico, as in most U.S. states, have mile-markers that start at zero at their southern or western origin or entry into the state; the numbers increase toward the north and east. For example, Interstate 25 begins at mile-marker zero at its origin at Interstate 10 near Las Cruces, and the numbers increase as you go north; Interstate 40 begins at mile-marker zero where it enters New Mexico at the Arizona border and the numbers increase as you head east. Exit numbers on highways match the mile-markers as closely as possible. But the numbering of highways can change from time to time, so make sure you have current highway information. As an example, the current U.S. Highway 550 from Bernalillo to Bloomfield was New Mexico Highway 44 before 2000.

Many of the county roads and even a few state highways mentioned in my books are unpaved. Some are good gravel roads, but others are rough and cross arroyos, and they can be difficult in wet, muddy, snowy, or sometimes even in dry conditions. Those roads require high-clearance or four-wheel-drive vehicles. In addition, many of the roads traverse open range, which means you can encounter cattle at any time. Slow is better than fast on such roads. Furthermore, some of these roads pass through private property. In most cases access is permitted as long as you stay on the road. I take closed but unlocked gates on county roads as permission to continue, but it is essential to close any gate you open as soon as you have passed through it. Gates usually are closed to prevent unwanted movements of animals. Whether a private landowner is legally permitted to block access on a county road is beyond my expertise, but I advise against forcing the issue. If I encounter a locked gate blocking access to a church, I try to find a person who will unlock it for me, a sometimes challenging and time-consuming but so far always rewarding endeavor.

Photographing churches is a delightful challenge. For my books, I have tried to represent each church by a single photograph of the exterior, with an interior photograph in some cases. This has meant omitting various interesting or pleasing aspects of many churches, but my aim here has been to present the best aspect of each church while also providing an illustration that helps you to identify the church.

Usually, a church looks best when the light is on the front. Some churches face south, and they are a photographer's dream, because they have good light most of the day. But more churches face east than other directions, and some even face north, which means they seldom have good light, and then only in summer. I have been lucky to find some remote churches that required difficult travel over rough roads bathed in glorious light on my first visit, but sometimes I have visited a church twice or even three times to get good light. In a few cases, I just accepted light that wasn't the best.

Another challenge can be presented by a church's surroundings, which might prevent one from getting to the best place for a photograph. These obstacles include fences, gates, telephone poles, trees (particularly when fully leafed), other buildings, ditches, vehicles, private property, unfavorable topography, and other things. You do the best you can.

Many small, rural churches are in need of funds for maintenance and restoration, so please consider donating to them if given an opportunity. And be prepared to meet many dogs, which seem to abound around old, rural churches.

For those interested in technical details, my main camera is a 20.2-megapixel Canon 6D with a Canon EF 24-105 mm f/3.5-5.6 IS STM lens. This provides wide-angle to medium-telephoto views. The camera also handles high ISOs well, so I never use flash inside any church. For harder-to-reach, more-distant churches, I use a Canon 100-400 mm f/4.5-5.6L IS II lens.

About Names and Dates

Correctly identifying the name of a church and its construction date has obviously challenged more people than only me. Let's start with names. Sometimes a church's name is written on or next to it, but sometimes it is nowhere to be seen. The challenge is increased when a church changes its name, which is not that rare, or when it has two names, or when it is referred to in English versus in Spanish. Some church names are quite common in New Mexico, so for example there are many churches named for San Antonio, San Isidro, San José, Nuestra Señora de Guadalupe, and others. In addition to church names, many place names also are repeated in New Mexico and hence names like San Miguel and San Mateo refer to more than one locality. In general, I have used the name as it appears on a church—if it appears—and I have used place names as they appear on highway signs or in the *DeLorme Atlas & Gazetteer: New Mexico.* I also have consulted historical documents, parishes, Internet sources, and local residents for church and place names.

Construction dates also are challenging to specify accurately. Sometimes a church will have a sign saying "Established on such and such a date," but that date might refer to the establishment of the parish or mission that the church belongs to and not of the building itself. Sometimes there is only a date, and that too might—or might not—refer to the date the building was constructed. Sometimes the date at the church conflicts with other information. For example, Santa Rosa de Lima Church in Blanco (page 30) has the date 1931 on its façade. However, the 1931 building was replaced by the current—albeit similar—building in 1986. It is for such reasons (as well as simple mistakes) that different sources give different names and construction dates for some churches. In addition, major renovations or even rebuilds often aren't noted on church signs. In this book, two dates separated by a slash (e.g., 1786/1990) indicate an initial build date and a date of major restoration or rebuilding.

It is a wonder that more errors aren't made. I have done my best to eliminate errors, by cross-checking sources; by asking questions of locals, parishes, diocesan historians, and others (please see the acknowledgments); and by reading as many documents as I can find. I have tried to be transparent about uncertainties. But despite my best efforts, it is likely that I too have made some errors. For those, I ask the reader's indulgence.

Changes

Churches are not timeless or eternal, although fortunately some of them can last for many centuries. But events occur: churches are affected by natural events such as earthquakes, tornadoes, floods, and fires; and by human-caused events, such as wars, changes in tastes, road-building, changes in technology, and fires. Churches get remodeled, refurbished, restored, painted, stuccoed, and receive other modifications. Some are even demolished. Stained-glass windows are added or replaced, steeples get added and removed, and other changes occur. As a result, any description or image of a church is valid only for the moment it was made.

Occasionally the changes can hinder identification of a church, but more often they just make it harder to determine when the church was built. When does a refurbishment or remodel become a rebuild, and when does a rebuild become a new church? Rather than being dogmatic, I have tried to describe the history of changes for those churches where the changes are noteworthy. But keep in mind that any church that you visit might look different from the illustrations in my books when you see it. This is why all the photographs in my books are dated.

Suggested Road Trips to See Old Churches

Finding old Catholic churches in New Mexico is a rewarding activity, because doing so takes you to some lovely places that you might not visit otherwise. In my book on central and southern New Mexico churches I suggested specific road trips to see churches, but there are so many historic Catholic churches in the region covered in this book—especially in Rio Arriba, Santa Fe, Sandoval, and Taos counties—that it is not feasible to suggest specific road trips. However, some highways or combinations of highways in particular have many churches along them. New Mexico highways 68, 75 and 76 (the High Road to Taos), 96, 111, and 519, and U.S. highways 64 and 84 are particularly rewarding routes. Albuquerque, Santa Fe, Abiquiú, and Gallup are great bases for expeditions to see historic churches in northwestern New Mexico.

The Challenge of Preserving and Restoring Old Churches

It should be clear from this and other books and from driving around the countryside that the survival of many historic Catholic churches in New Mexico is far from assured. Indeed, dozens if not hundreds have disappeared over the past four centuries, for a variety of reasons. Frank Graziano (see reading list) addressed this issue in detail. In its simplest terms, the problem results from lack of funds for maintenance and repair, and that results from the depopulation of rural communities, the decline in adherence to Catholicism, conversion to other denominations, and improved transportation. The last factor might not be obvious. Before the 1930s, travel in rural areas was difficult, and so people in small communities built churches where they lived rather than travel to a more-distant one. Now transportation is much easier, and there aren't enough priests to serve all the churches, so parishioners can get to the parish church.

Graziano discussed an additional challenge for obtaining adequate funding, namely the tension between parish and diocesan administrations, which own the mission churches, but which don't have the funds, or the willingness to provide the funds, to maintain them; and the remaining congregation members of the mission churches, who regard them as "their" churches. The parishes also require the missions' congregations to pay for insurance, making funds that might be used for maintenance and repair unavailable. The topic is critical for understanding the genesis of the funding problem, and I refer the reader to Graziano's book. He did discuss possible solutions, and these considerations led him to found *Nuevo Mexico Profundo* (see below).

A consistent refrain I have heard from residents of small New Mexico settlements is that they have great emotional attachment to the church they grew up in, the church where their parents were married and they were baptized. This motivates their commitment to maintaining and restoring these historic churches, but younger parishioners, who have experienced services only in their parish church, have less emotional attachment to the local church. Sometimes younger family members continue to care for the church, even if they live far away, like the Mora family and the Capilla de San Antonio in Cieneguilla (page 104), but demographic and economic trends continue to present a challenge.

It seems likely that not all small, rural, Catholic churches in New Mexico will endure. There just are not sufficient resources for all of the churches that need them. And restoring a church once is not enough: it needs to be maintained. If it is not, it will need restoration again. But there is hope for many of them, and that hope lies in part in the organizations mentioned below.

Many individuals and organizations are interested in preserving New Mexico's history, culture, and architecture, including its old Catholic churches, but, as described above, not much money is available in many cases. Preserving old churches often depends on community and family efforts. Many churches have a *mayordomo* or *mayordoma*, an individual who takes responsibility for taking care of and maintaining the church. Historically, these people were elected from the congregation or community each year, but today many of them maintain the role for years, or even decades, because nobody is available to take their place. They sometimes can help organizing fundraising and restoration efforts. Many small churches have collection boxes and the money collected often is used, at least in part, for maintenance and repair. Some more-formal organizations are listed below, and if they are not directly involved in funding or aiding preservation efforts, they often know who is. Websites are current at the time of publication of this book.

Archdiocese of Santa Fe Office of Historic-Artistic Patrimony and Archives, www.archdiosf.org/archives

Cornerstones Community Partnerships, www.cstones.org

Historic Santa Fe Foundation, www.historicsantafe.org

New Mexico Historic Preservation Division, www.nmhistoricpreservation.org

Nuevo Mexico Profundo, www.nuevo-mexico-profundo.org

Architecture, Artwork, and Vandalism in Historic Catholic Churches

Religious art—including architecture, visual arts, and music—represents some of the greatest of humankind's achievements. For example, the great European cathedrals, 15th century Italian paintings and sculptures, and much religious music are unsurpassed. While more modest in scale and scope, New Mexico's churches include some deeply moving art and stunning architecture. They include the much-photographed and painted San Francisco de Asís in Ranchos de Taos (in my third book) and the gorgeous Nuestra Señora de Asunción in Zia Pueblo (pages 150-151); and the beautiful altar screens in the churches at Truchas, Las Trampas, Santa Fe (several illustrated in this book), and elsewhere. But they also include more-modest buildings and artwork. Although unappreciated and in some cases destroyed by Archbishop Jean Baptiste Lamy in the latter half of the 19th century and some others earlier, these modest churches and their statues and paintings reflect New Mexican culture with deep roots in Spain and Mexico. Fortunately, many of them have been preserved and restored. For an in-depth look at the history and evolution of New Mexican church art, see Cash (1999) in the reading list.

In addition to the art described above, some of New Mexico's churches have a remarkable combination of Indigenous and traditional Catholic imagery. St. Mary Catholic Church in Tohatchi (Navajo; pages 34-35) is a wonderful example; two others are St. Joseph's Apache Mission Church in Mescalero (Mescalero Apache; pages 70-71 in my book covering central and southern New Mexico) and Blessed Nativity of the Virgin Mary Catholic Church in Encinal (Laguna; page 47, interior not illustrated). The placing of Indigenous imagery in New Mexico Catholic churches has not always been without controversy, although it usually is celebrated today. Recently, a beloved Indigenous-inspired eight-foot-tall painting of the Apache Christ by Franciscan artist Robert Lentz was removed from St. Joseph's in Mescalero by a new priest who considered the image to be paganistic. That sparked great dismay and concern among the congregation and the tribe. The painting has since been returned and the priest no longer serves there, but emotional and spiritual damage was done. It is gratifying that the United States Conference of Catholic Bishops recently has recognized the importance of Indigenous approaches to Catholicism: (United States Conference of Catholic Bishops, 2024, reading list): "The survival of Indigenous communities is a testament both to Indigenous Peoples' enduring strength and to the power of God's grace. Drawing upon their innately sacramental worldview and reverence for Creation, Indigenous Catholics in the United States have embraced the Gospel despite these tragic stories, which could easily have hardened their hearts against God and those in the Church. Healing and reconciliation can only take place when the Church acknowledges the wounds perpetrated to her Indigenous children and humbly listens to them as they voice their experiences." This is a striking and welcome departure from the attitudes that led to the Pueblo Revolt of 1680, and which persisted among many church officials well into the 20th century.

The people who create church art are called *santeros* and *santeras* in New Mexico. They appeared as local, vernacular artists (all male) in the 18th century largely because it was too expensive and cumbersome to import church art from Europe or Mexico, although a few pieces did come to New Mexico that way. While some people had artistic training, many did not, and they evolved distinctive styles. Several of them, like the Laguna Santero and José Rafael Aragon (usually referred to simply as Rafael Aragon), became famous. In addition to still being found in some churches, their work is found in museums and private collections. Cash (1999, reading list) described the work of these artists in great detail, including much historical sleuthing to properly attribute pieces to their actual creators.

In the first half of the 19th century the art of *santeros* really flourished, but after New Mexico became part of the United States in 1848 the composition of the population and their lifestyles started to change and the golden age of New Mexican *santeros* came to an end. By the 1880s the railroads made access to New Mexico from other parts of the country easy, and inexpensive, mass-produced church art was brought to New Mexico by the car-load, reducing demand for the *santeros*' work.

By the latter part of the 20th century, conservation and preservation and a new appreciation for local arts led to a revival of local church art, and today restored and even new artwork is being placed in churches and museums, and is sold in retail outlets and studios. As in the earlier times, some contemporary *santeros* and *santeras* have become well known and their art is collectible. In addition to Marie Romero Cash, mentioned above, Felix López, Gustavo Victor Goler, Nicholas Otero, and Jerry Sandoval are contemporary *santeros* who contributed their talents and expertise to the restoration of historic churches in Las Trampas, (pages 84-85), Córdova (pages 72-73), and Truchas (pages 76-77).

Sadly, time, the environment, and carelessness have taken their toll on church buildings and the art they contain. It is demoralizing to read how churches have been destroyed by misguided attempts to protect them, for example by adding pitched metal roofs without taking care to first strengthen the church, leading to the building's collapse; or by stuccoing exterior adobe walls and wallpapering interior ones, leading to fatal water damage. In some cases, fine old paintings have been discovered under coats of housepaint. But far more demoralizing is reading about arson, theft, and vandalism. Churches have been burned, or razed when they could have been restored; statues and paintings have been stolen; and some churches and their artwork have been vandalized. It is difficult for me to understand the motivation for such crimes. The art by famous *santeros* is valuable but difficult to sell because it's so well known. That of relatively unknown artists is much less valuable monetarily despite its great sentimental value to the local congregation. In addition, many fine church artists offer their work for sale at legitimate retail outlets or at their own studios, and so it's not necessary to steal it. But it is easy to understand one of the consequences of these crimes: most rural churches in New Mexico are now locked.

What can you, dear reader, do about the situation? You can be aware. Make sure you respect any church you visit. Make sure you don't touch any artwork or take flash photographs inside a church (or any interior photographs without permission). If you buy historical church art, make sure the seller can provide appropriate documentation of its provenance. Your presence at a rural church might deter some crime, if only temporarily. And please consider donating to each church's restoration fund and the organizations mentioned above.

Addendum

After my third book was published, I learned about two historic Catholic churches in the northeast region. San Juan Bautista in Miera is in Union County and Santo Niño in Lower Colonias is in San Miguel County. They are included here, on pages 164 and 165.

Acknowledgments

More people helped me in this endeavor than I could have imagined when I started. I am enormously grateful to all of them. The Reverend Matthew Keller of Gallup provided much helpful information on churches in the Diocese of Gallup and joined me on a memorable excursion to find one of them. The Reverend Dale Jamison gave me a tour of the lovely interior of St. Mary Catholic Church in Tohatchi. Murt Sullivan and the Torrance County Archaeological Society extended a field trip, allowing me to photograph the ruin of Our Lady of Guadalupe Church in Guadalupe (page 155) and Santo Niño Church in Casa Salazar (page 156), both far down a usually rugged dirt road in Sandoval County (it had been graded shortly before our trip, making travel surprisingly easy). Gilbert Lujan gave me a tour of San Isidro Church in Santa Fe (page 103). Alfonso Chacon opened and showed me the interior of Nuestra Señora del Carmen in Cañon Plaza (page 49). Danny Gonzales of Seboyeta and Paul Pino of Laguna Pueblo provided helpful information about churches in their parishes. The Pueblo of Zia gave me permission to photograph Nuestra Señora de Asunción Catholic Church (pages 150-151). In particular, Executive Administrative Assistant Ursula Toribio put me in contact with the right members of the pueblo government and Governor Ben Shije guided me to and around the church. Monica Murrell of the Santa Ana Preservation Department provided much helpful information on the history of Santa Ana de Tamaya church (page 161). The foreman of the renovation of the Bishop's Lodge Resort and of Archbishop Lamy's Chapel kindly gave me a tour of the property. Debbie Gachupin of Jeméz Parish gave me information about churches in the parish and Pauline Chacon of San Tomás el Apostól Parish in Abiquiú helped me with identifications and locations of mission churches in that parish. Maria Ortega of St. Athony's Parish in Questa and Scott and Gail Buchanan of Red River provided helpful information. John Taylor continued to provide information on specific churches near the Rio Grande. As he did for my previous books, Frank Graziano provided information and encouragement. His Nuevo Mexico Profundo tours provided access to several historic Catholic churches. Bernadette Sanchez (Archdiocese of Santa Fe) and Gretchen Brock and Bridget Barela (New Mexico Historic Preservation Division) provided much helpful historical information. The Archdiocese of Santa Fe granted me permission to photograph the interiors of several historic churches. Gary Gum of Las Cruces told me how to find a couple of historic churches. Larie Mora opened her family's Capilla de San Antonio (page 104) and encouraged photography. José Villegas provided insight and historical information on the community of Cieneguilla. Father Adrian Sisneros of St. Joseph's Parish gave tours of the churches at Galisteo, Cerrillos, and Golden. The parishes of St. Anthony in Pecos, San Isidro in Agua Fria, and Santo Niño in Tierra Amarilla were helpful in providing information about churches in their parishes. Douglas Ash, docent at El Rancho de Las Golondrinas, provided historical insight into many aspects of the culture and history of Catholics in New Mexico. Marie Romero Cash continued to provide encouragement and information. Rebecca Anthony and Linda Marie Carroll of La Galeria at the Shaffer have encouraged my work and were among the first to carry my books. Architect Jon Dick of Santa Fe has enlightened me on many architectural details. Members of the Facebook group *Abandoned, History, Landscapes & Wildlife of New Mexico* have also been helpful. I thank Carl Condit and James Smith of Sunstone Press for turning my writings and photographs into beautiful books.

I also am grateful to many other individuals I have met in my travels who have generously shown me and told me about their churches, and pointed me toward others I was not aware of. Their kindness and pride in their churches have been an inspiration.

Finally, my wife Sheila David provided advice, support, encouragement, patience, and company. She came with me on many of my "churching expeditions," as we call them, and encouraged me to find good churches when she did not accompany me. She advised me on photographing individual churches and helped me choose among the photographs afterwards. I am more than grateful for those gifts from her.

Churches By County

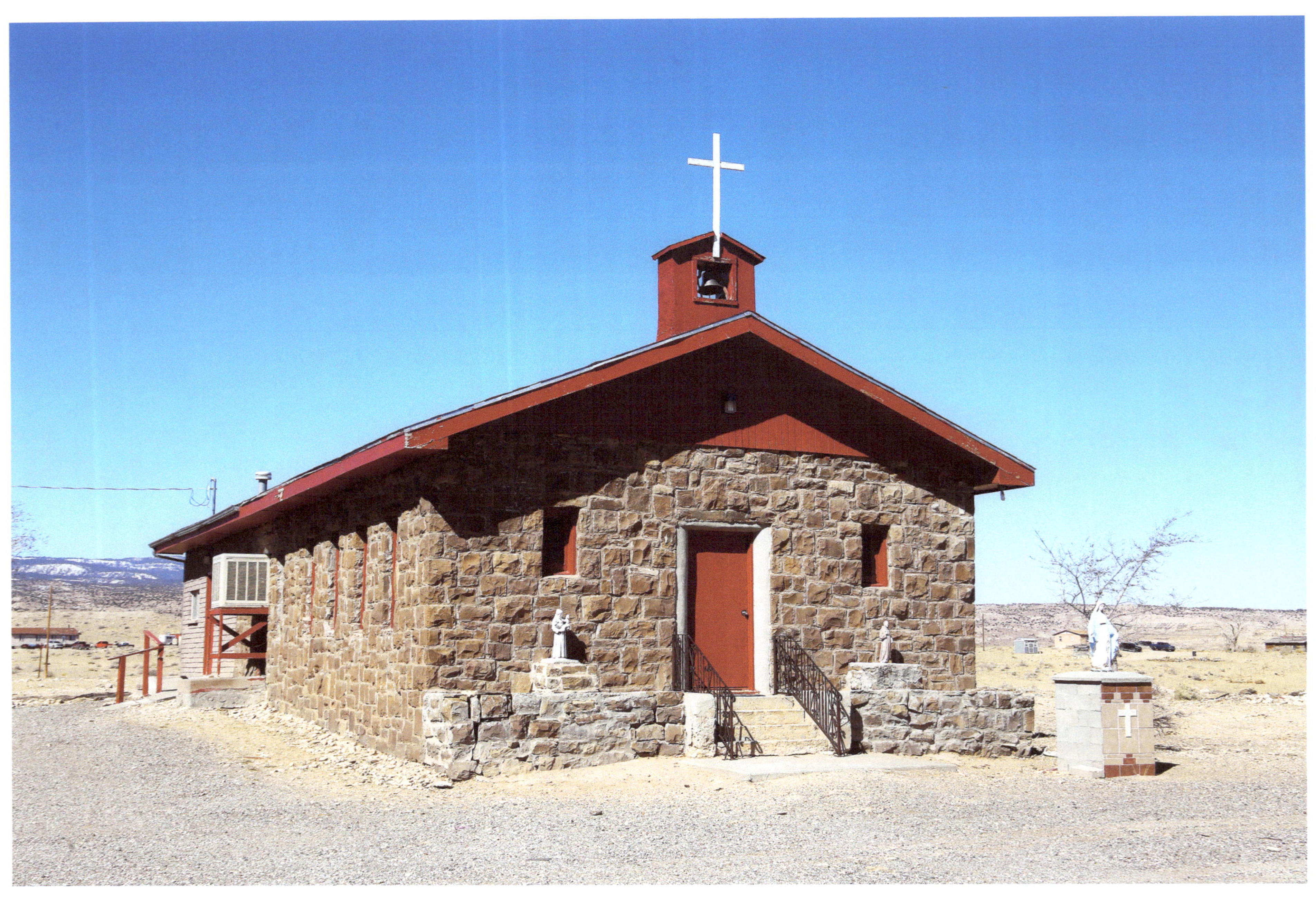

St. Anthony's Catholic Church, Naschitti, San Juan County. 1935. This stone church is near the school on the west side of U.S. Highway 491. Photograph taken in 2022.

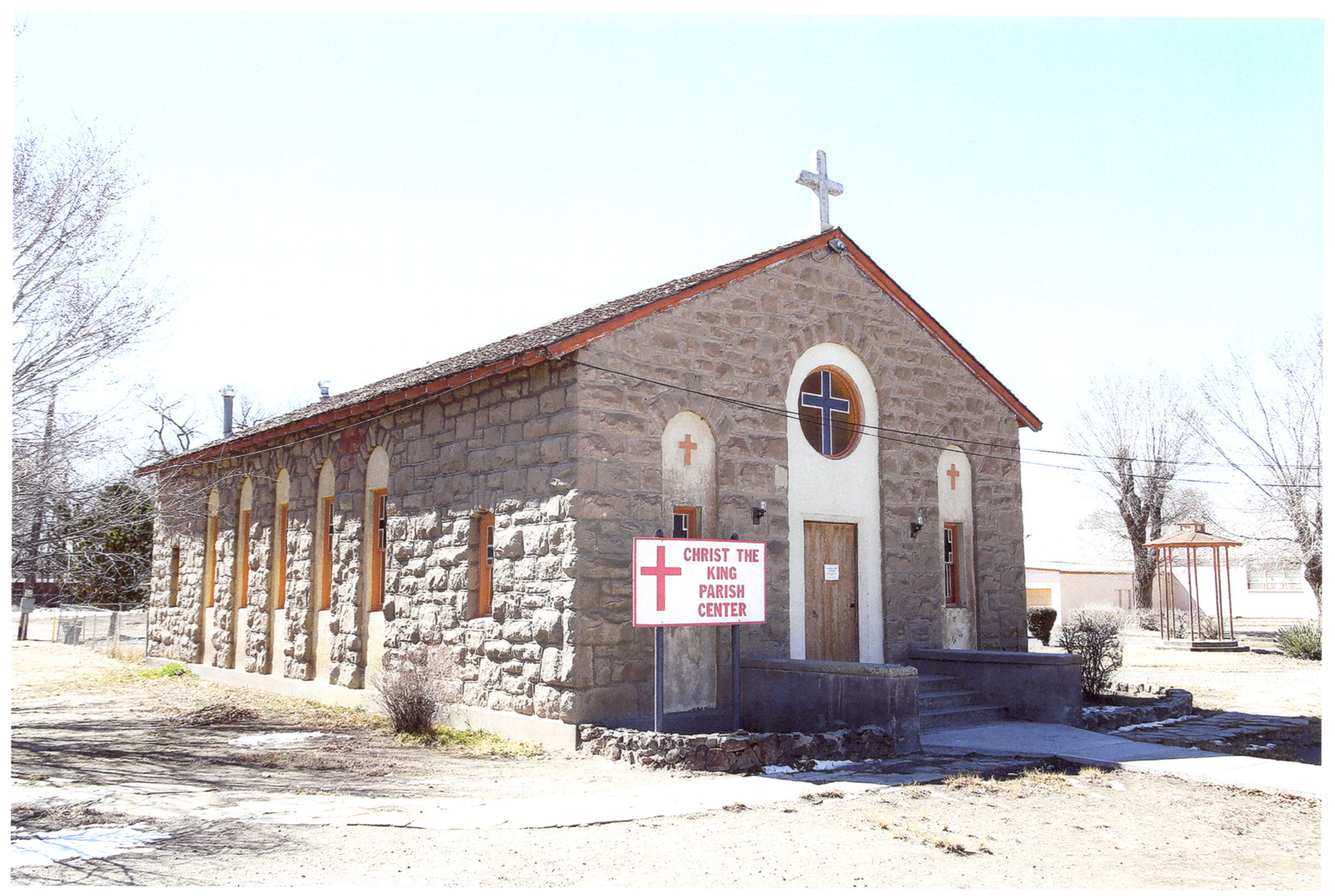

Christ the King Catholic Church, Shiprock, San Juan County. 1935. Another stone church, now the parish hall; it is across the parking lot from the new church. On the south side of U.S. Highway 63. Photograph taken in 2022.

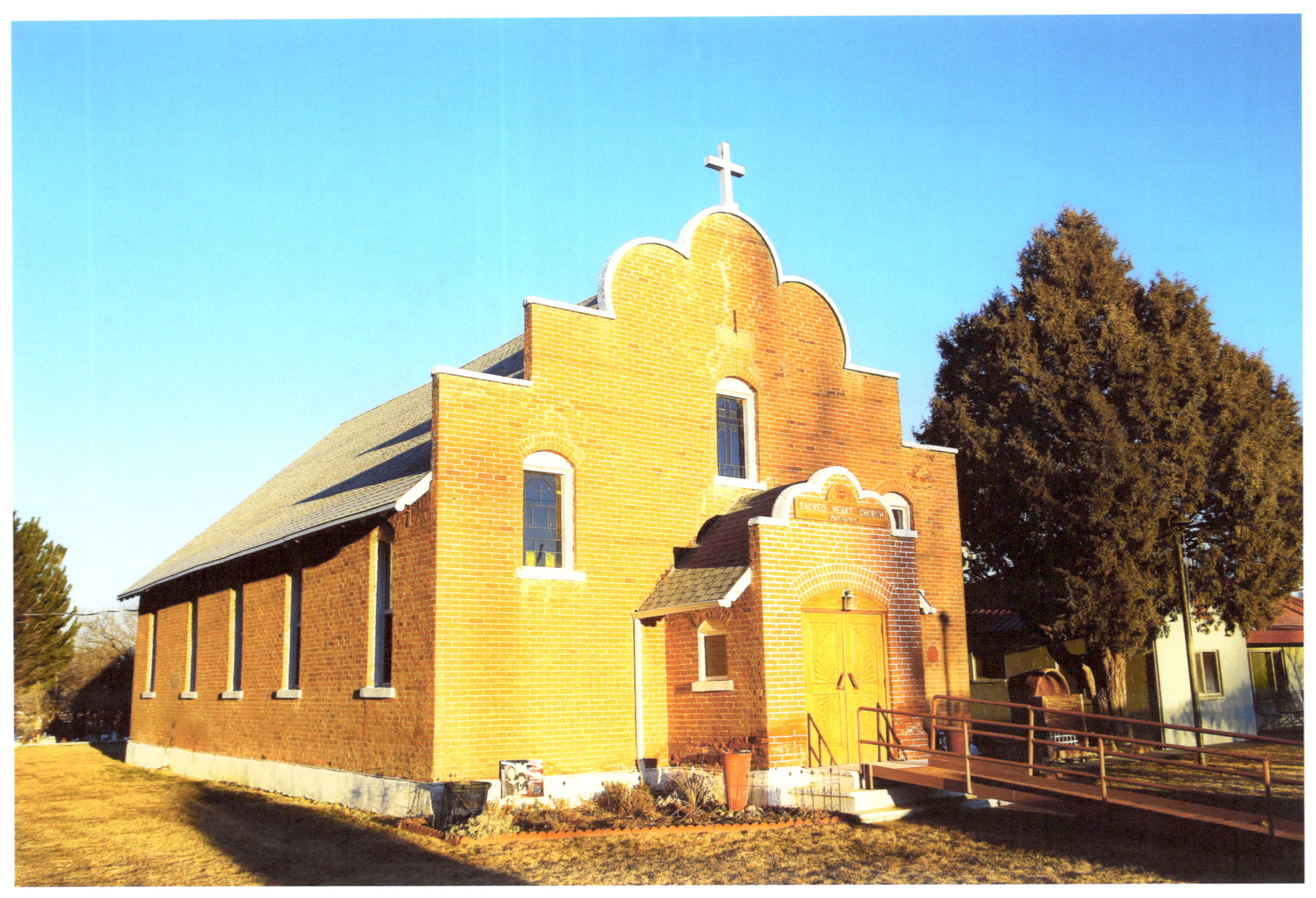

Sacred Heart Catholic Parish Church, Waterflow, San Juan County. 1917. This California-mission-style brick church is at 9 Road 6820. Photograph taken in 2022.

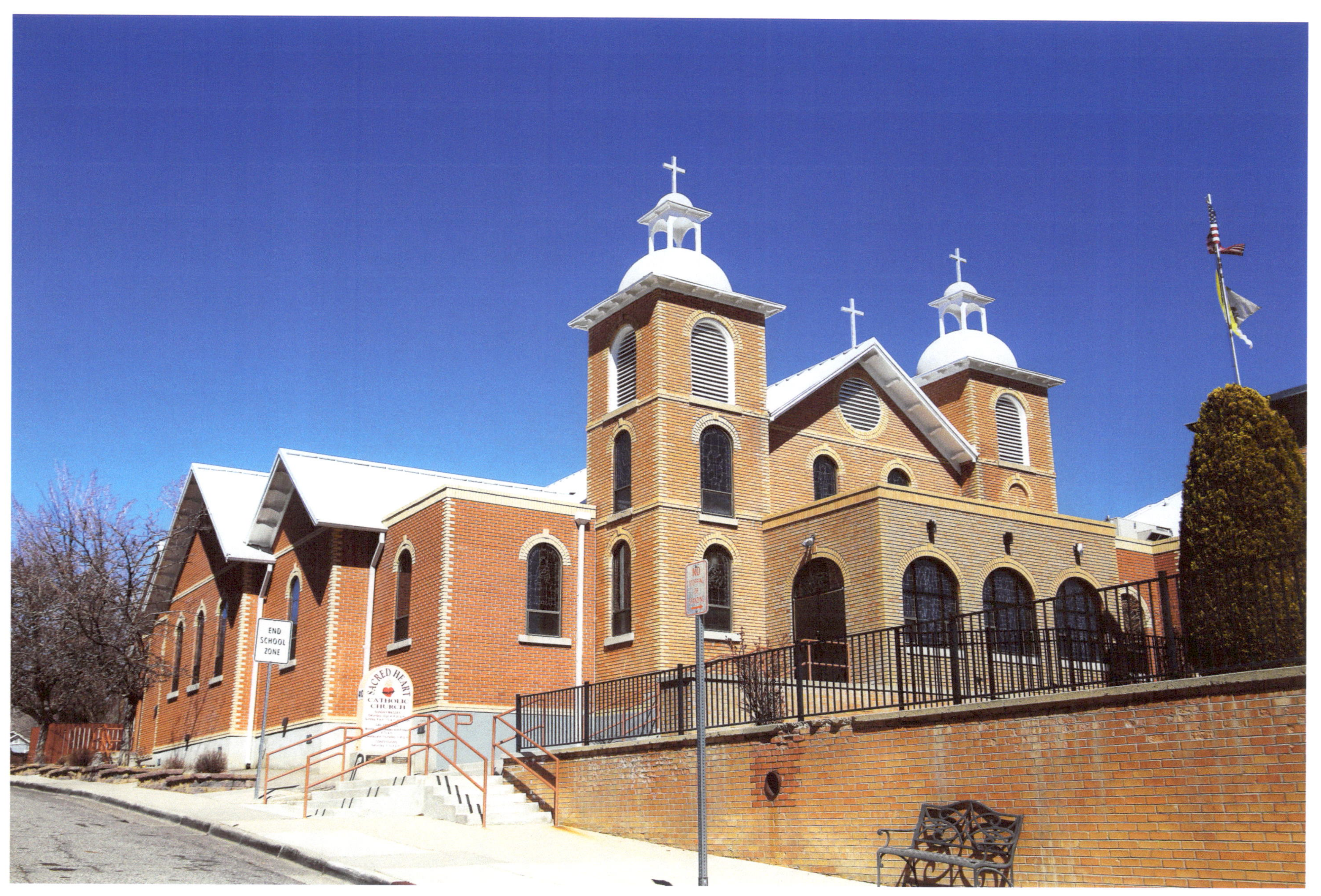

Sacred Heart Catholic Church, Farmington, San Juan County. 1929. This large, handsome, brick church, the parish church, is at 414 North Allen Avenue. Photograph taken in 2022.

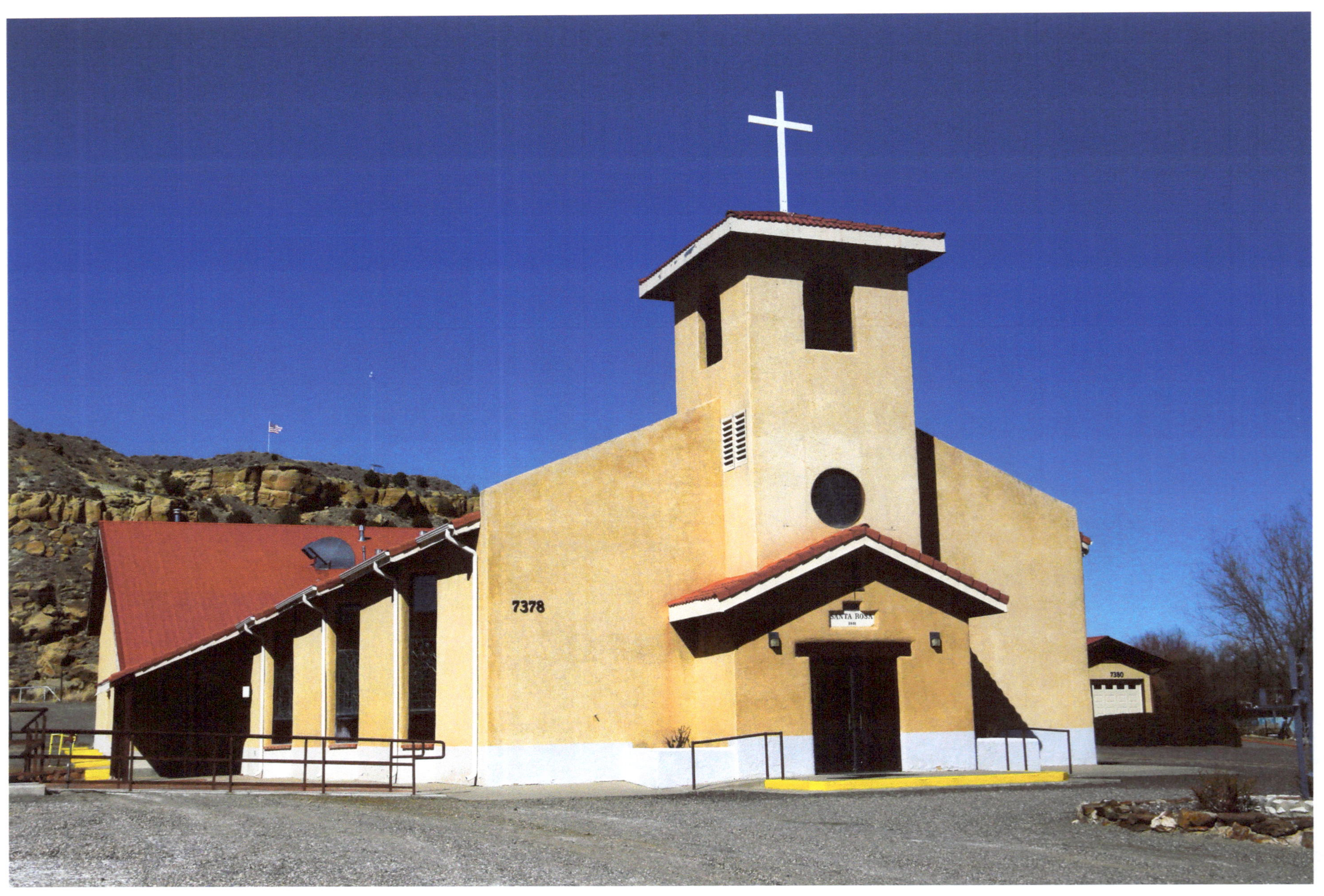

Santa Rosa de Lima Catholic Church, Blanco, San Juan County. Despite the date of 1931 on the front of this fairly traditional church, it was built in 1986, but it is quite similar to the 1931 church it replaced. At 7378 U.S. Highway 64. Photograph taken in 2022.

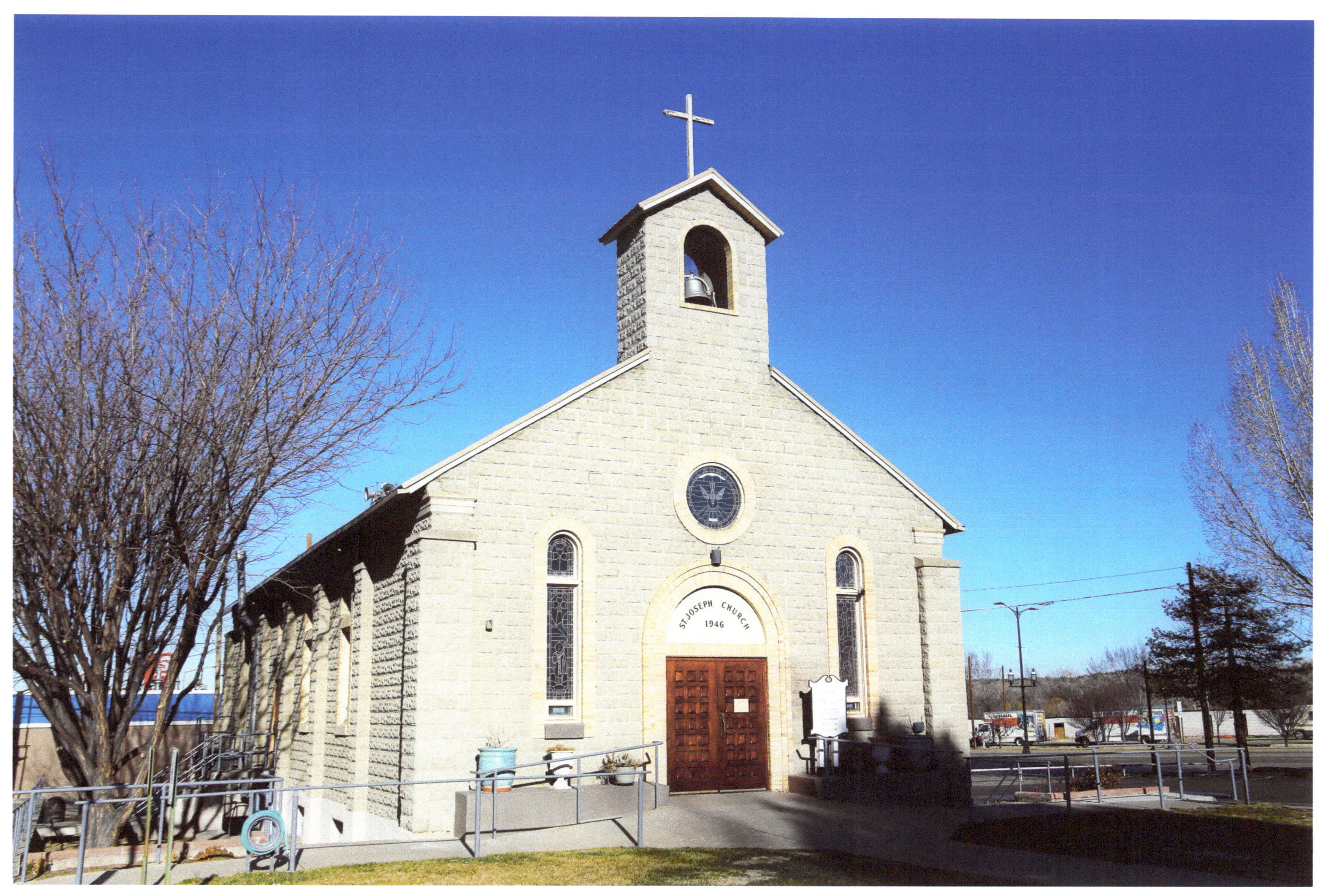

St. Joseph Catholic Church, Aztec, San Juan County. 1946. The stone church is at 424 North Mesa Verde Avenue. Photograph taken in 2022.

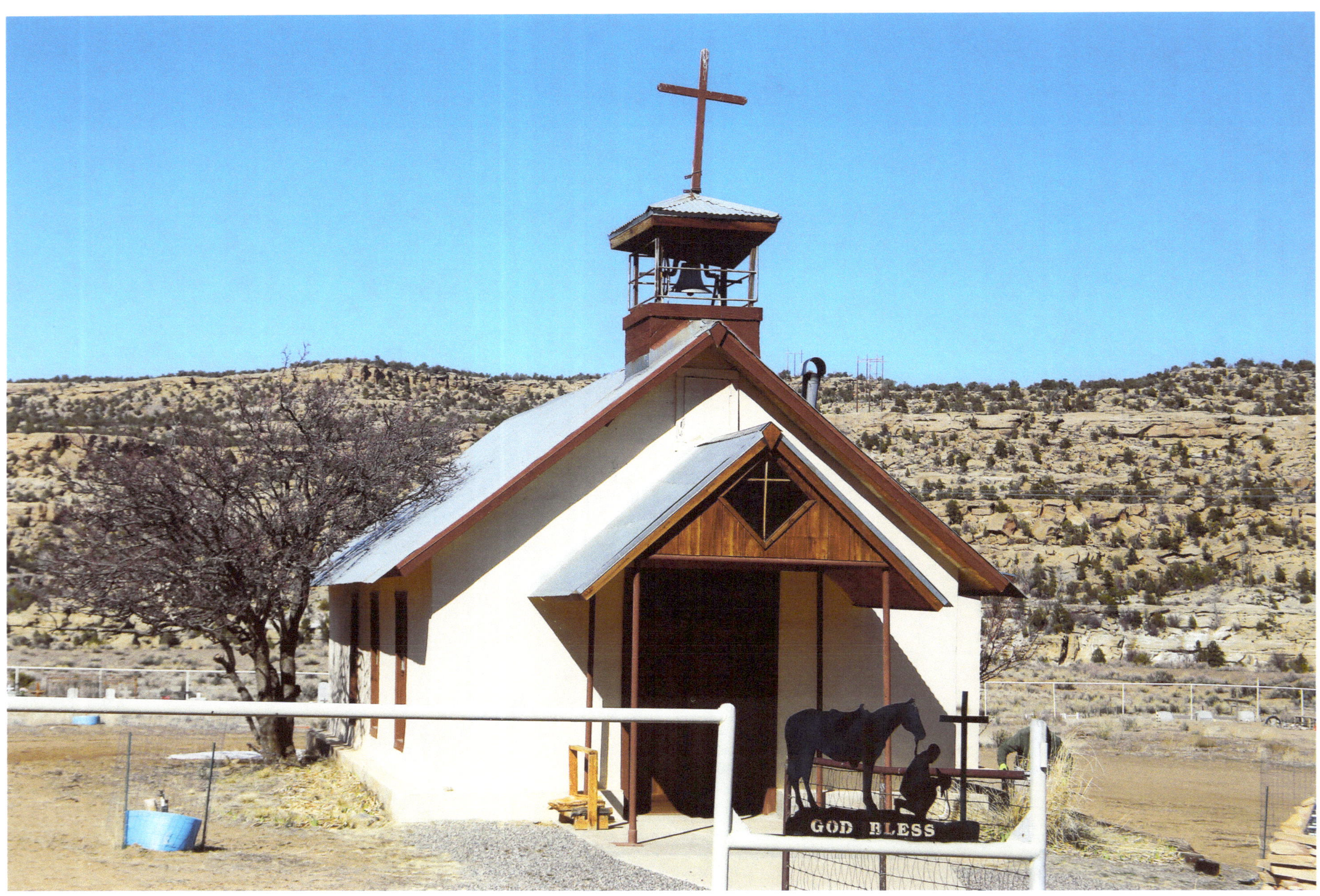

Our Lady of Guadalupe Catholic Church, Navajo Dam, San Juan County. 1920. This traditional church was not directly affected by the filling of the reservoir behind the dam, which was completed in 1963. After 11.6 miles on New Mexico Highway 111 off U.S. Highway 64, take the Texas Hole Day Use exit (bring a fly rod). Photograph taken in 2022.

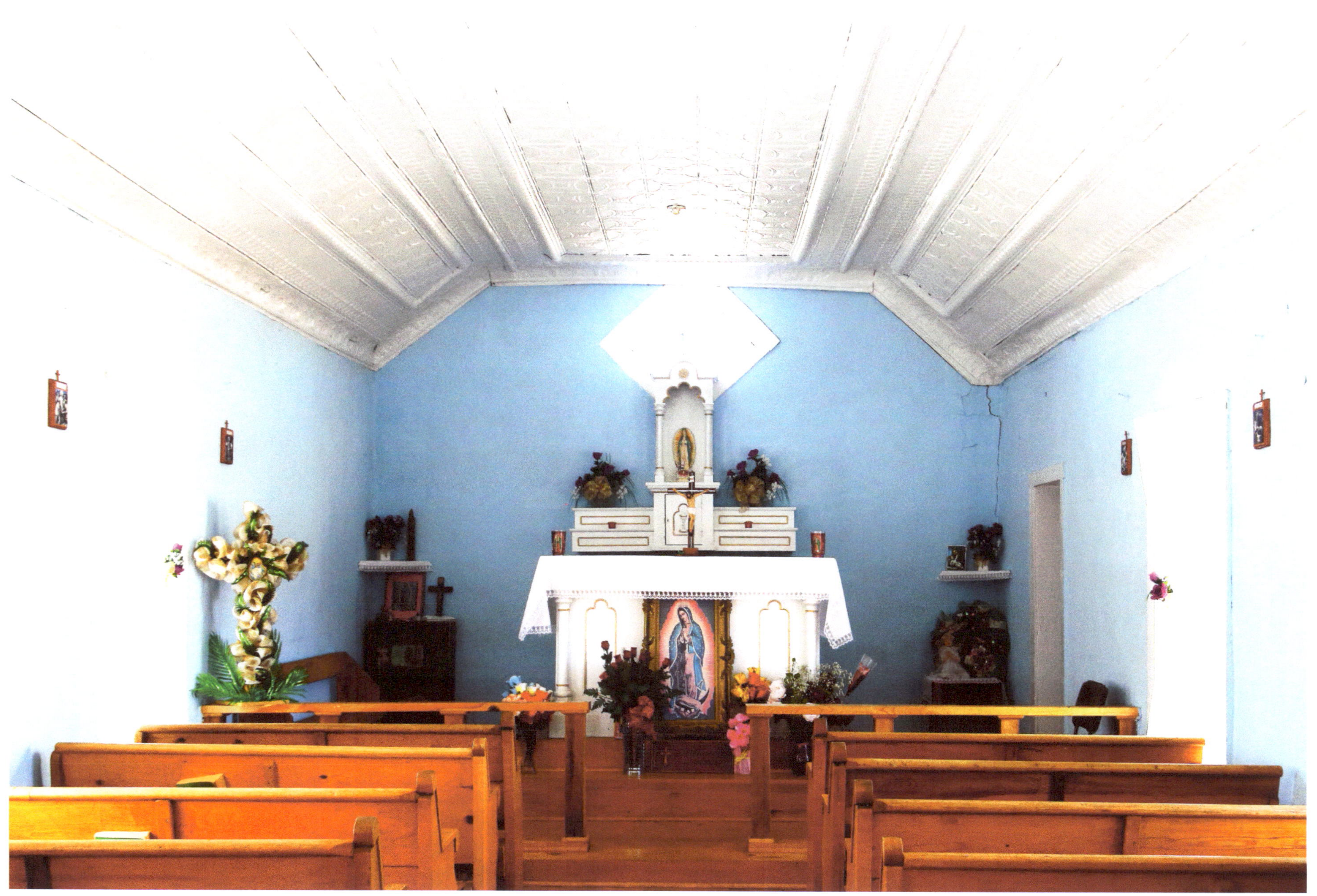

The beautifully maintained interior of Our Lady of Guadalupe Church in Navajo Dam. Photograph taken in 2022.

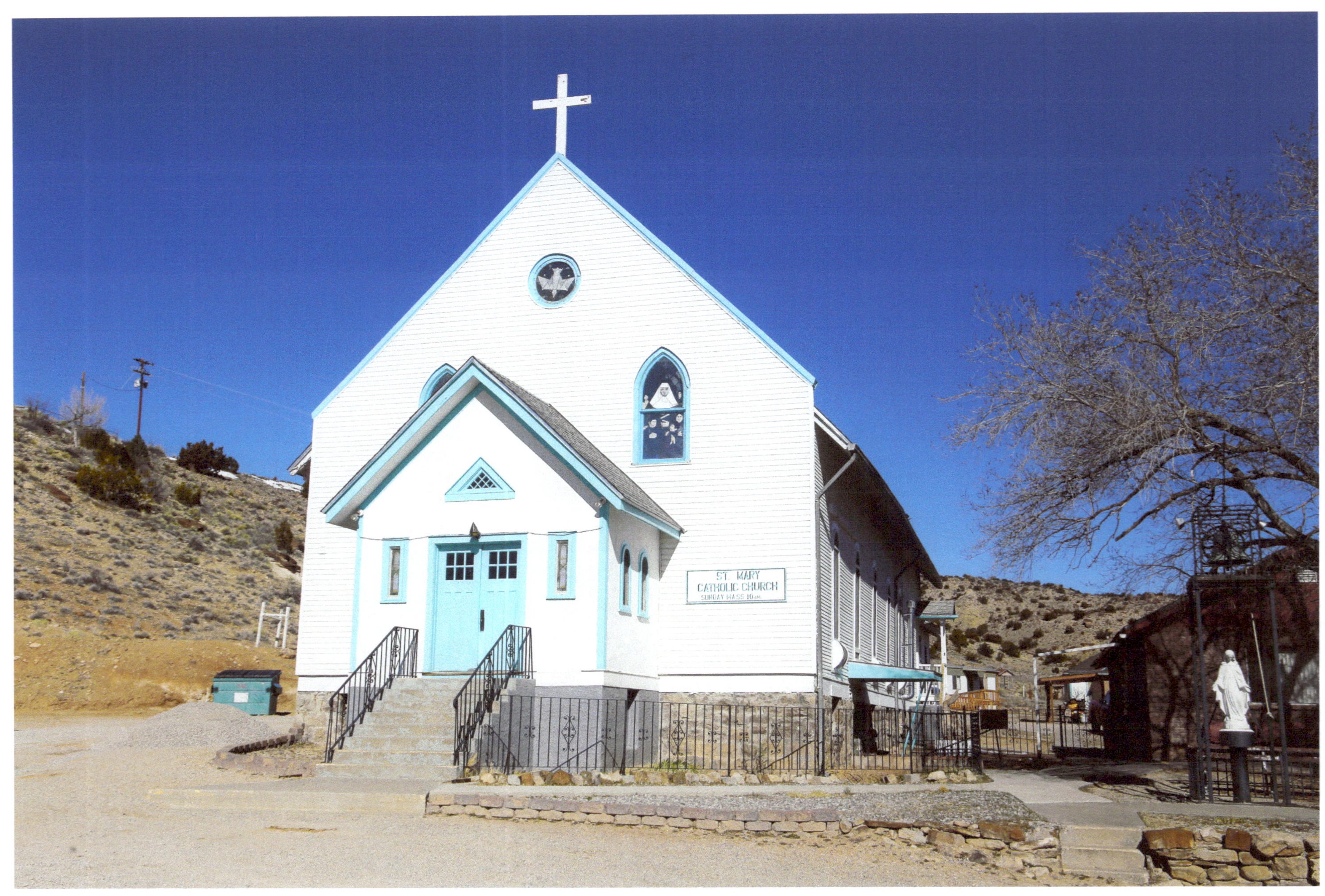

St. Mary Catholic Church, Tohatchi, McKinley County. 1920. This attractive, neo-Gothic wooden church has been well maintained. On Indian Service Road 108 three-quarters of a mile from its junction with U.S. Highway 491. Photograph taken in 2022.

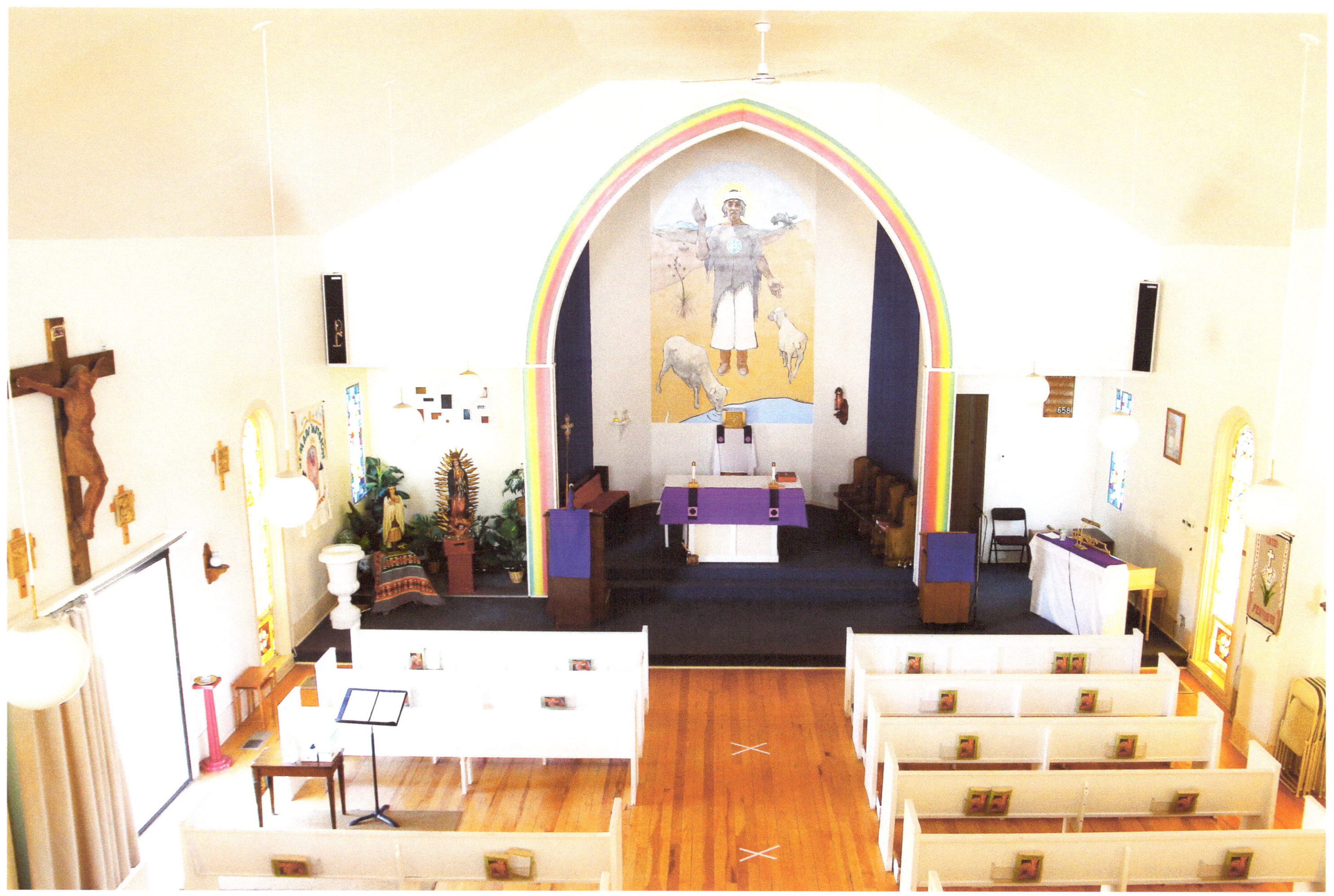

The lovely interior of St. Mary Church in Tohatchi. The Navajo Good Shepherd behind the altar (signed by D. Rogers, 1989), Christ on the cross, Mary in Indian clothes, and Our Lady of Guadalupe are a striking blend of Navajo and traditional Catholic imagery, reminiscent of the blended imagery in St. Joseph's Apache Mission Church in Mescalero (in my second book). Photograph taken in 2022.

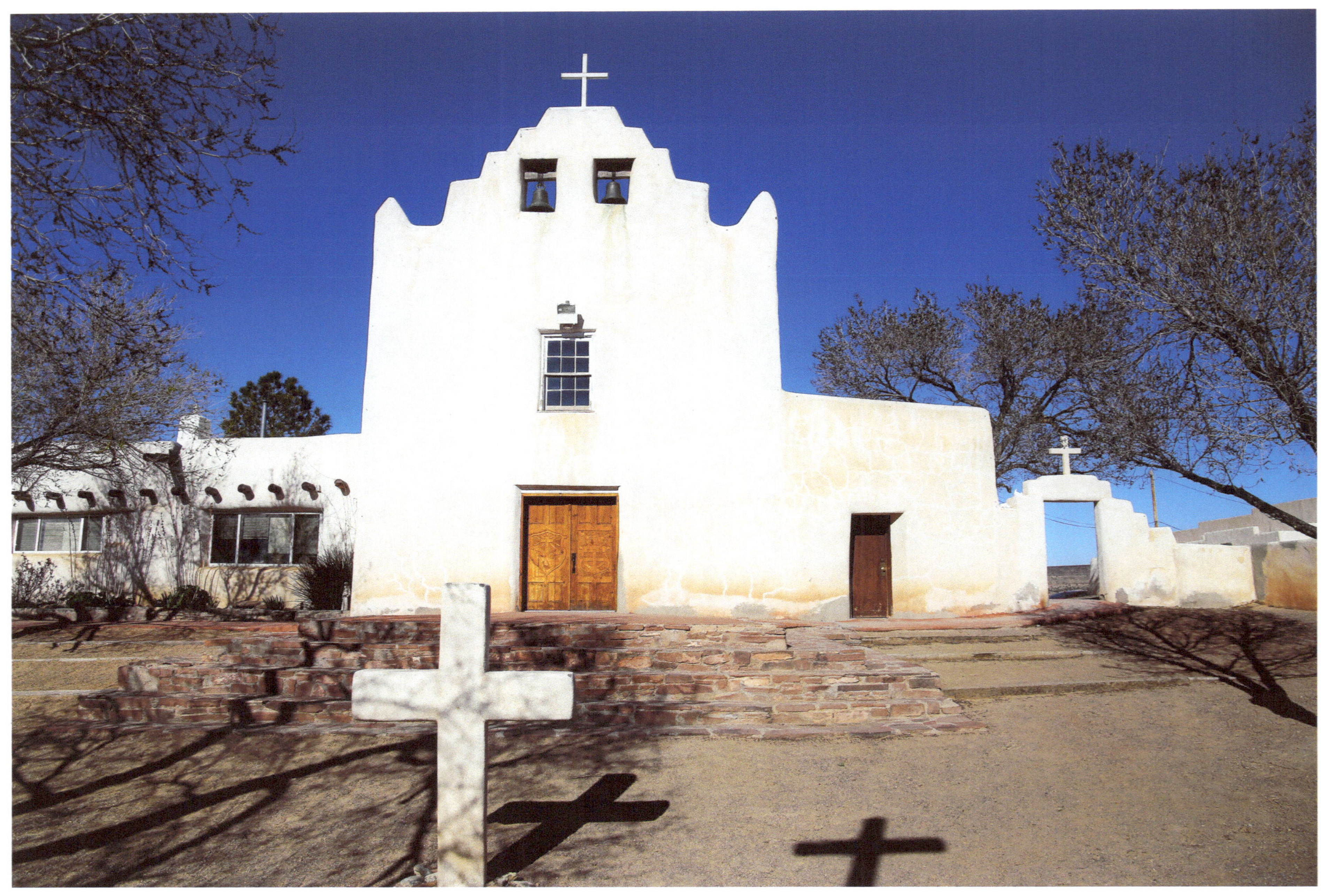

San José de Laguna Catholic Church, Laguna Pueblo, Cibola County. 1706. This stunning church, built of field stone, adobe, mortar, and plaster, is one of the finest mission churches in New Mexico, with glorious murals inside. In the plaza of the pueblo on Capital Road. Photograph taken in 2020.

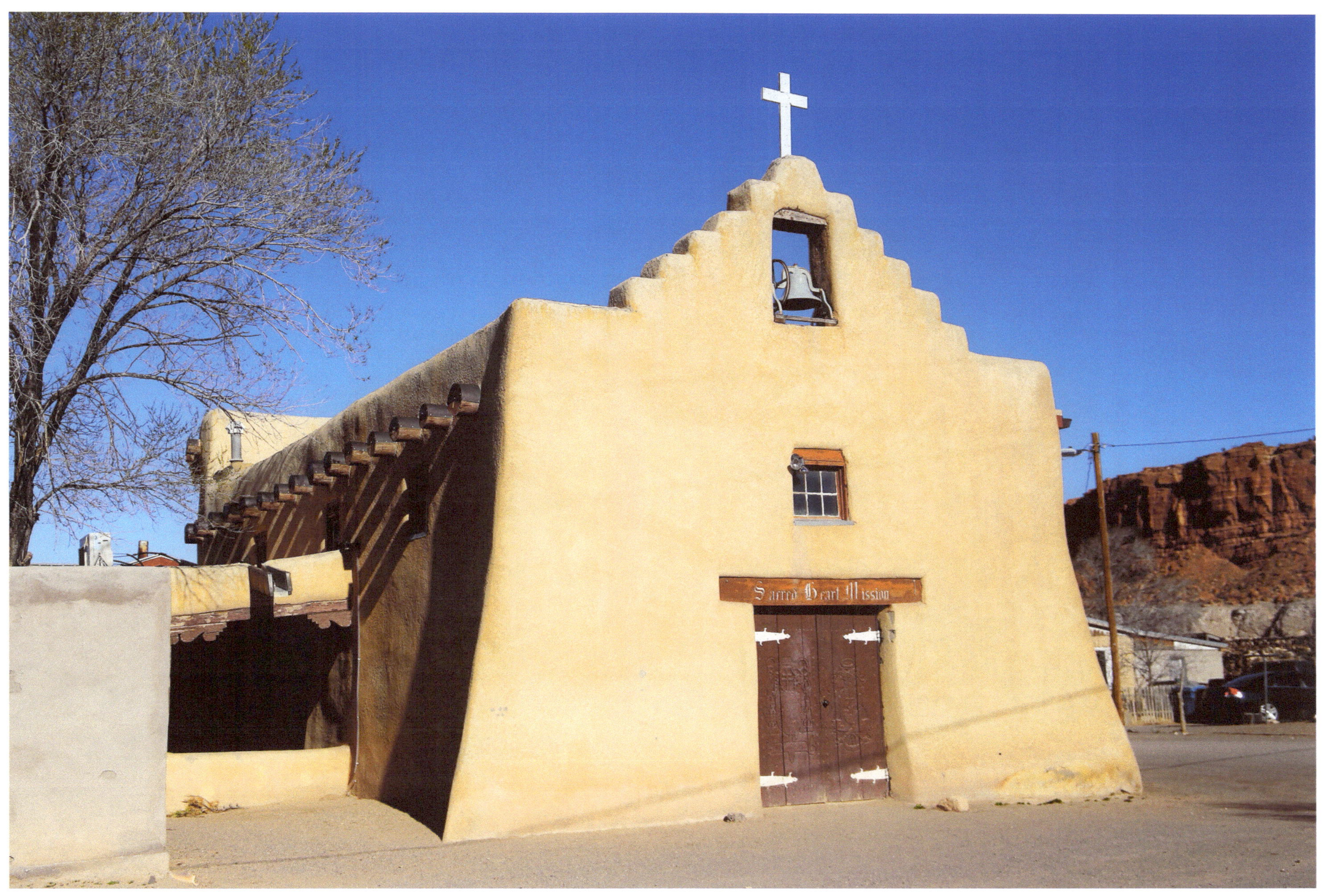

Sacred Heart of Jesus Catholic Church, Mesita, Cibola County. 1936. The façade of this fine adobe church was designed by John Gaw Meem. At Indian Service Road 53 and Church Road. Photograph taken in 2020.

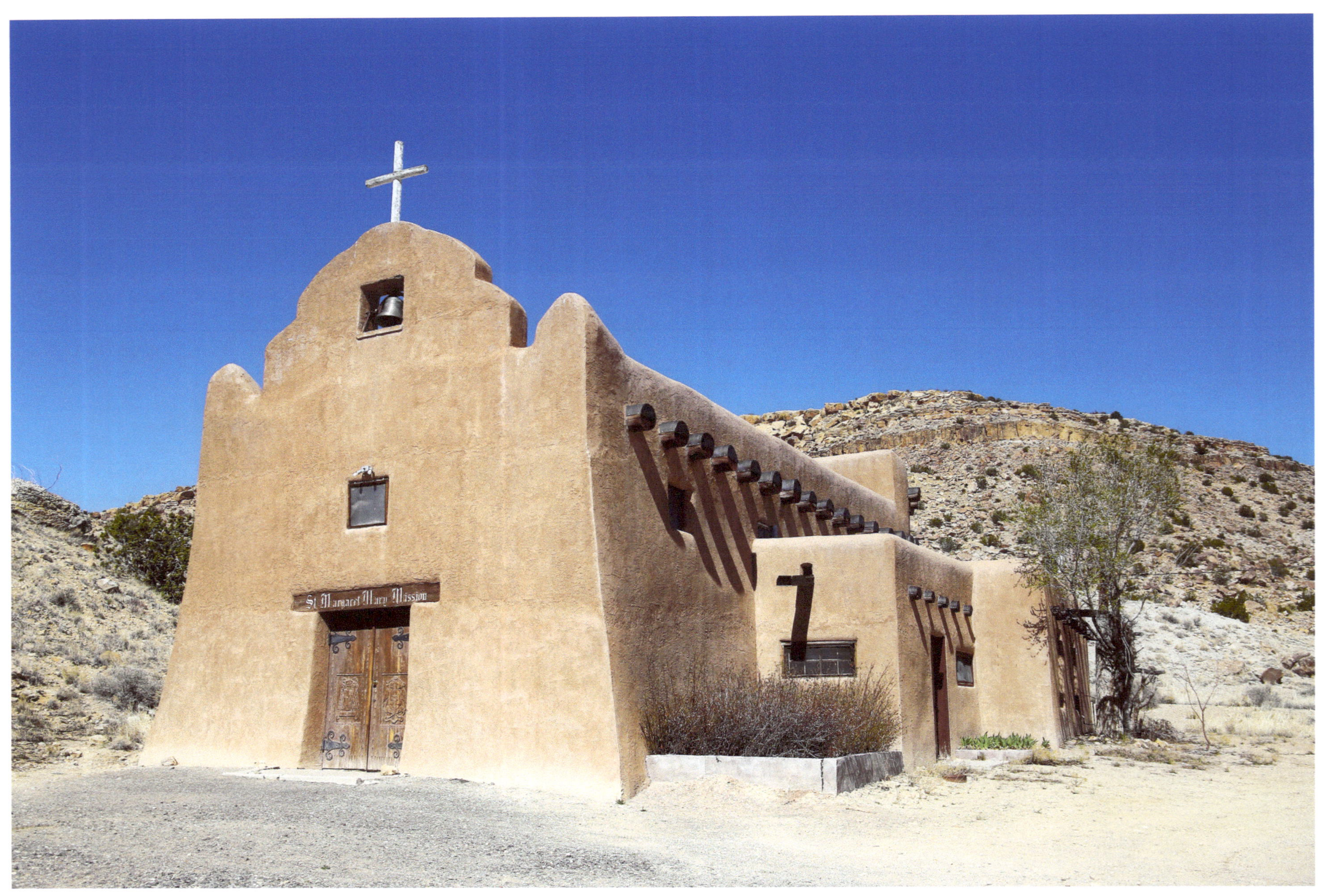

Catholic Mission of St. Margaret Mary, Paraje, Cibola County. 1935. One of several in the region designed by John Gaw Meem, this striking adobe church has a marvelous setting. Indian Service Road 243 or Acorn Road from New Mexico Highway 124 to the end of Paraje Road.
Photograph taken in 2020.

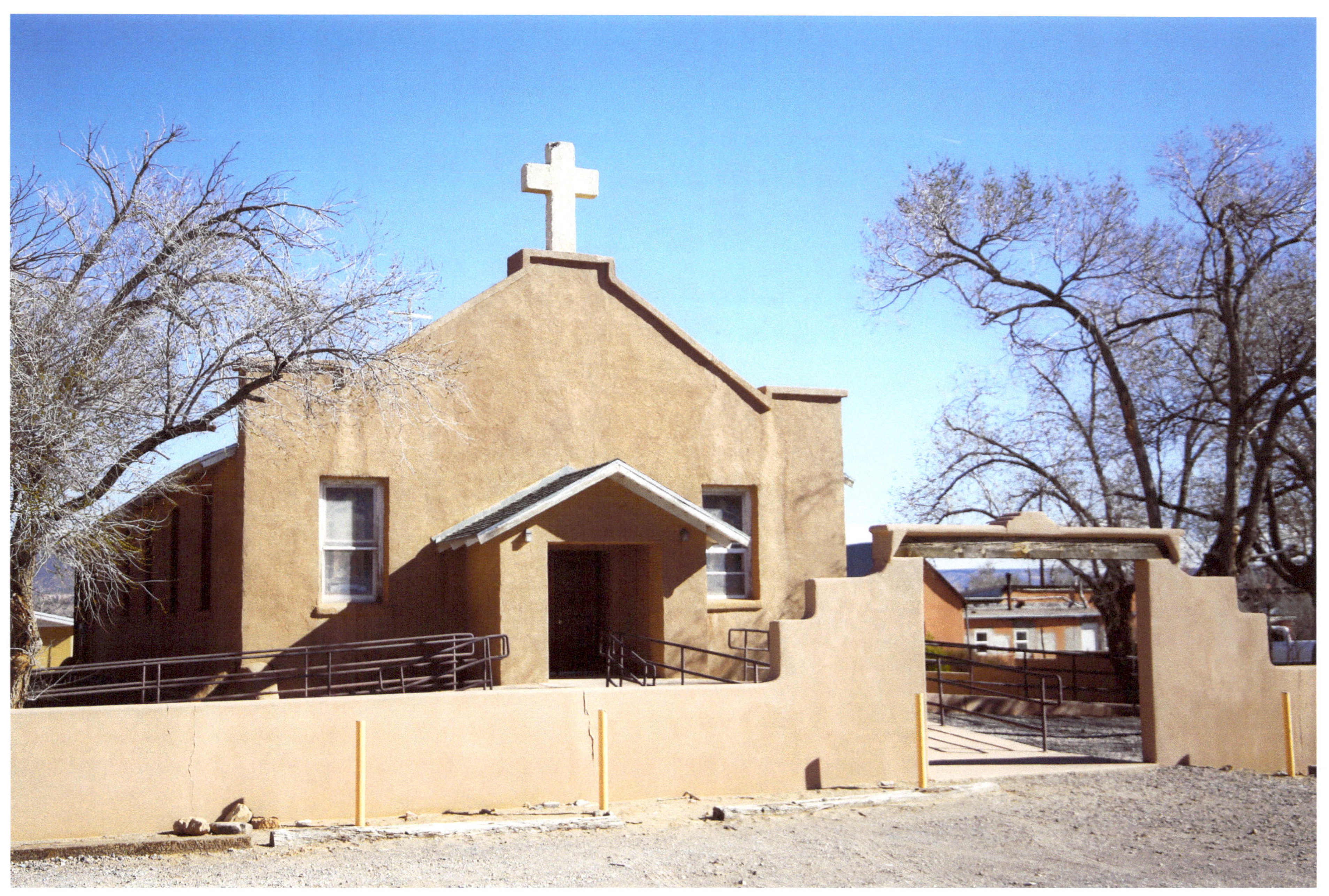

St. Elizabeth of Hungary Catholic Church, Paguate, Cibola County. 1920. This adobe church seems more modern than it is. At 23 St. Elizabeth Road. Photograph taken in 2020.

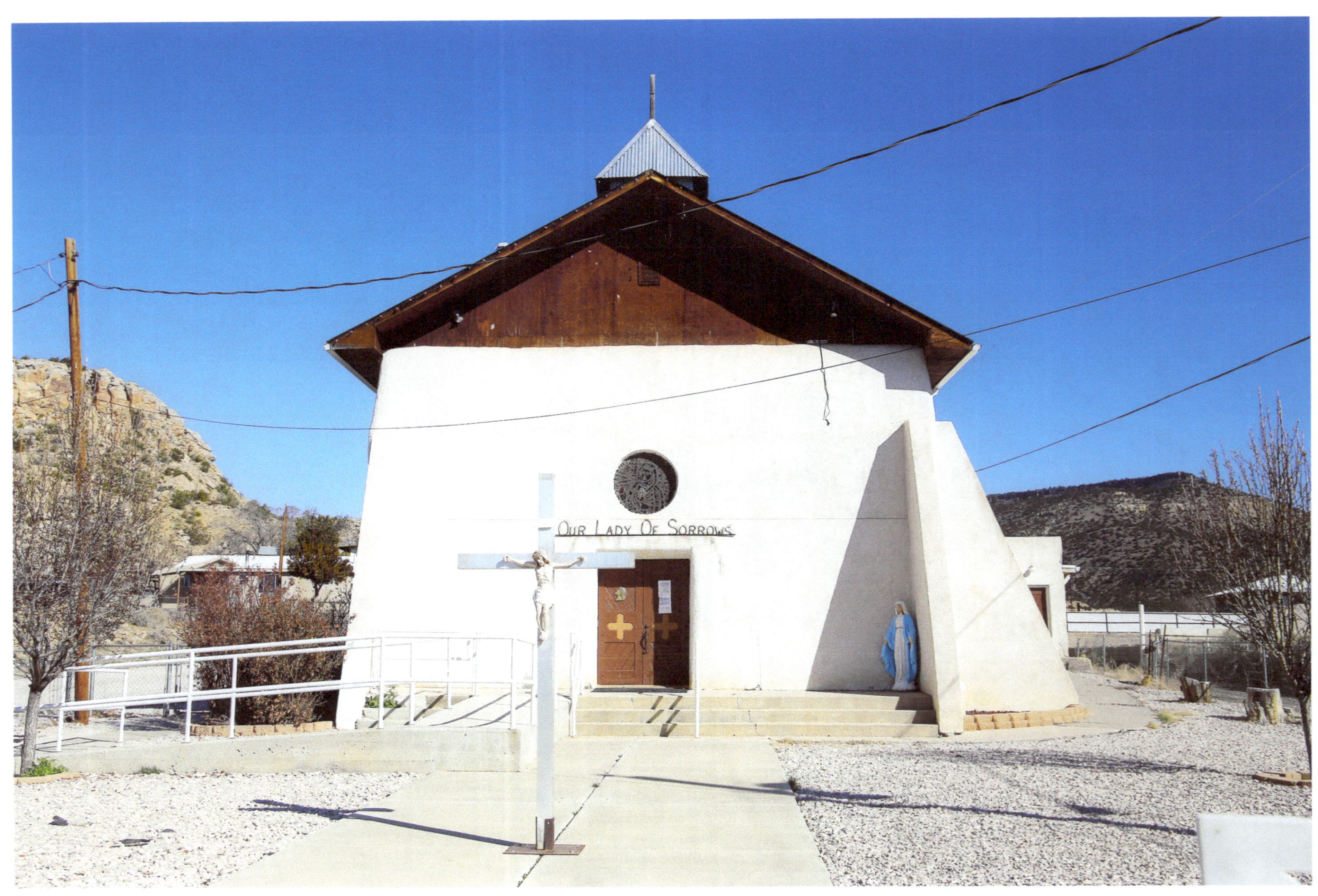

Our Lady of Sorrows Catholic Church, Cebolleta (Seboyeta), Cibola County. 1820. This is a fine, old church constructed of stone and whitewashed. On New Mexico Highway 279. Photograph taken in 2020.

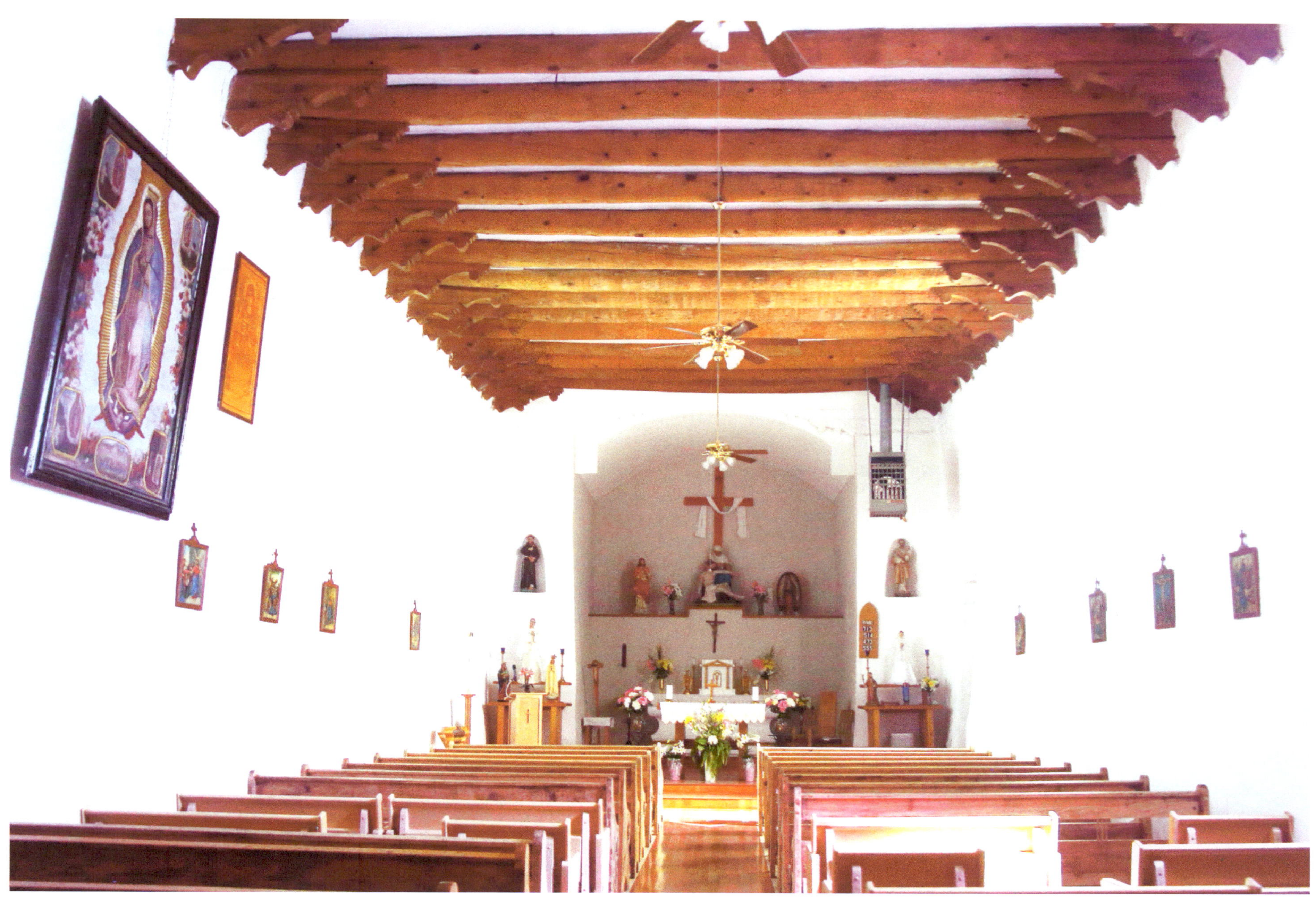

Interior of Our Lady of Sorrows. As is common in older New Mexico churches, the corbels are hand-carved. The large image of Our Lady of Guadalupe is striking. Photograph taken in 2023.

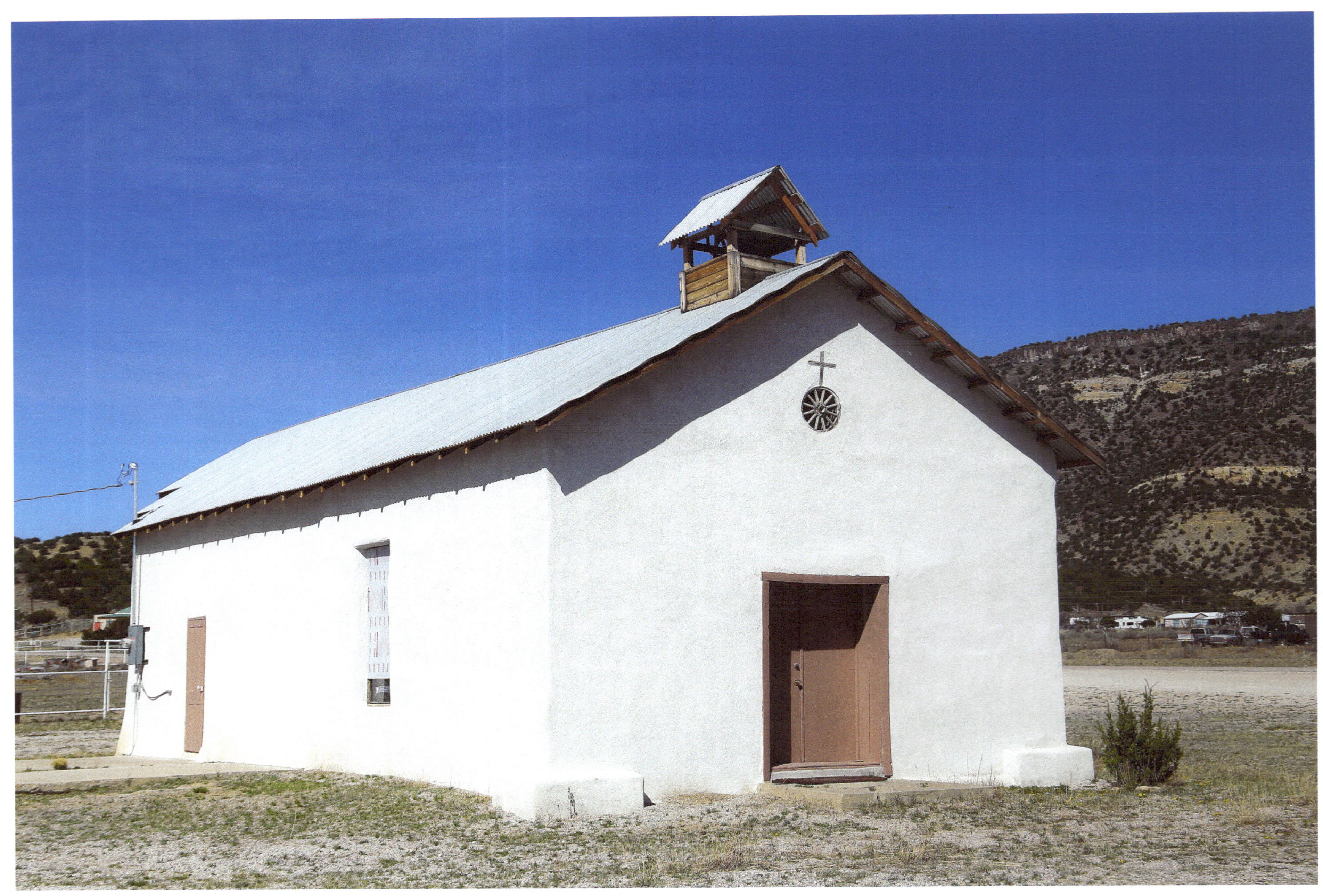

Our Lady of Loretto Catholic Church, Bibo (Cebolletita), Cibola County. Around 1900. The adobe church is currently undergoing much-needed restoration. On New La Joya Loop (County Road 5). Photograph taken in 2023.

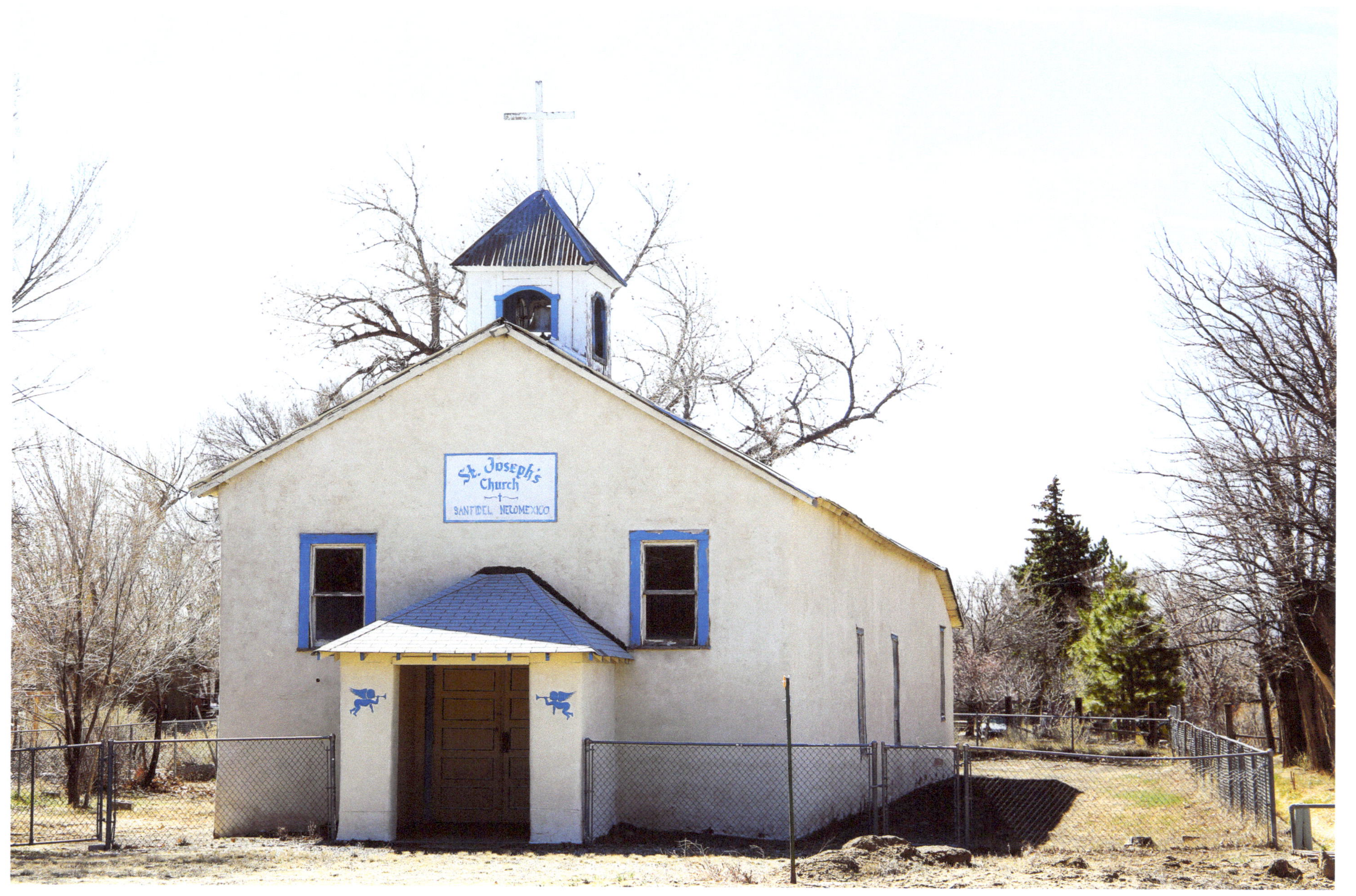

St. Joseph's Catholic Church, San Fidel, Cibola County. 1920. This charming church has cherubs on each side of the vestibule. Exit 100 north from Interstate 40 then left on Old Route 66/New Mexico Highway 124. Photograph taken in 2020.

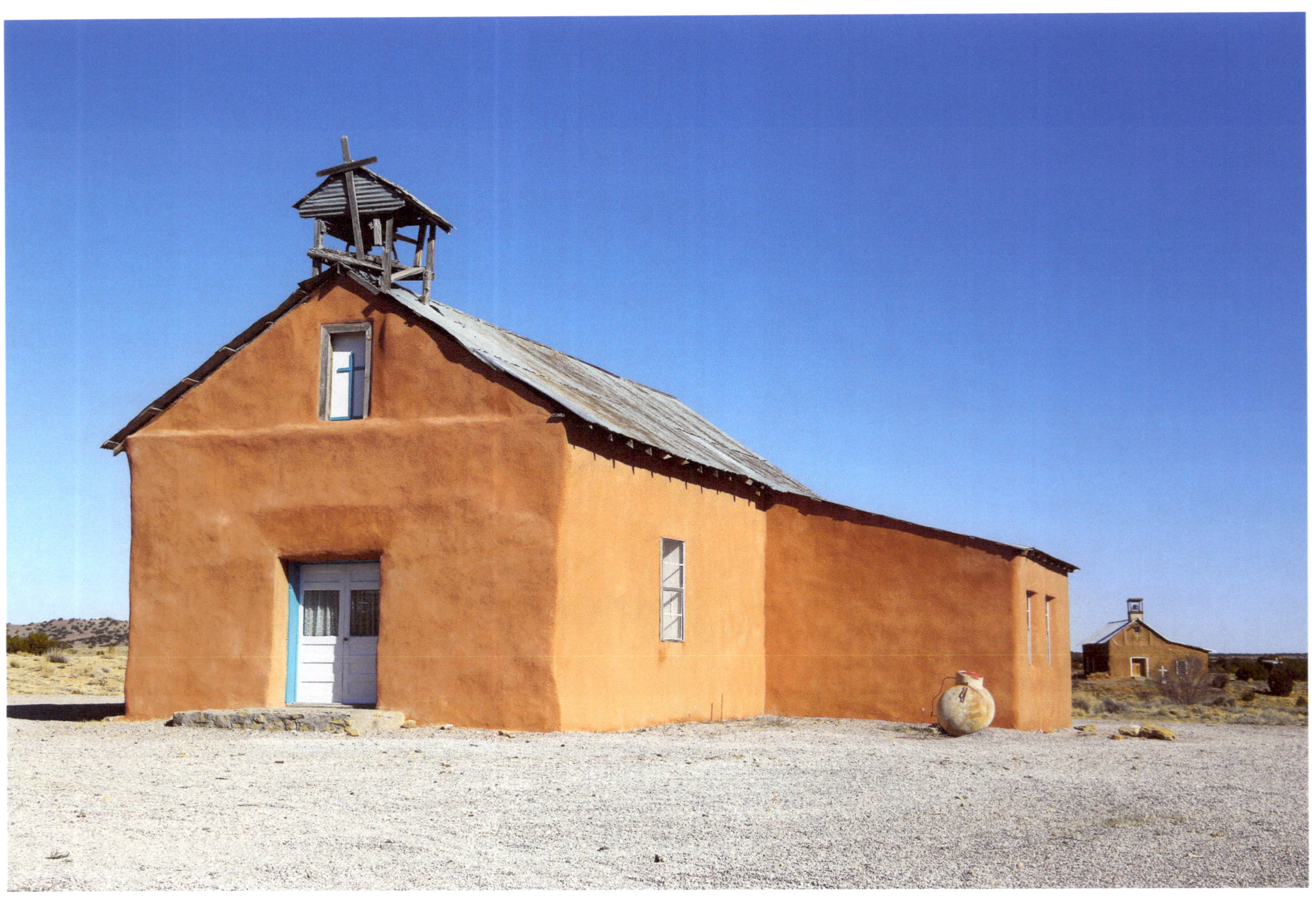

Santa Rosalia Catholic Church, Moquino, Cibola County. Around 1900. Santa Rosalia of Palermo was proposed as the patron saint of evolutionary studies by ecologist G.E. Hutchinson in 1959. The morada of the Penitente Brotherhood can be seen behind the lovely adobe church in this 2021 photograph. About 1.3 miles down Moquino Llano Road from New Mexico Highway 279.

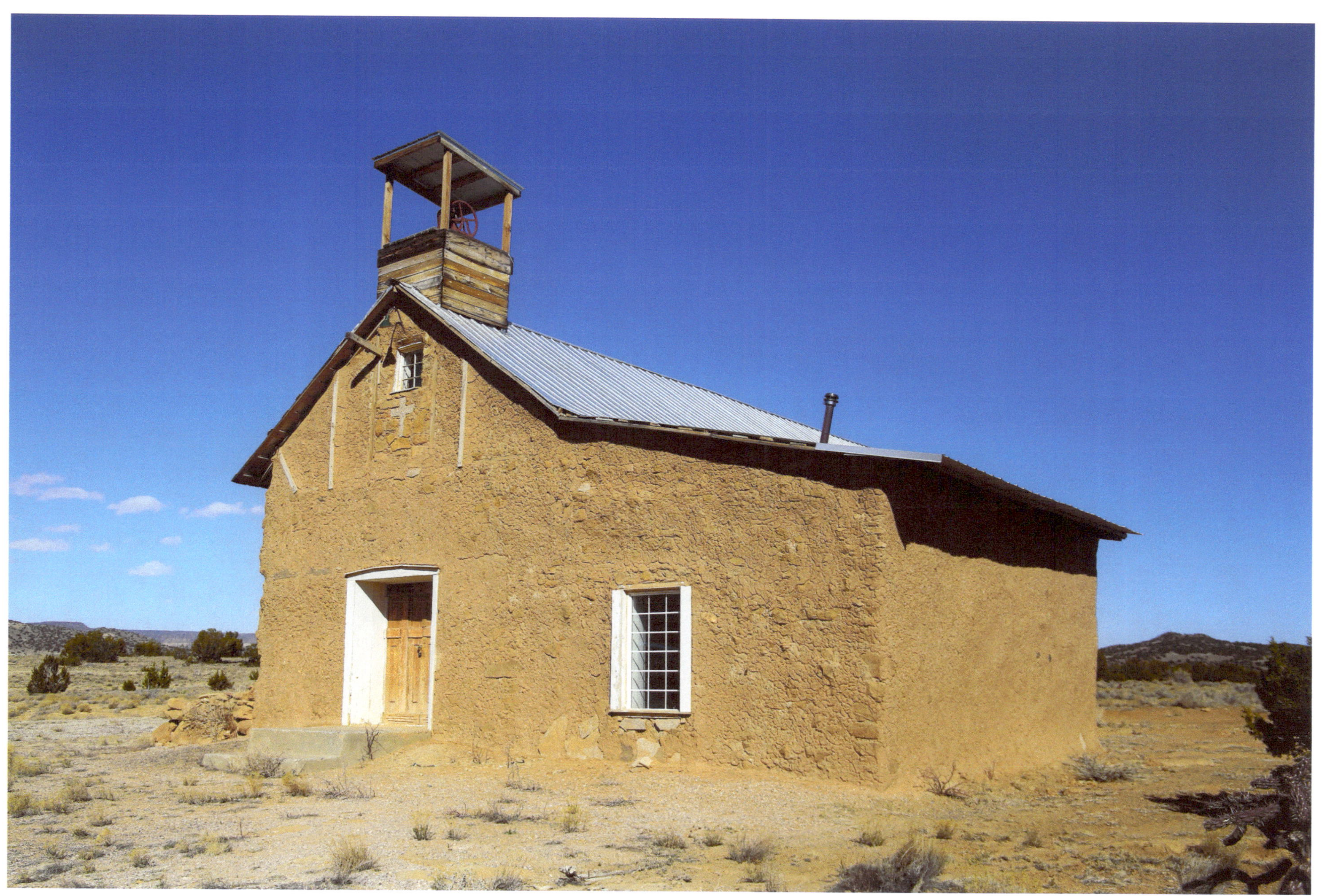

The very church-like La Morada de Moquino de Nuestro Padre Jesus de Nazareno in Moquino, Cibola County. This adobe Penitente Brotherhood morada likely was built around 1900. About 300 yards east of Santa Rosalia Church. Photograph taken in 2021.

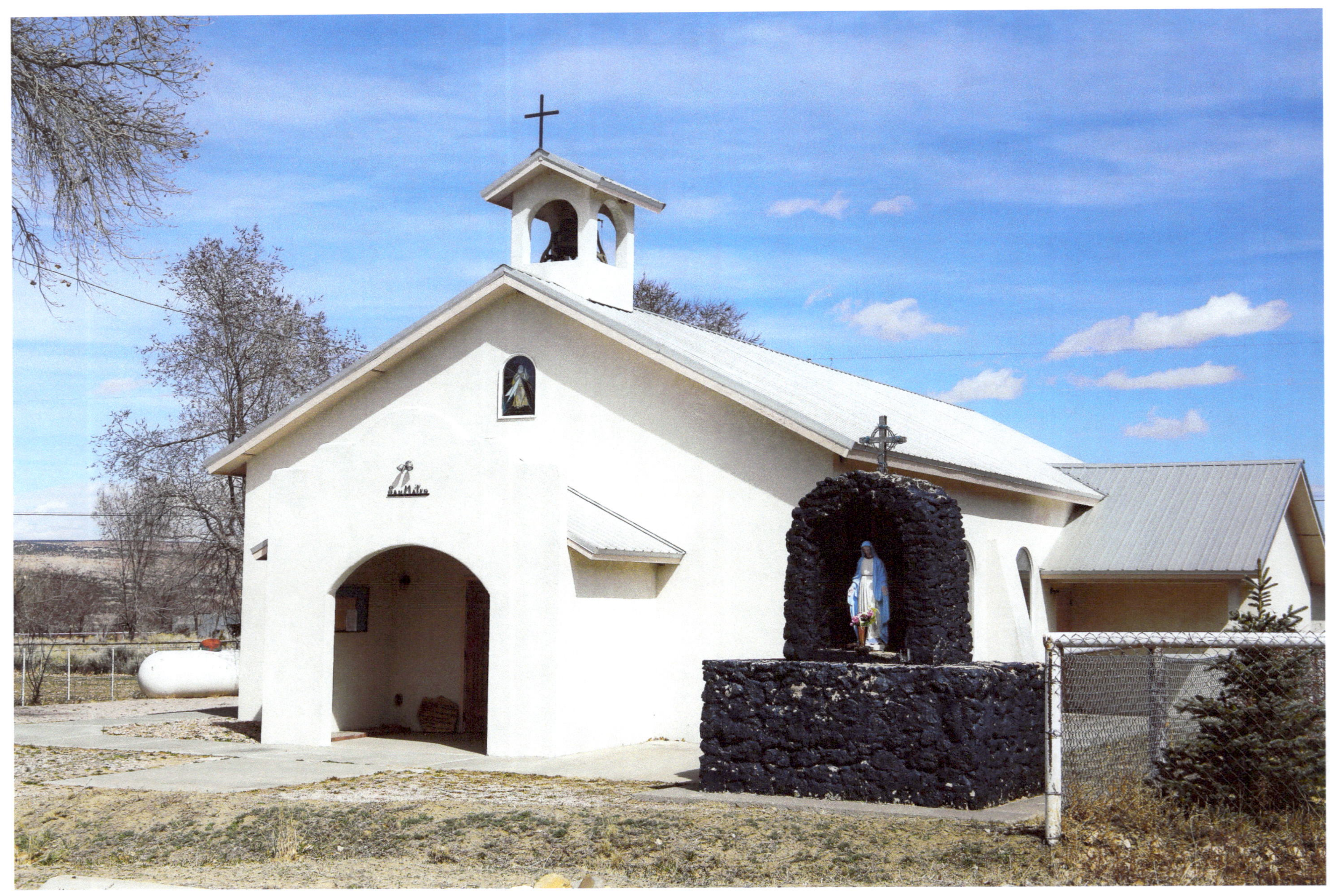

San Mateo Catholic Church, San Mateo, Cibola County. Early 2000s. When the old church burned in 2004, a new one was built that was faithful to the spirit of the old one. Take New Mexico Highway 605 into the town. Photograph taken in 2020.

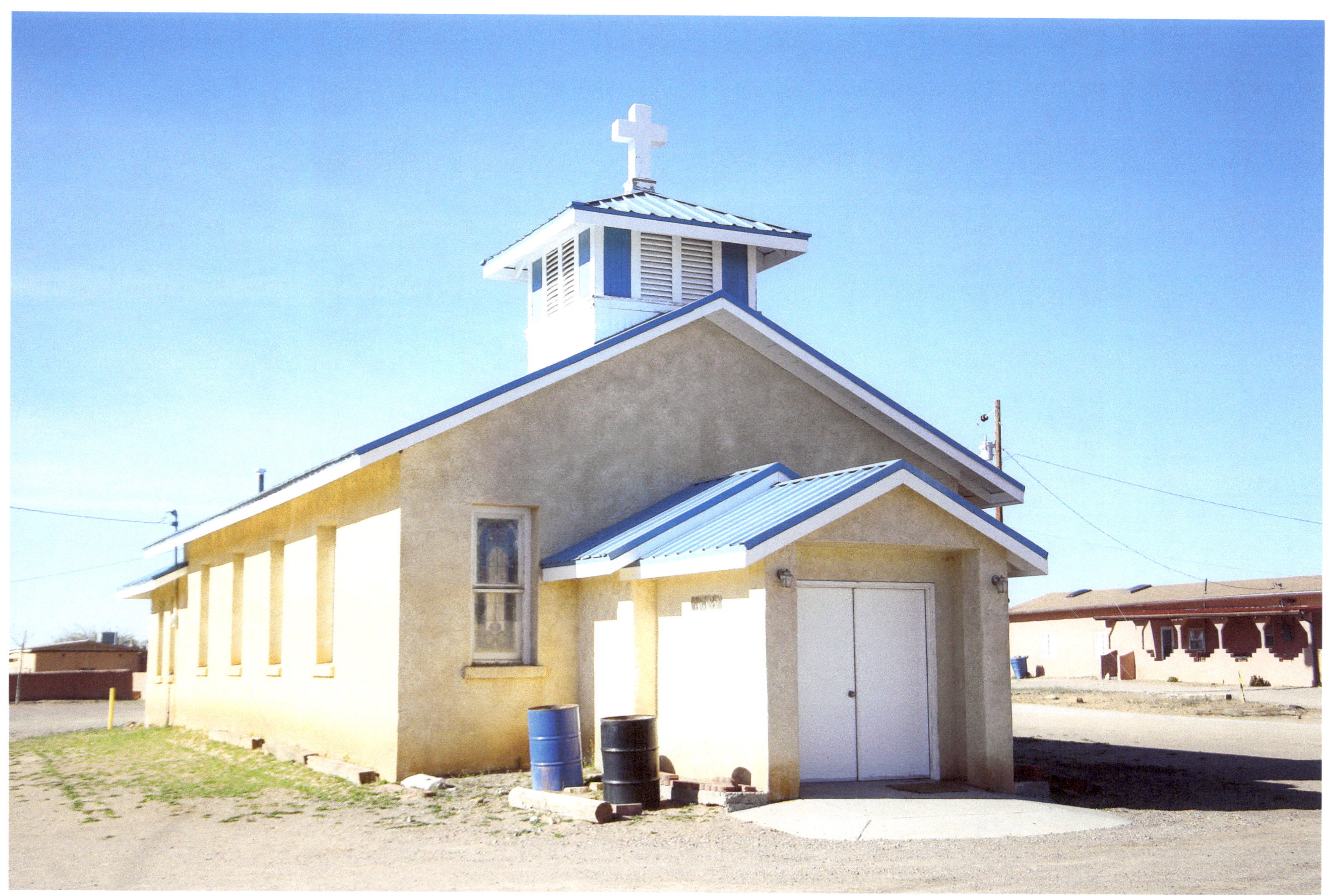

Nativity of the Blessed Virgin Mary Catholic Church, Encinal, Cibola County. 1921. Traditionally designed, the interior of the church (not pictured) includes some Puebloan as well as traditional Catholic imagery. From New Mexico Highway 124 take Encinal Road to Mt. Taylor Vista Road to Village Road. Photograph taken in 2023.

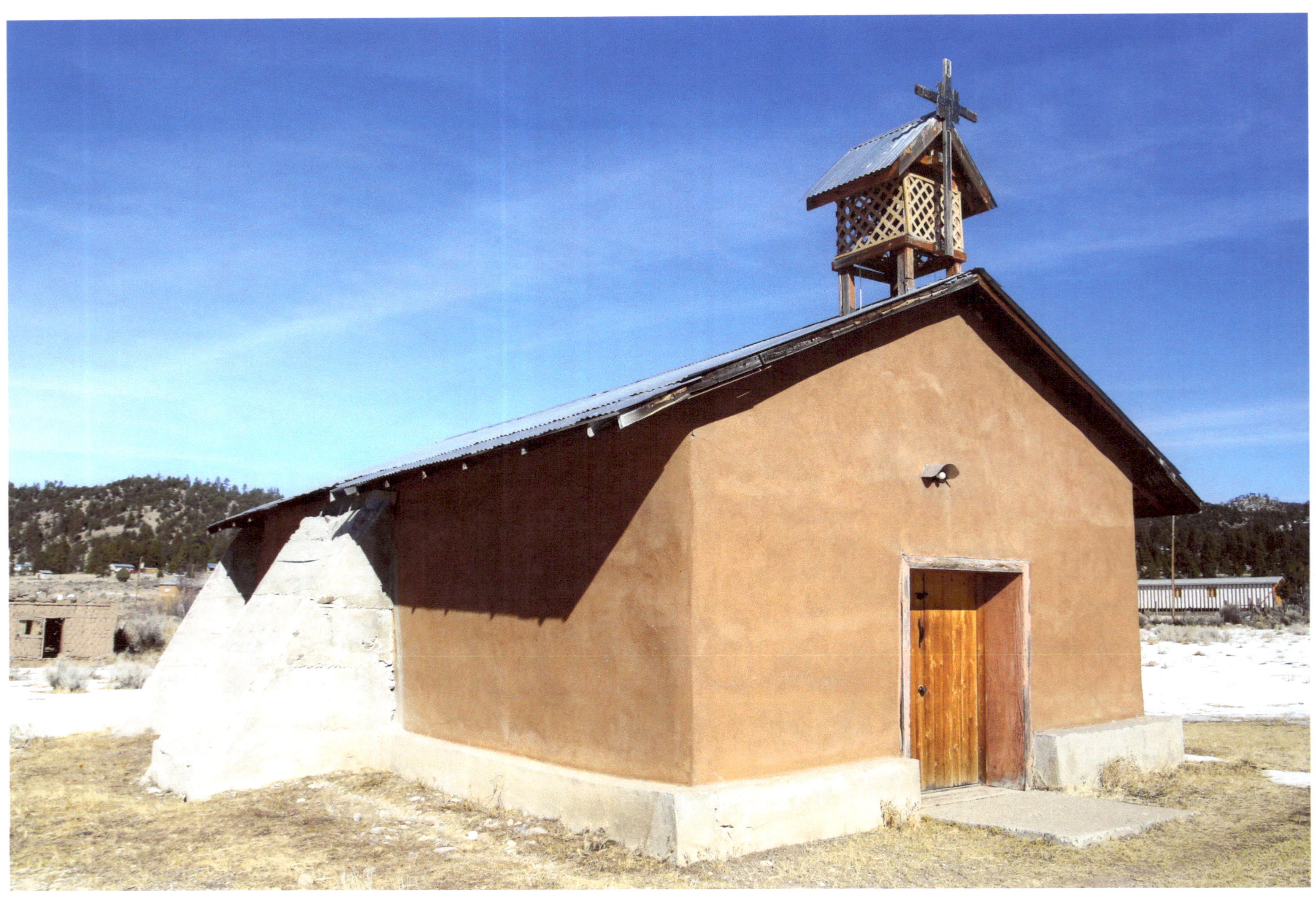

Nuestra Señora del Carmen Catholic Church, Cañon Plaza, Rio Arriba County. 1896. This isolated, small adobe church is just off New Mexico Highway 111. The concrete buttresses were added later. Photograph taken in 2023.

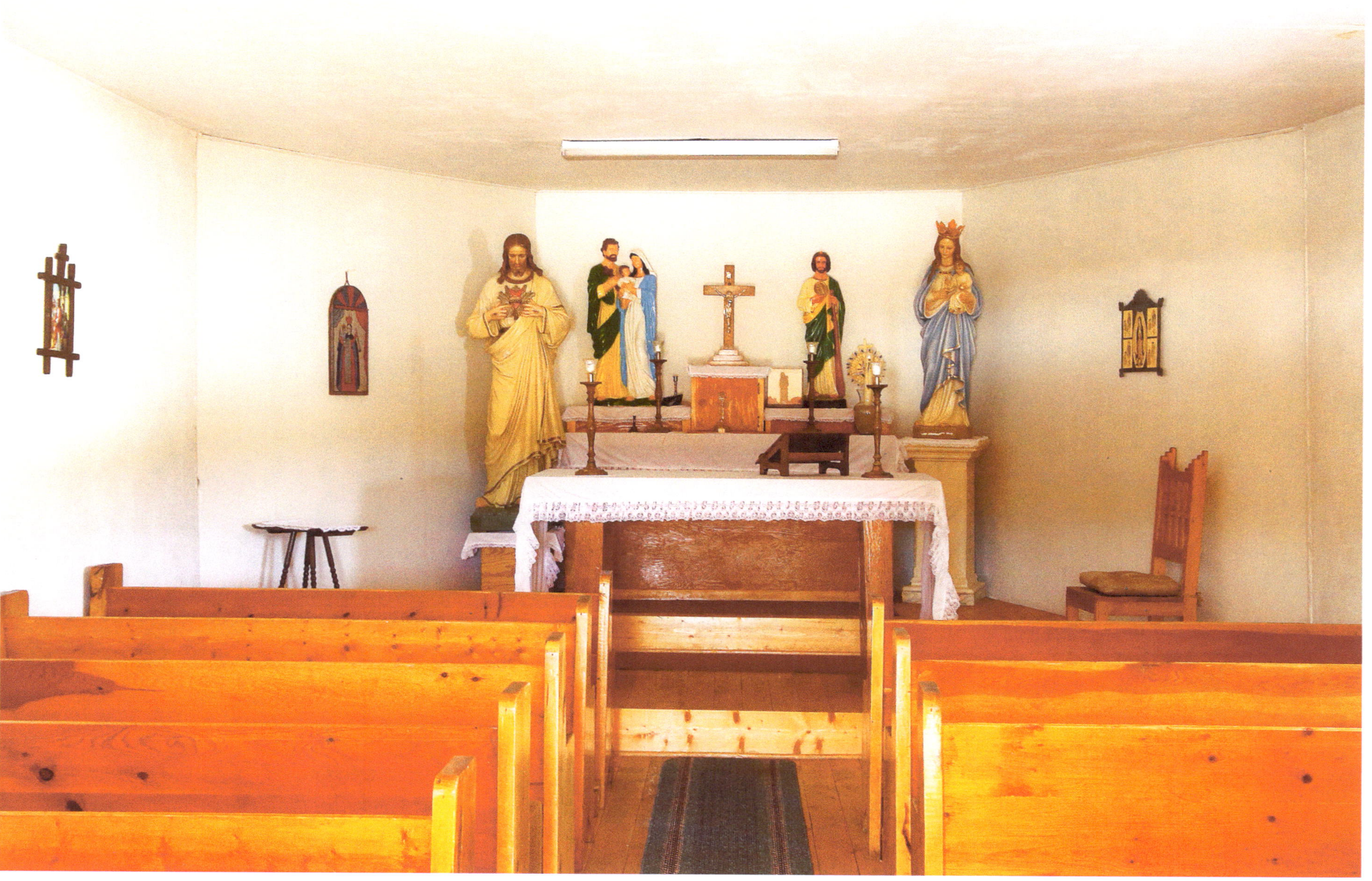

The interior of Nuestra Señora del Carmen in Cañon Plaza. The bultos (statues) in this modest church are plaster of Paris rather than hand-made, although the two retablos on the wall are by the late *santera* Anita Romero Jones, sister of contemporary *santera* Marie Romero Cash. The church is not currently used for services. Photograph taken in 2023.

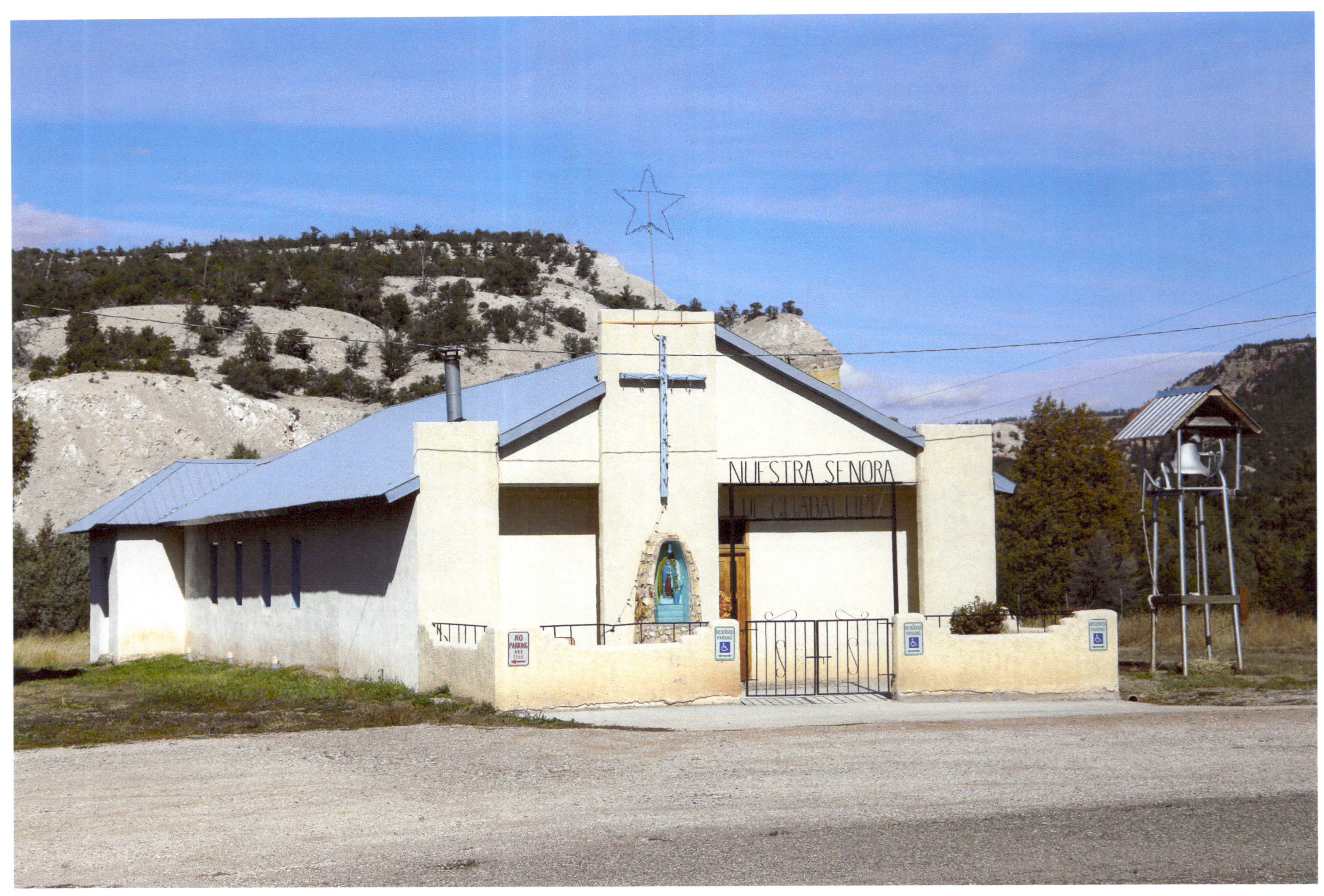

Nuestra Señora de Guadalupe Catholic Church, Gallina, Rio Arriba County. 1954. Notice the free-standing bell tower in front of the adobe church. On New Mexico Highway 96. Photograph taken in 2021.

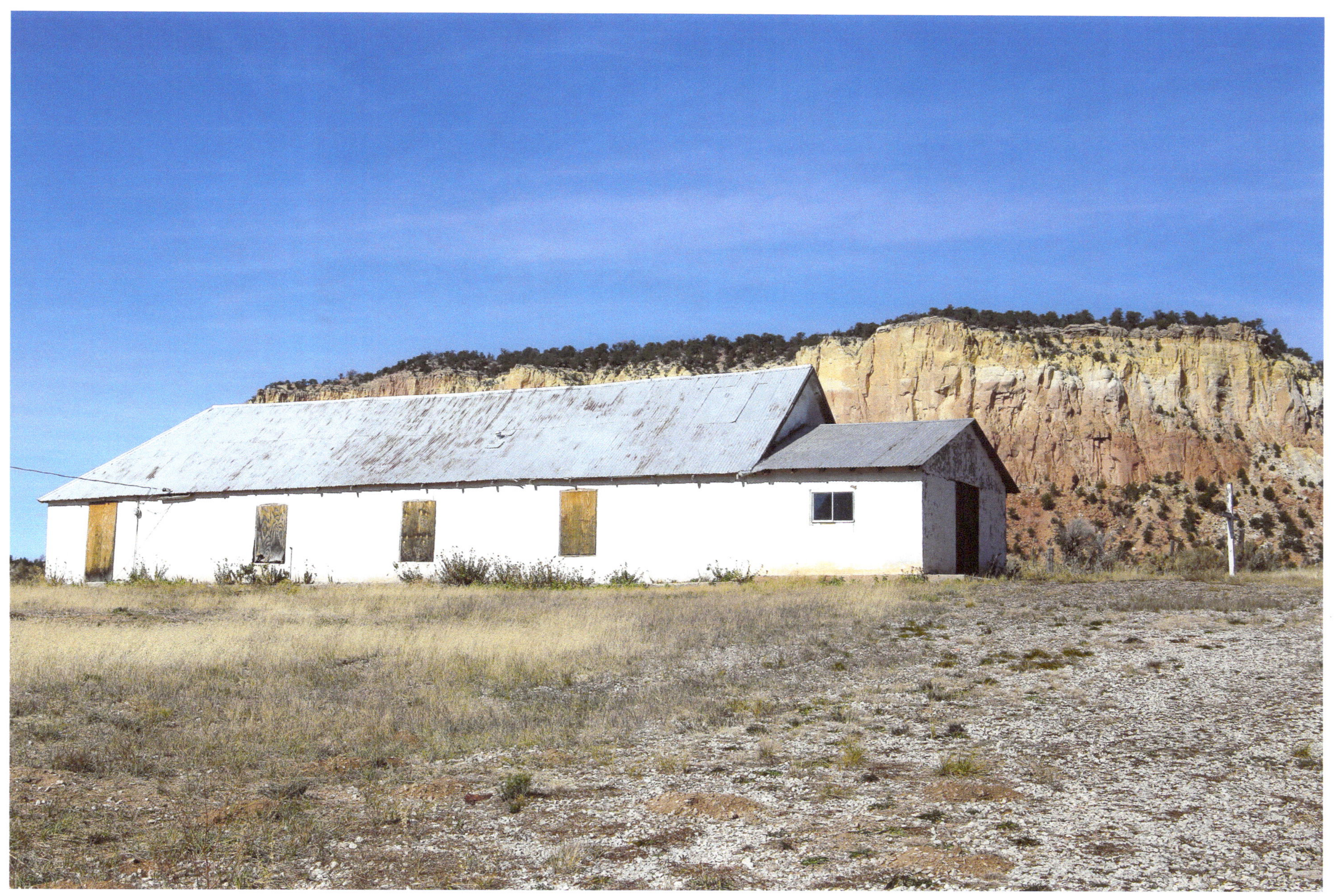

Santo Niño Catholic Church, Capulín, Rio Arriba County. 1920. The adobe church is no longer used and a free-standing bell-tower seen in earlier photographs was not present recently. Six hundred yards north of New Mexico Highway 96 on County Road 422. Photograph taken in 2021.

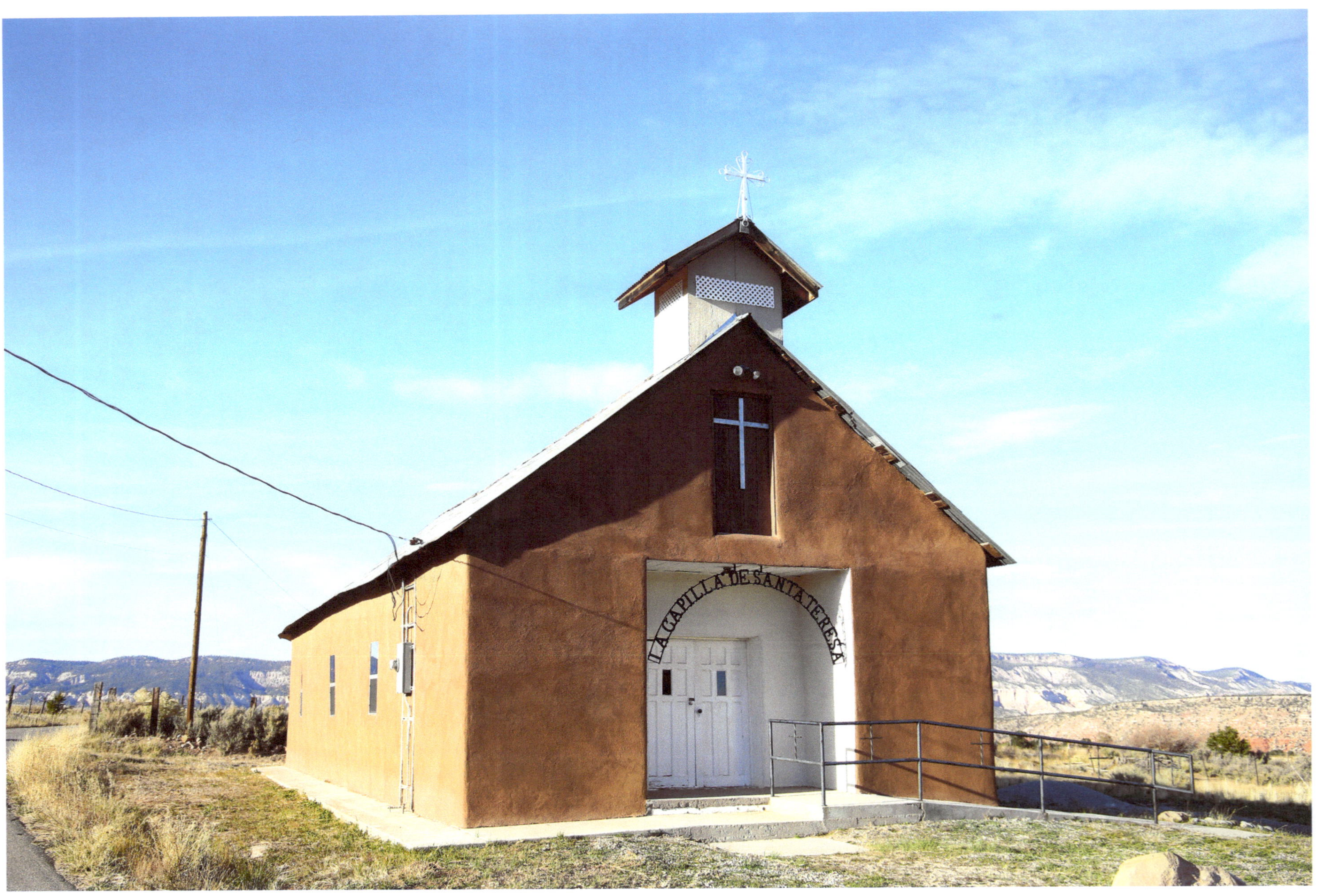

La Capilla de Santa Teresa, Mesa Poleo, Rio Arriba County. Around 1900. The charming adobe church is well maintained. Between mile markers 29 and 30 on New Mexico Highway 96 take County Road 172 south 0.3 mile, then left 2.2 miles on County Road 426/313 to the church. Photograph taken in 2021.

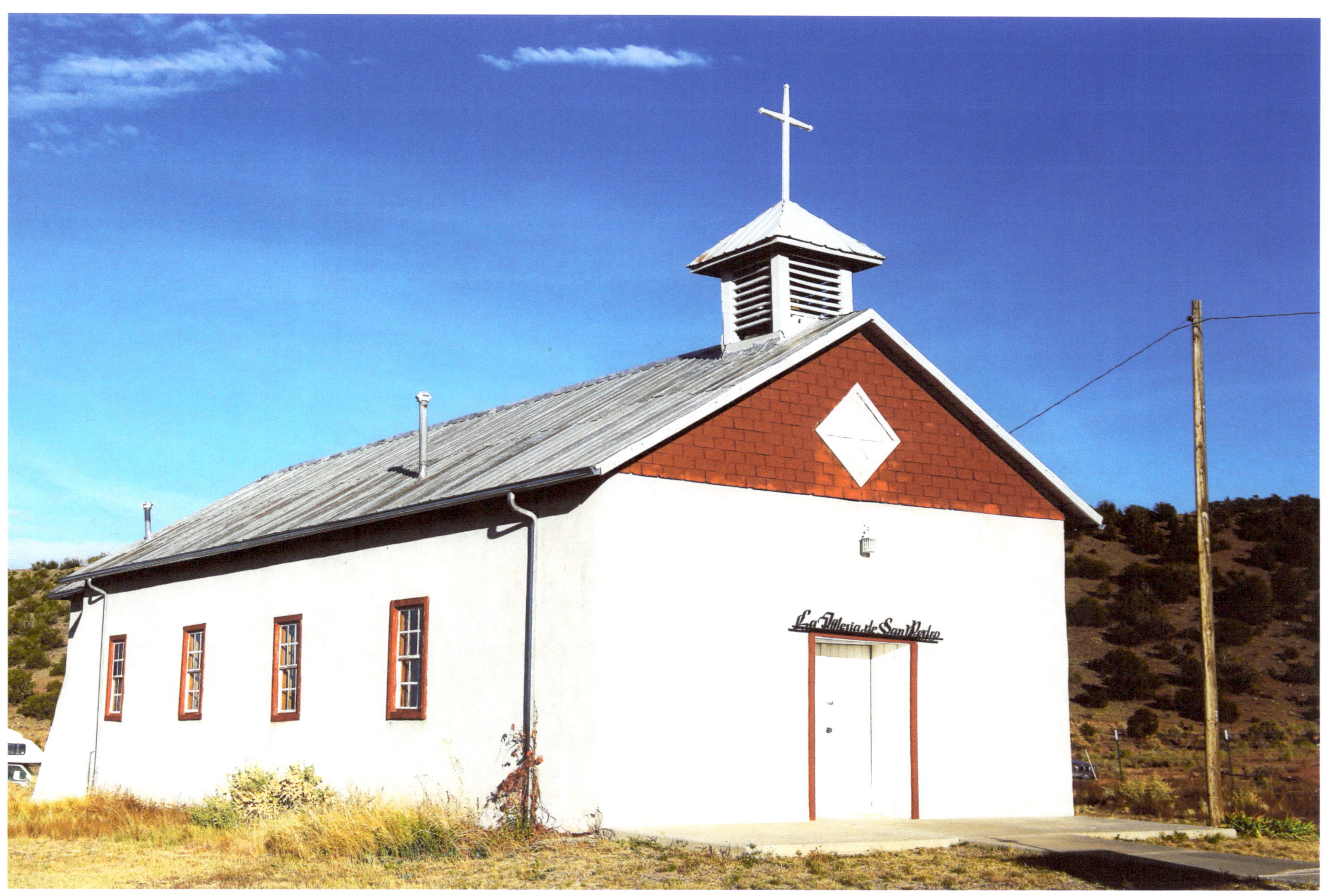

San Pedro Catholic Church, Youngsville, Rio Arriba County. Around 1900. A nice example of a northern New Mexico vernacular church. From New Mexico Highway 96 take County Road 201 1/3 mile to the church. Photograph taken in 2021.

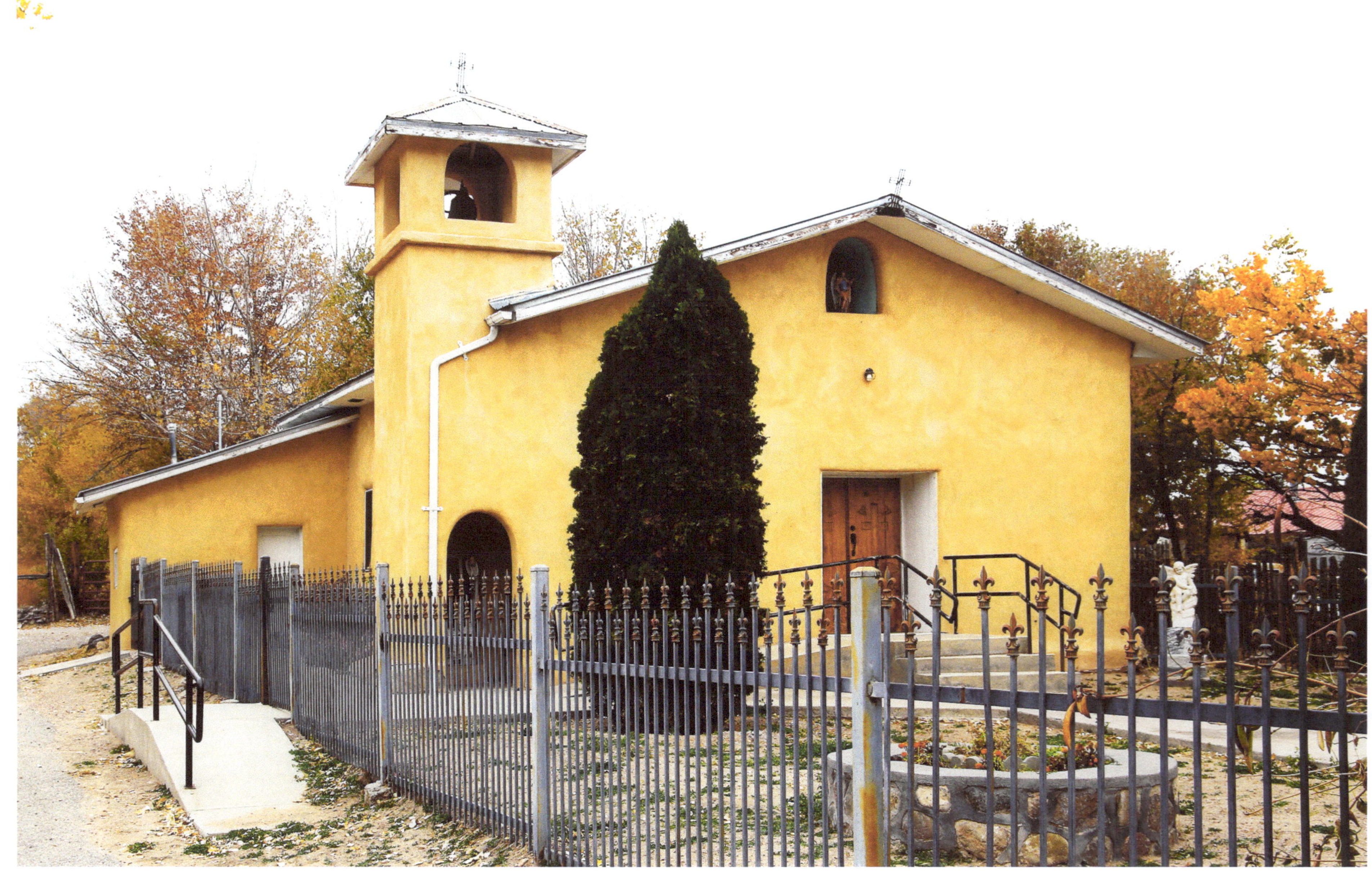

San Miguel Catholic Church, Cañones, Rio Arriba County. 1859. The adobe church seems to have been recently stuccoed. Just south of mile marker 45 on New Mexico Highway 96, take County Road 194 three miles south to the church. Photograph taken in 2021.

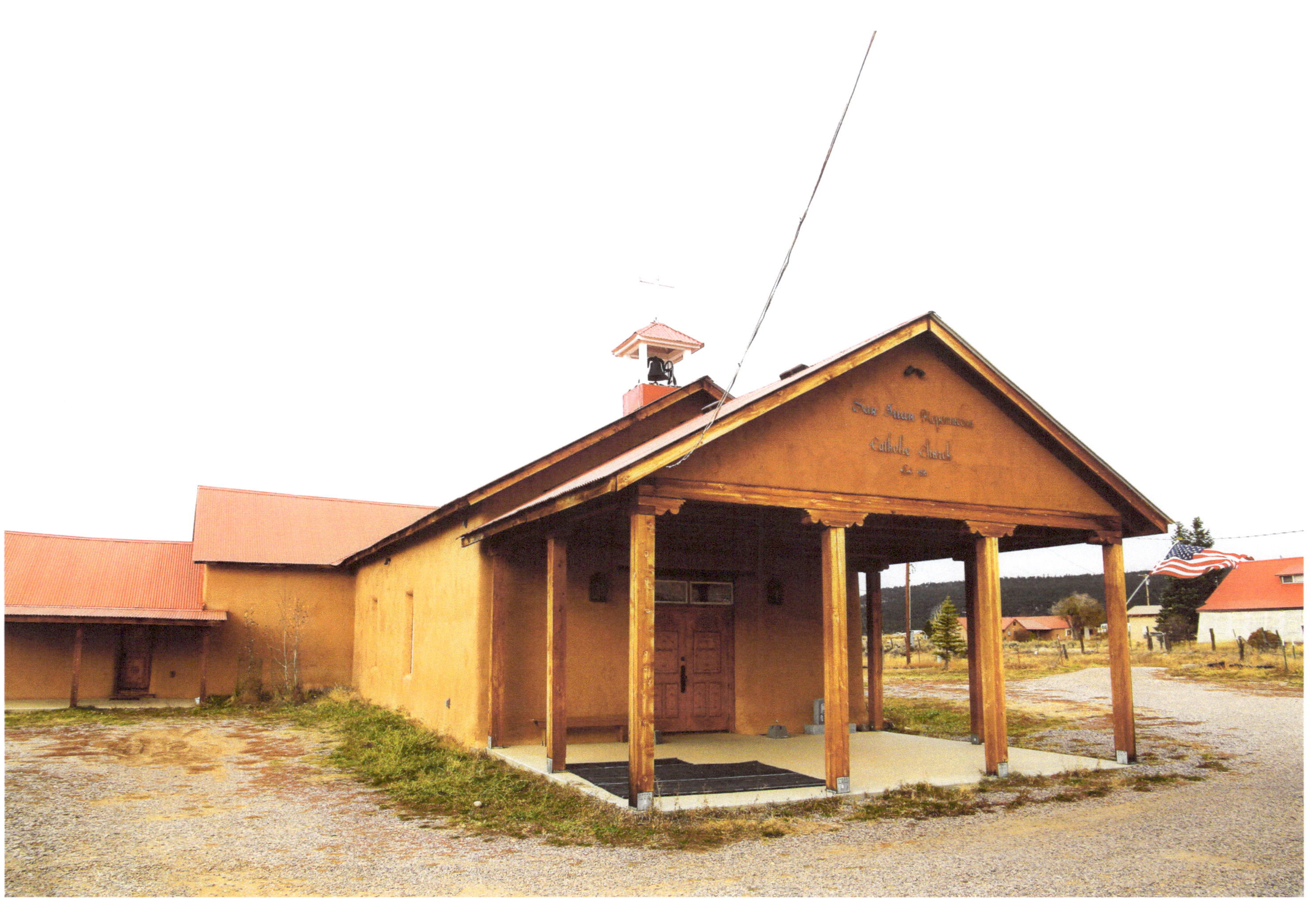

San Juan Nepomucemo Catholic Church, Canjilon, Rio Arriba County. 1878. The oversized portico detracts from the adobe church's otherwise pleasing architecture. On New Mexico Highway 115 3.3 miles west of U.S. Highway 84. Photograph taken in 2021.

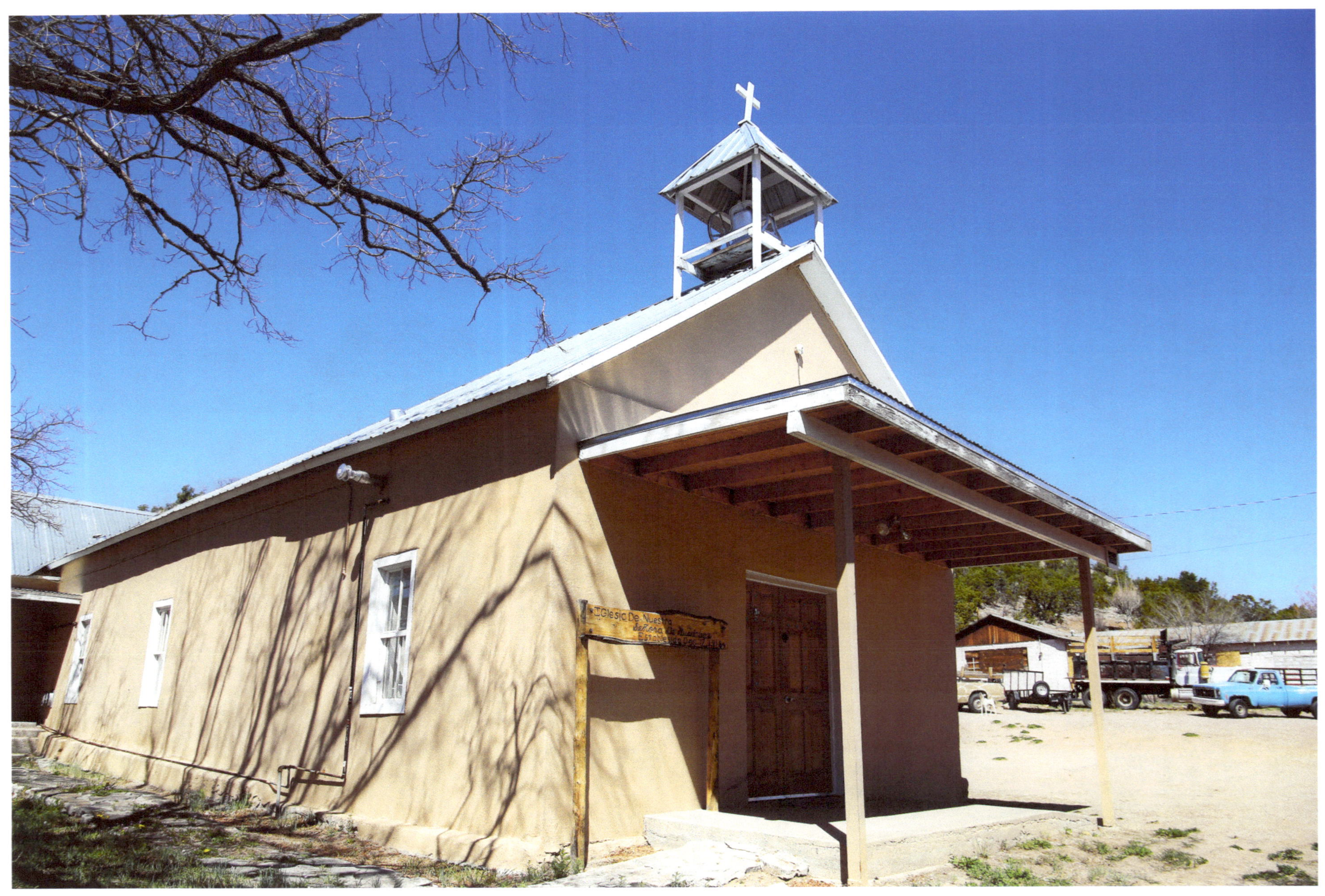

Iglesia (Catholic Church) de Nuestra Señora de Guadalupe, La Madera, Rio Arriba County. 1918. "La Madera" means the wood, and this area is well wooded. At the junction of New Mexico highways 111 and 519. Photograph taken in 2021.

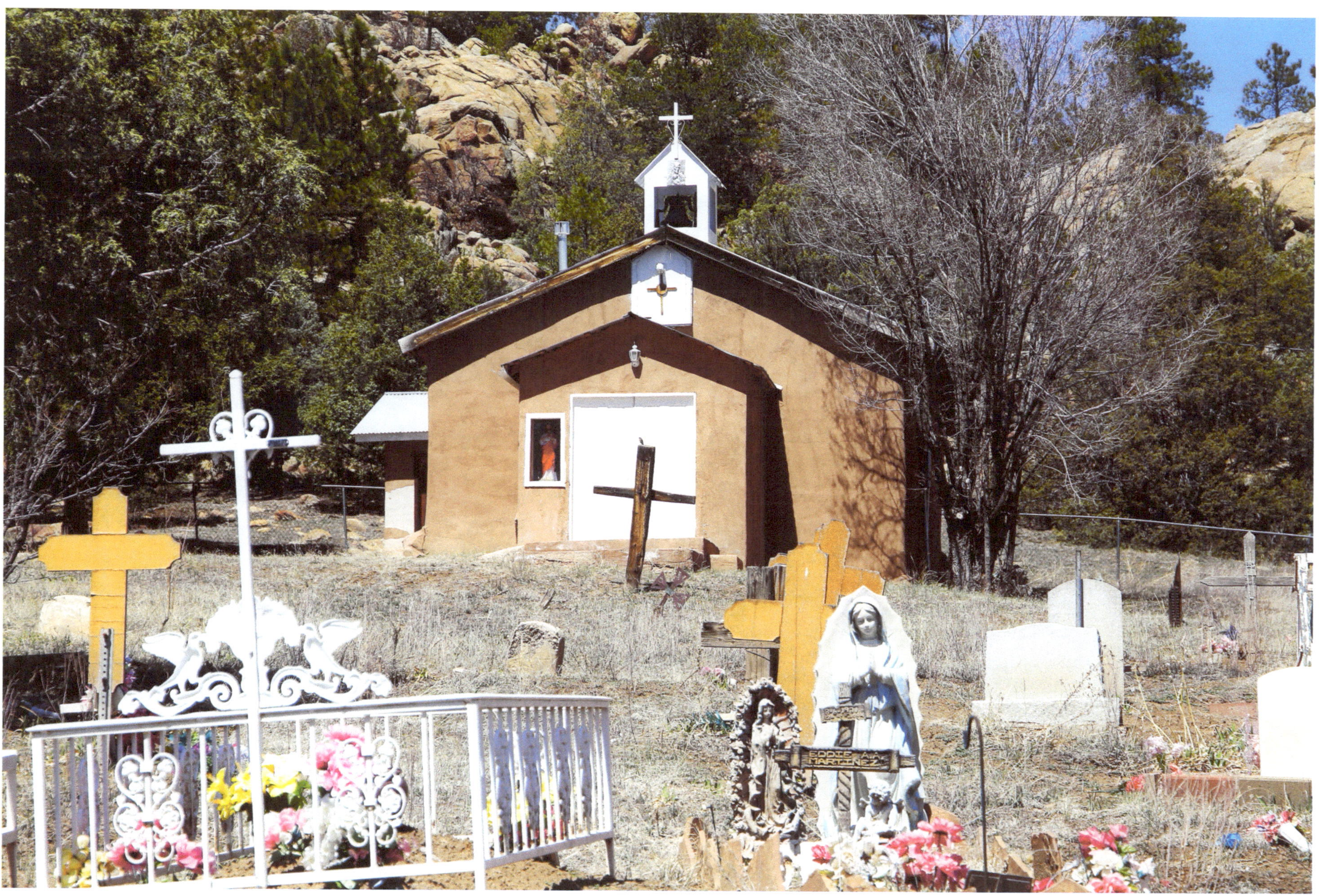

San Luis Gonzalo Catholic Church, Las Tablas, Rio Arriba County. 1899. This traditional adobe church has a colorful cemetery in front with many more monuments and statues than are shown here. On County Road 271 less than a mile west of New Mexico Highway 519. Photograph taken in 2021.

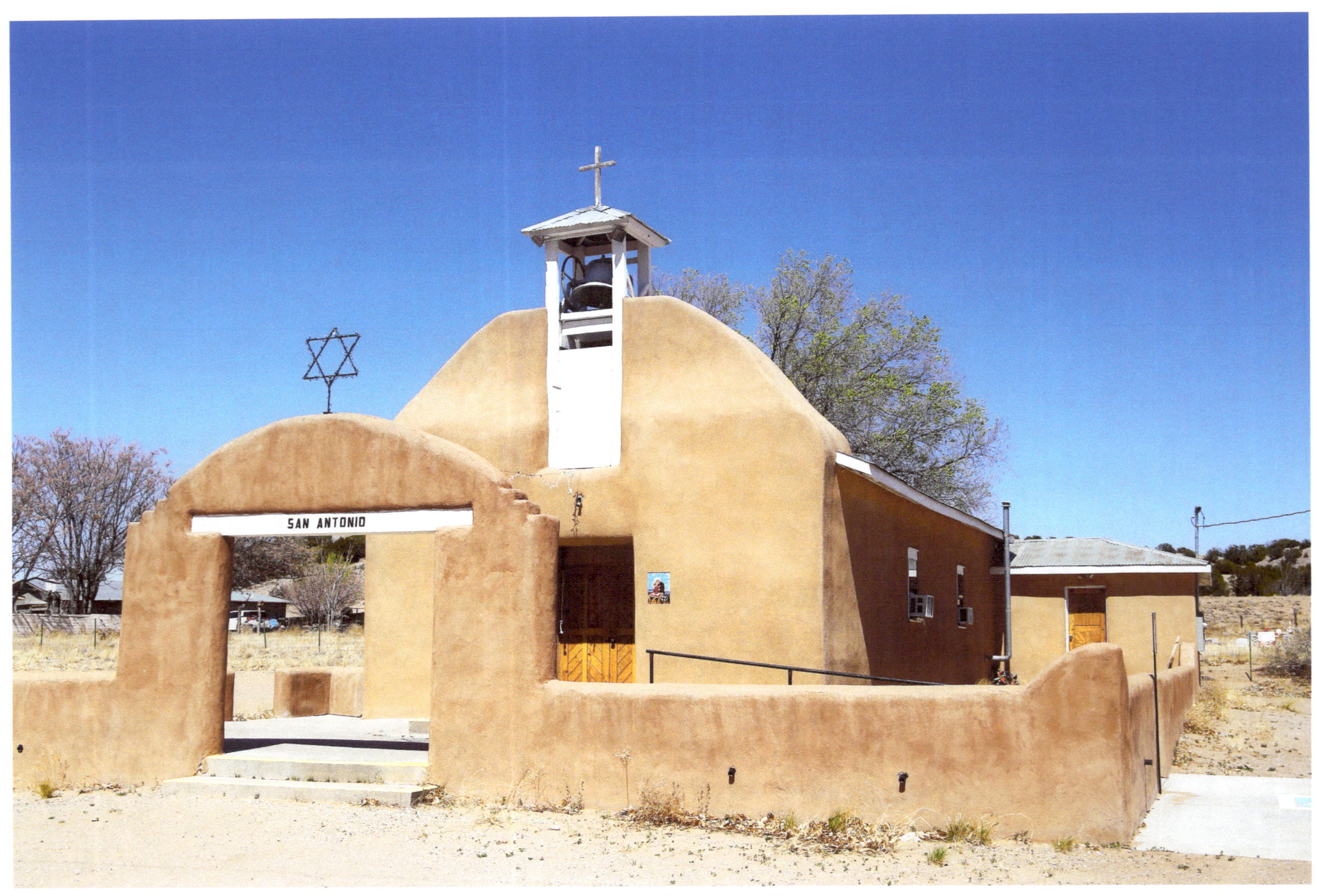

San Antonio de Padua Catholic Church, Medanales, Rio Arriba County. 1950. The adobe church is quite traditional despite its relative recency. From U.S. Highway 84 take New Mexico Highway 233 north across the Chama River, then half a mile west on County Road 142. Photograph taken in 2021.

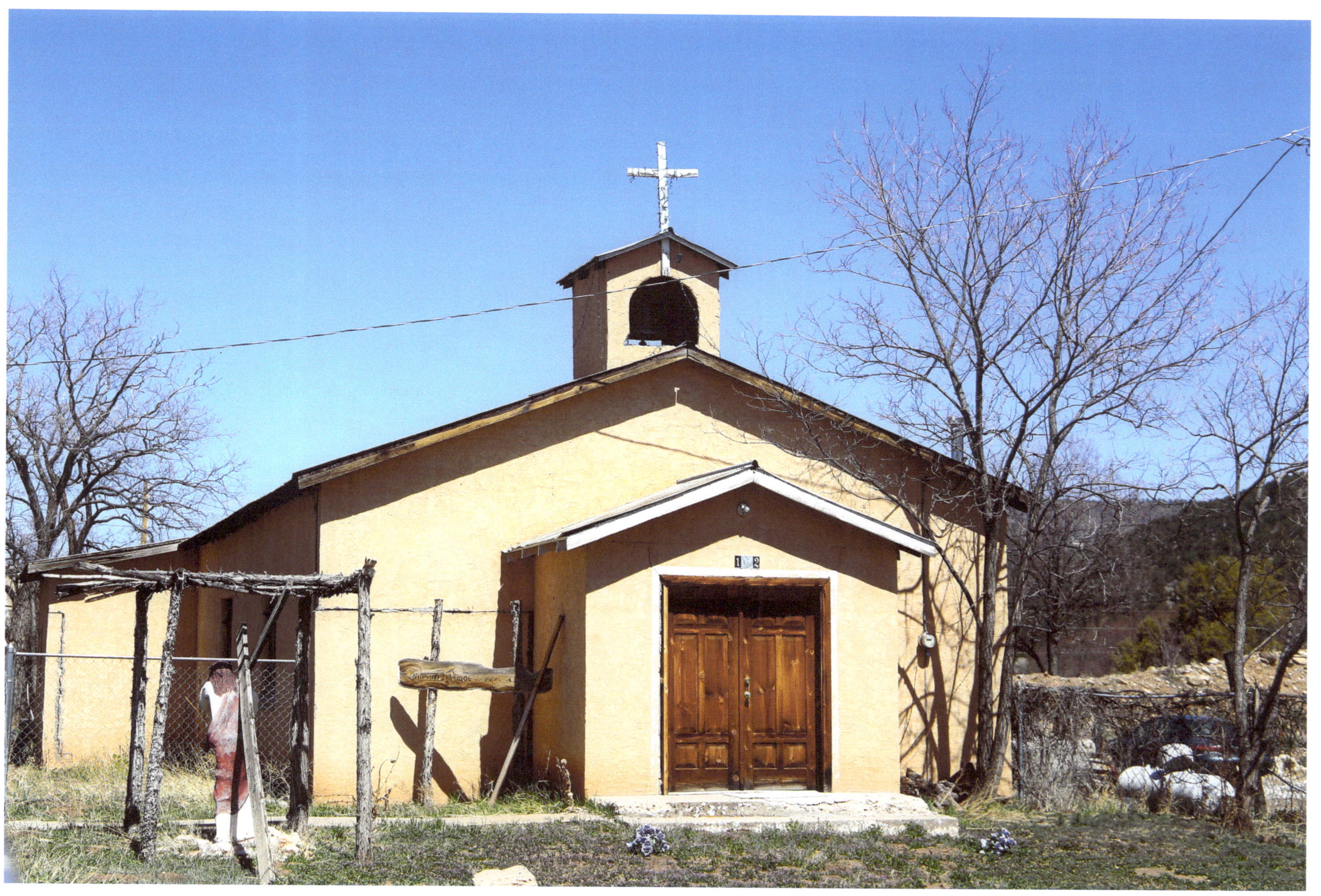

Divina Pastura (Divine Shepherdess) Catholic Church, Petaca, Rio Arriba County. 1950. At the lower left of the image a figure of Christ is carrying a cross. About ten miles north of La Madera on New Mexico Highway 519. Photograph taken in 2021.

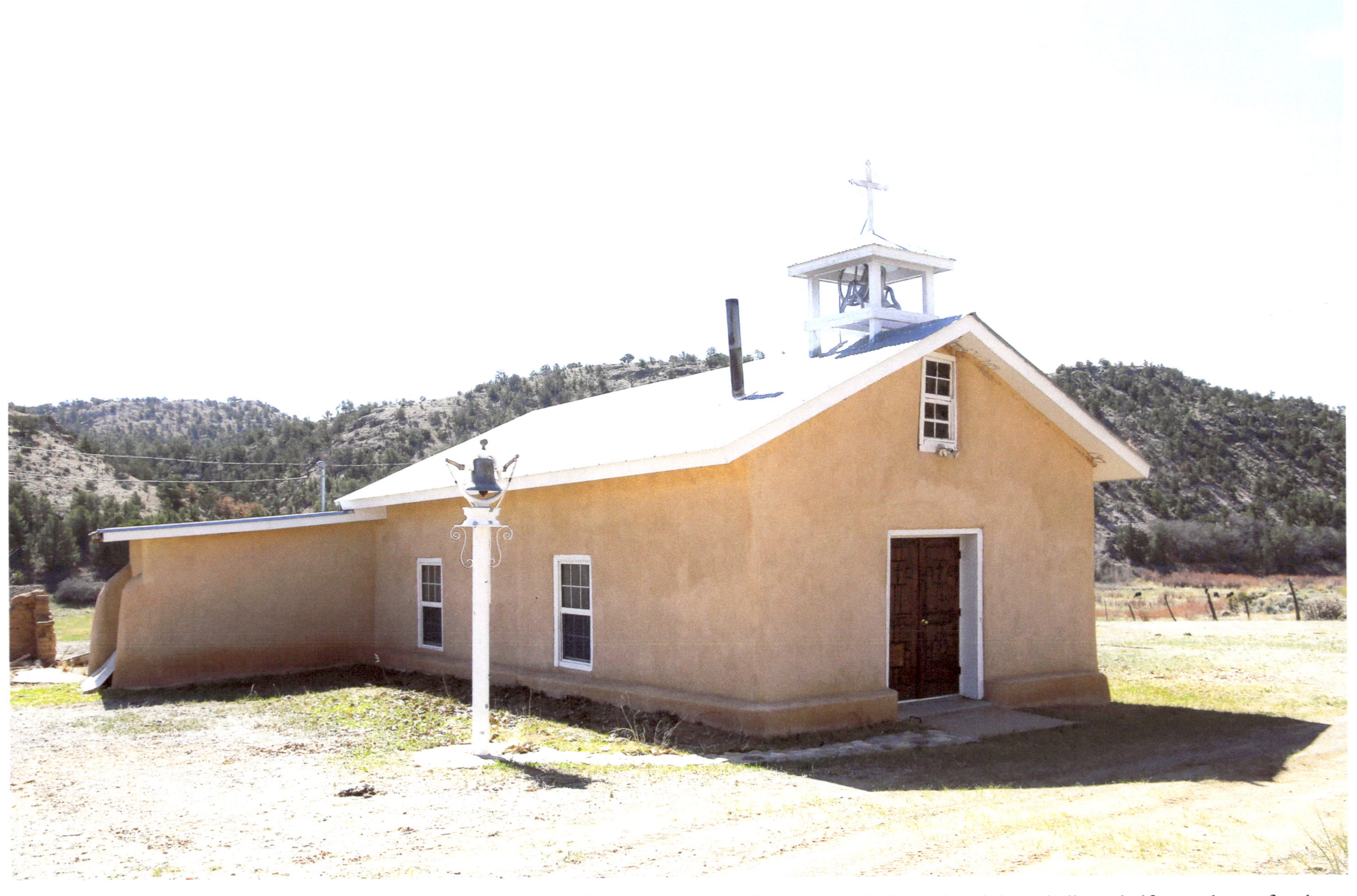

San Antonio de Padua Catholic Church, Servilleta Plaza, Rio Arriba County. 1880. This renovated adobe church has a bell in a belfry on the roof and one in a separate bell tower. Take New Mexico Highway 519 about 3.5 miles north of La Madera, then right 2.5 miles on Forest Road 376. Photograph taken in 2021.

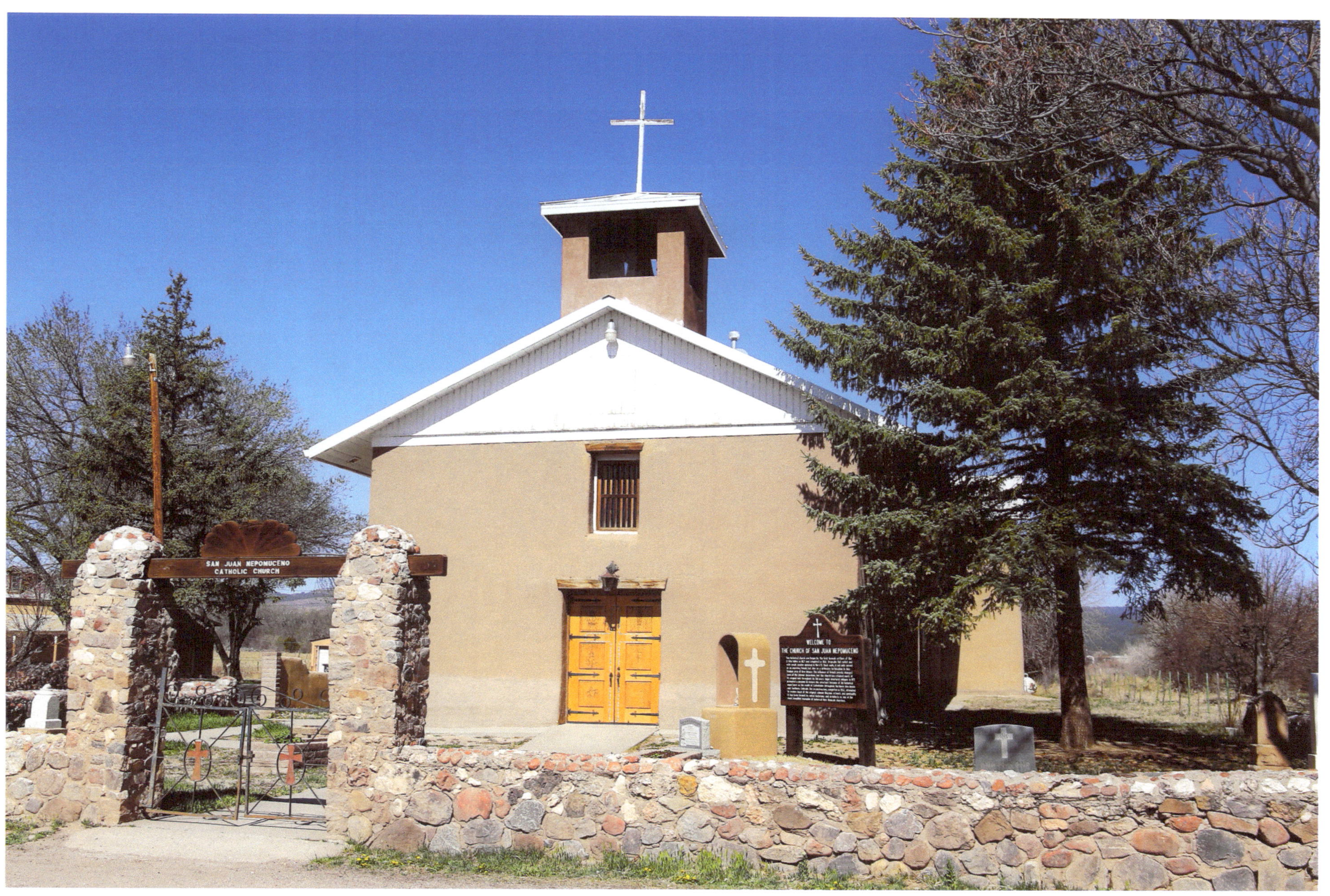

San Juan Nepomucemo Catholic Church, El Rito, Rio Arriba County. 1827–1832. The reconstruction of this handsome adobe church was completed in 1982, and includes an altar screen created by contemporary *santera* Marie Romero Cash. The church is on New Mexico Highway 554. Photograph taken in 2021.

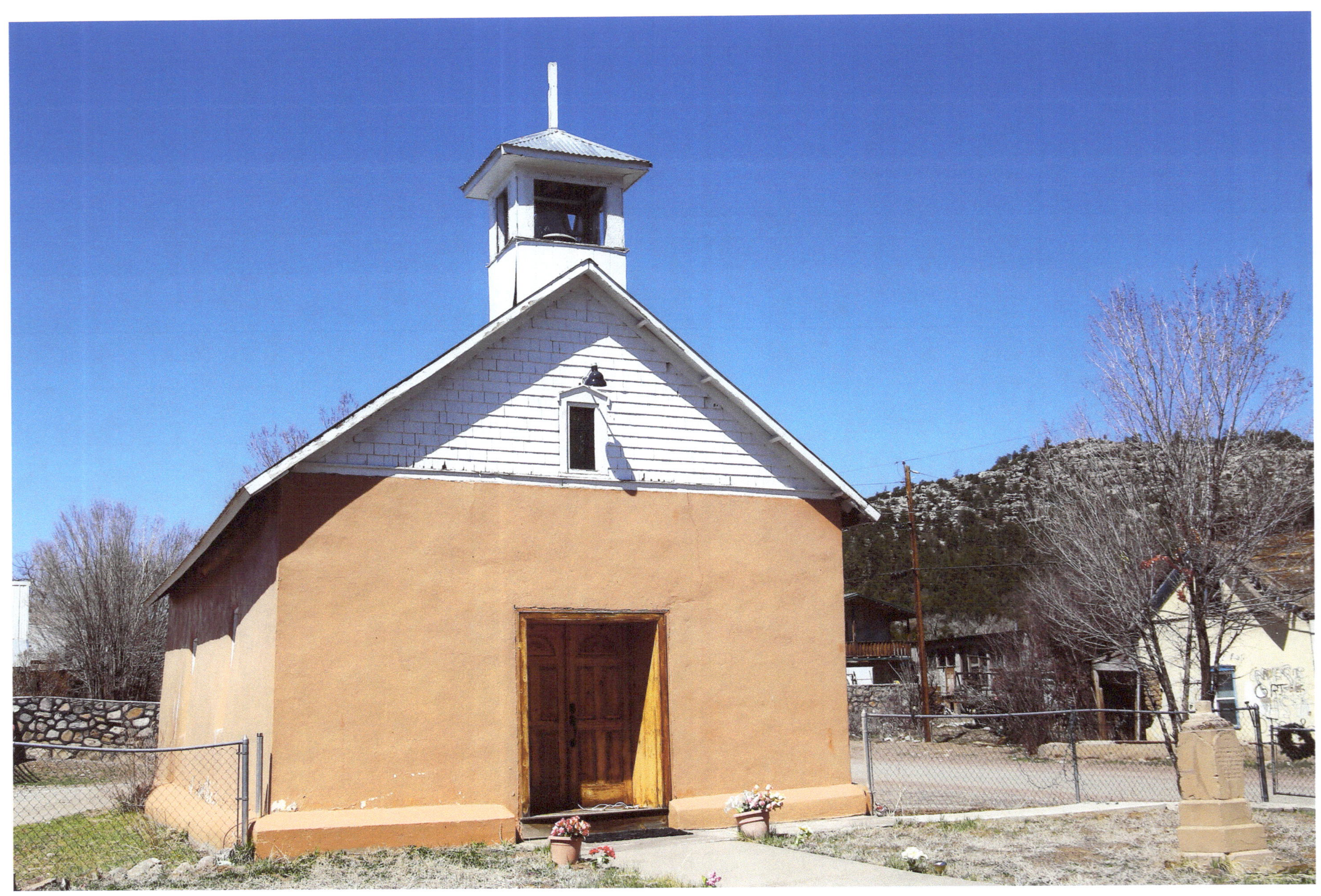

Nuestra Señora de Dolores Catholic Church, Vallecitos, Rio Arriba County. 1880. This traditional adobe church is about 15 miles north of La Madera, just west of New Mexico Highway 111 in the village center. Photograph taken in 2021.

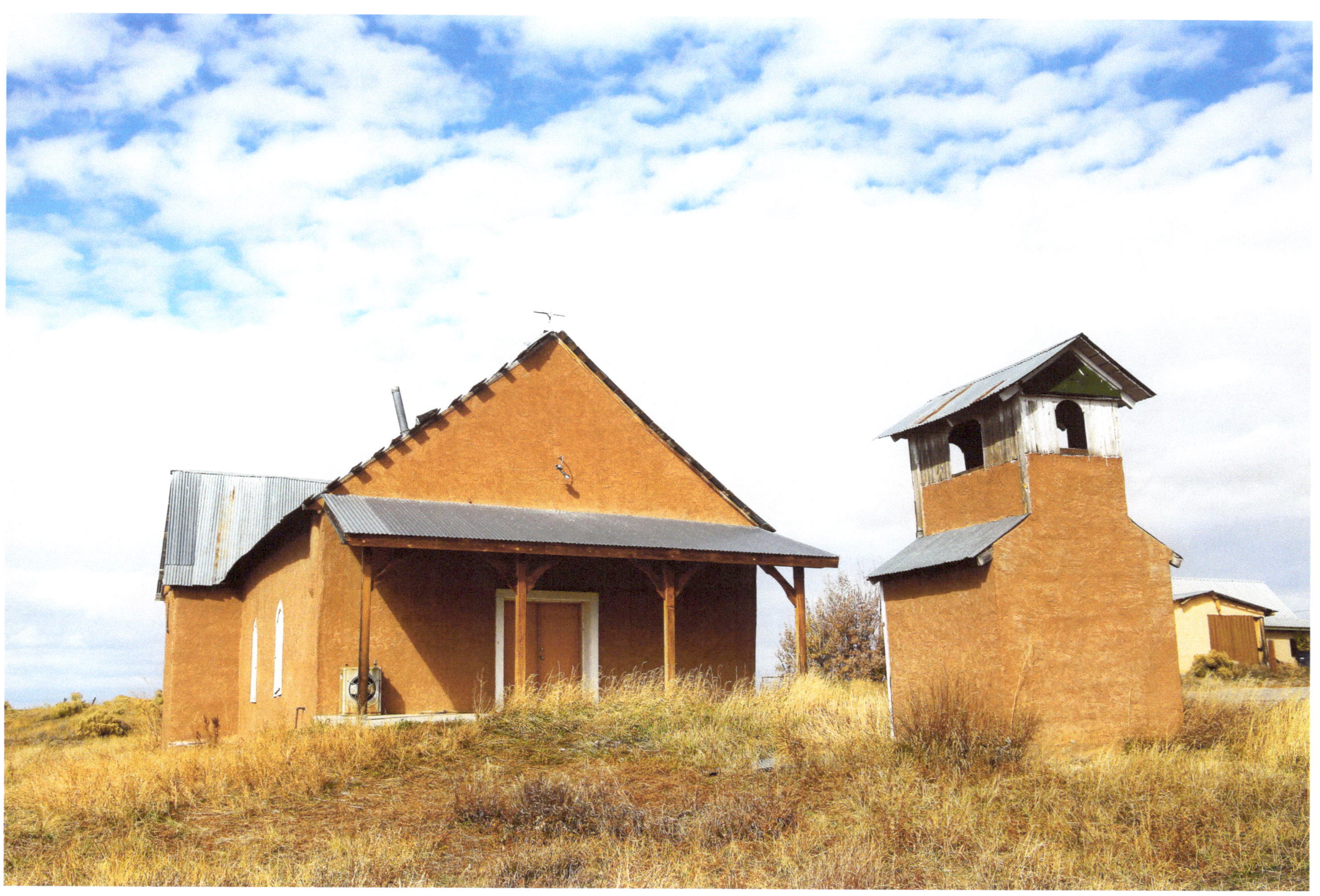

San Joaquin Catholic Church, Ensenada, Rio Arriba County. Around 1910. The adobe church has a separate bell tower. The building has been condemned and might not survive much longer. Take New Mexico Highway 162 to New Mexico Highway 573 3.3 miles to the church. Photograph taken in 2021.

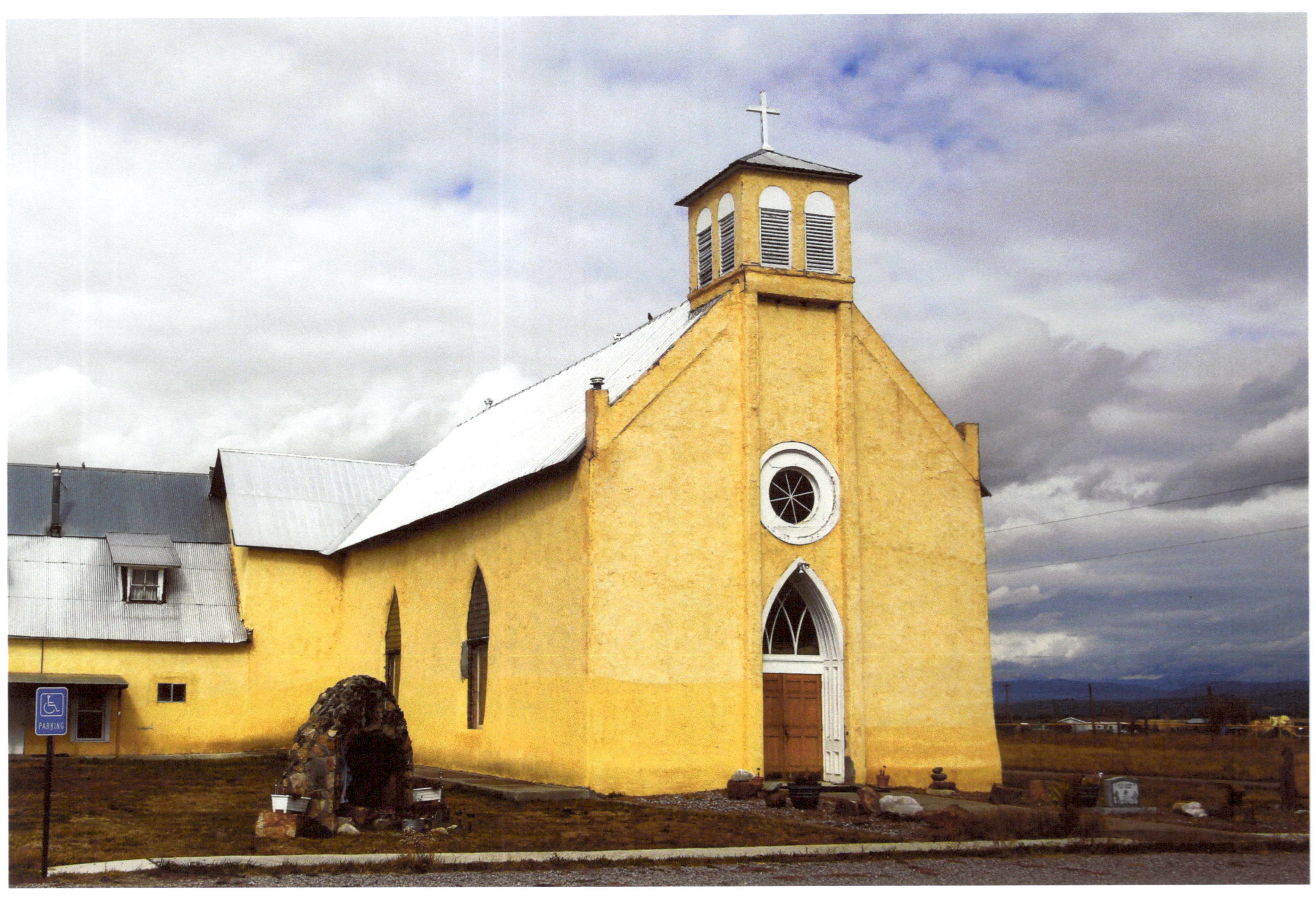

Santo Niño Catholic Church, Tierra Amarilla, Rio Arriba County. 1907. The adobe church has neo-Gothic elements. From New Mexico Highway 531 take New Mexico Highway 162 then left on County Road 323. Photograph taken in 2021.

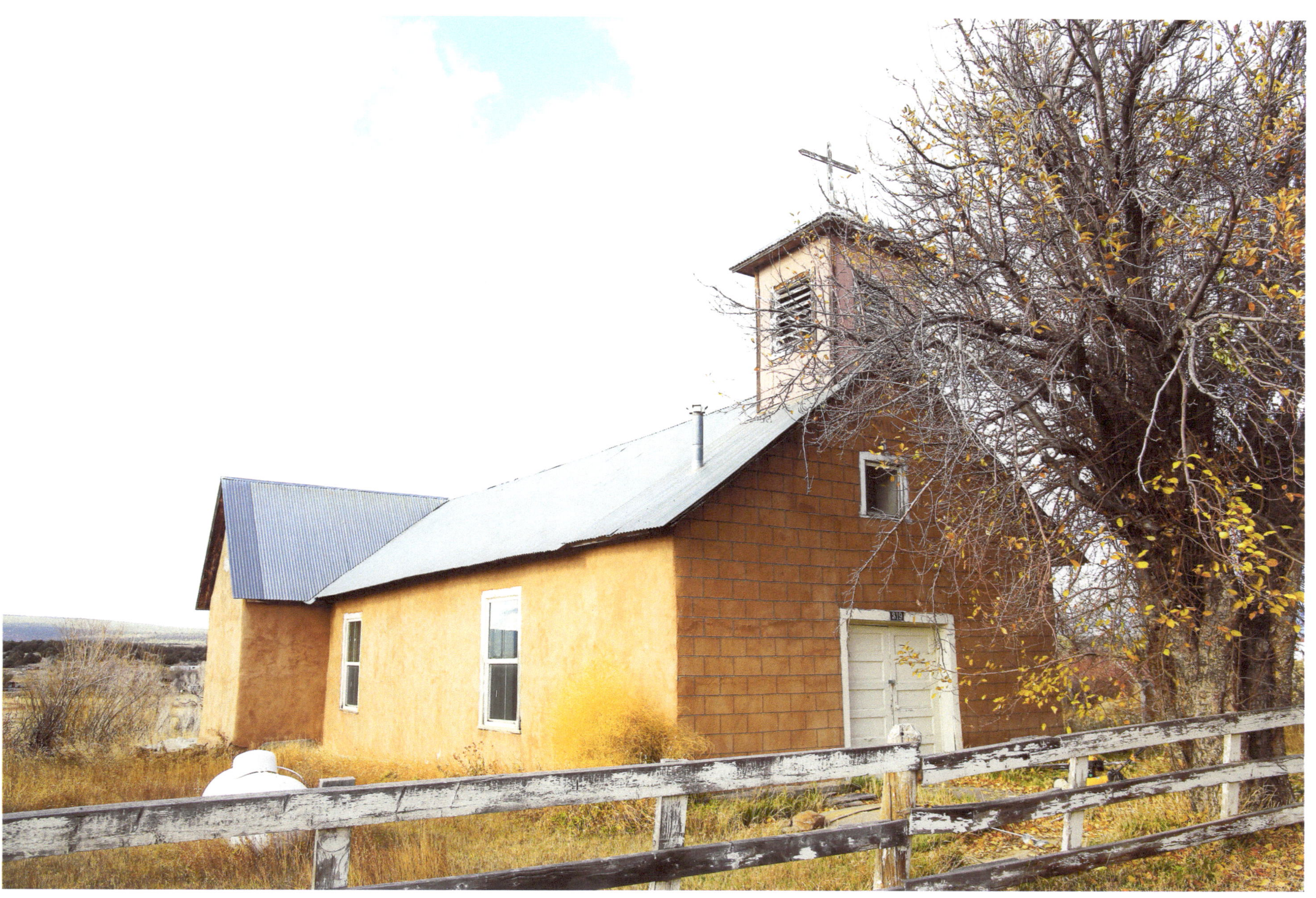

San Miguel Catholic Church, La Puente, Rio Arriba County. 1914. Notice the uncovered adobe bricks on the front of the church. From U.S. Highway 84/64 take New Mexico Highway 531 east to New Mexico Highway 112 then 1.2 miles to the church. Photograph taken in 2021.

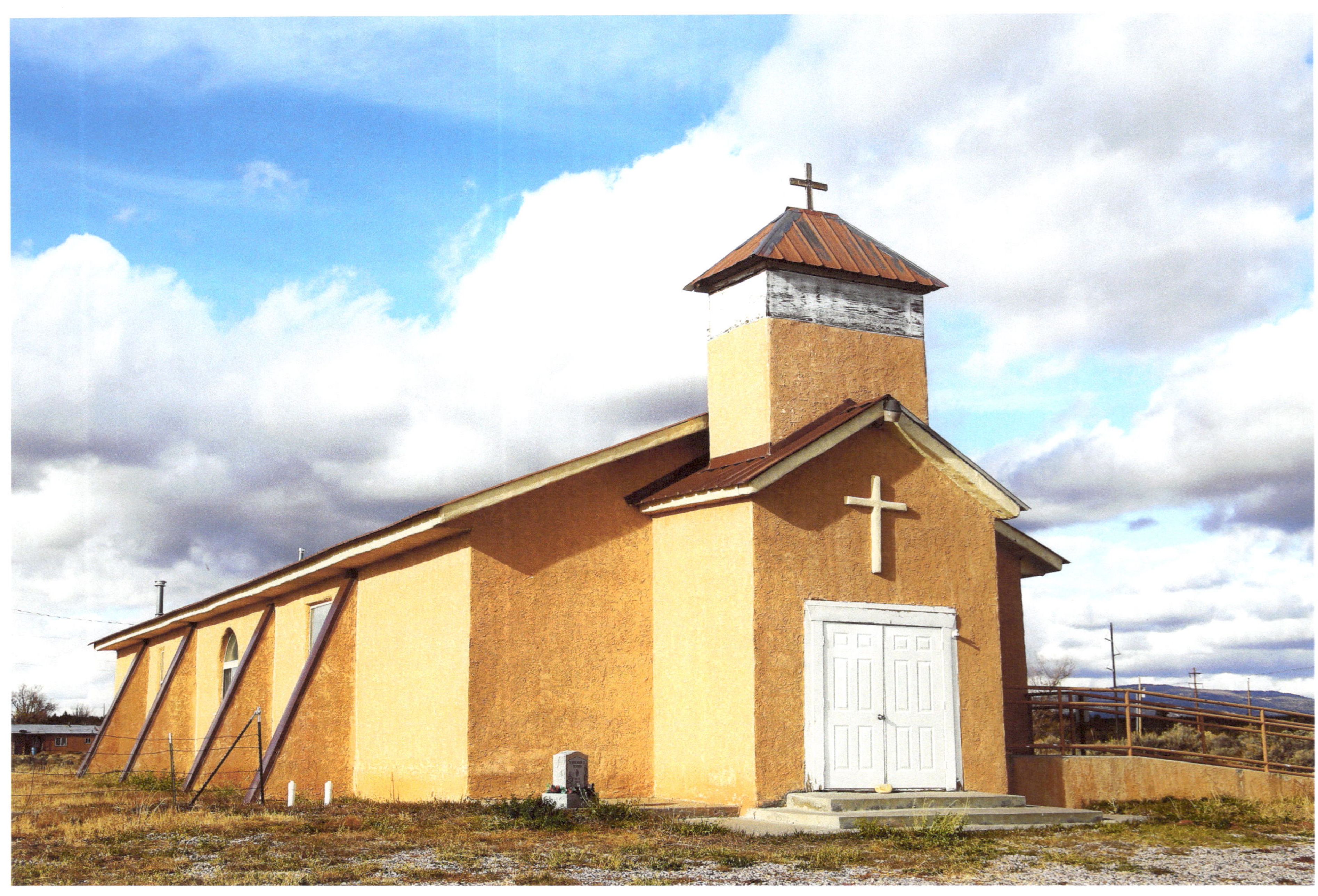

Santo Niño Catholic Church, Cebolla, Rio Arriba County. 1949. This church replaced a more-beautiful adobe church, demolished in 1945, the subject of a famous painting by Georgia O'Keeffe. On County Road 310 just off U.S. Highway 84. Photograph taken in 2021.

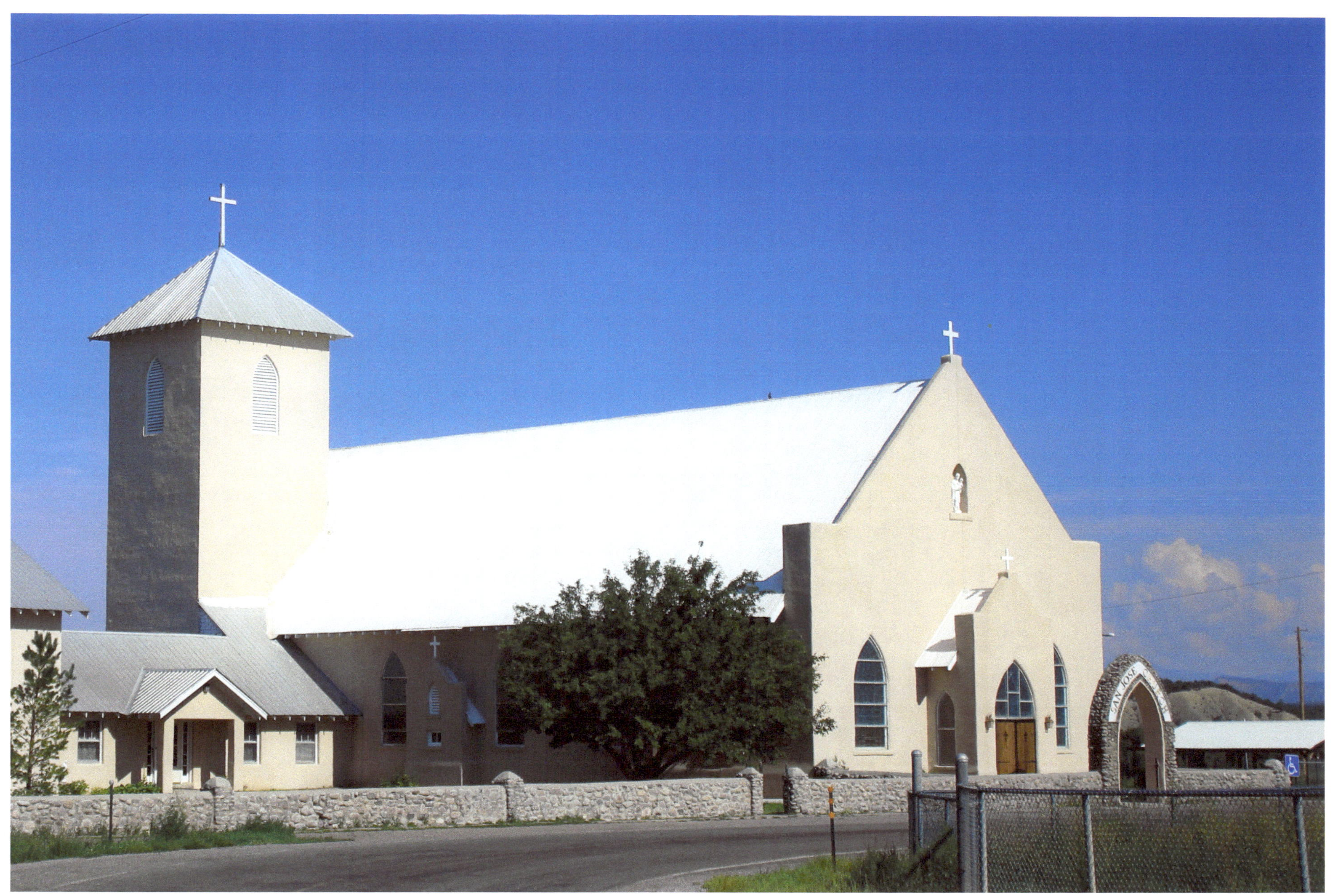

San José Catholic Church, Los Ojos, Rio Arriba County. 1935–1950. The original church, built in 1883, was demolished in 1930. Beginning in 1935, it was rebuilt, but not completed until 1950. On New Mexico Highway 514. Photograph taken in 2013.

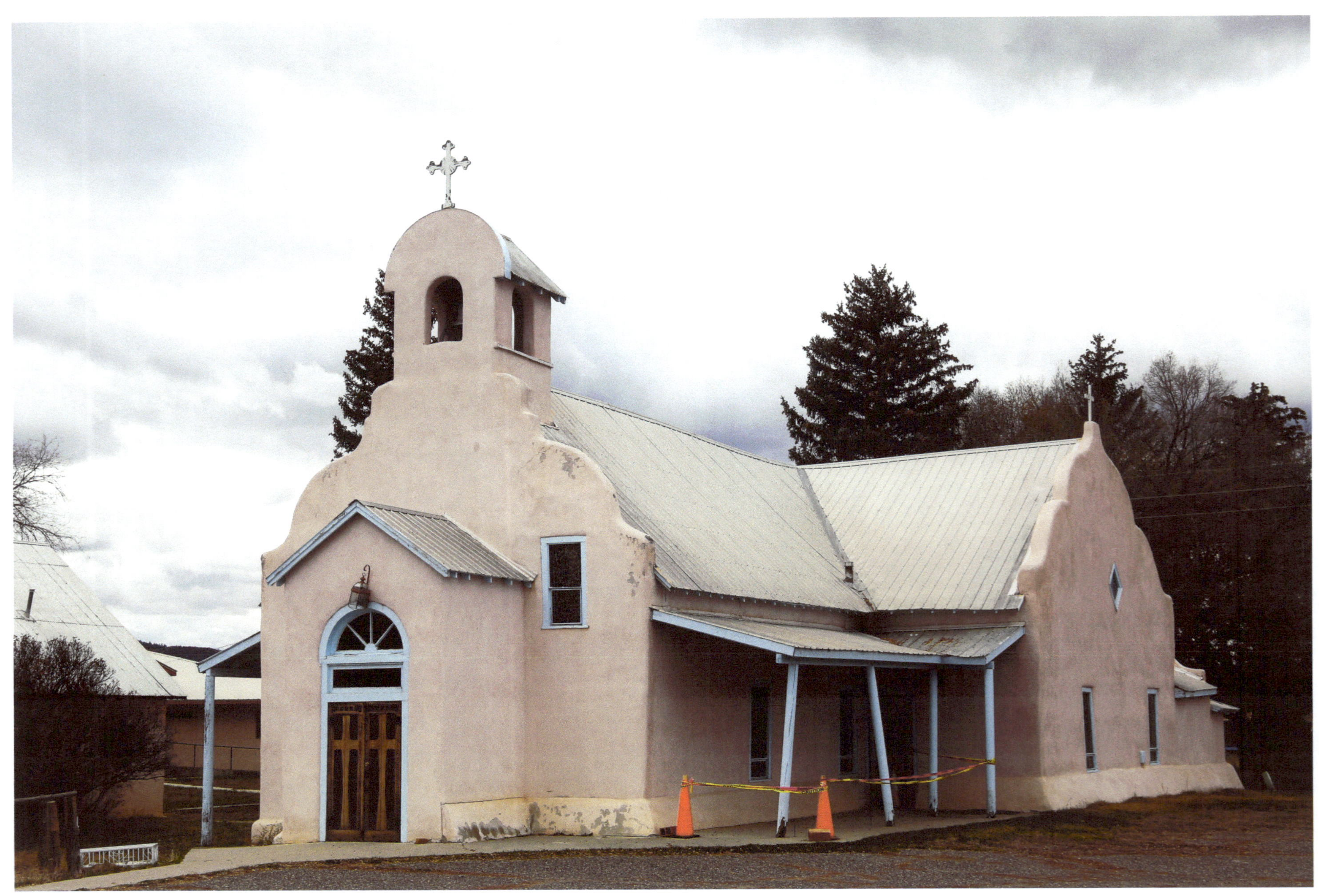

St. Francis of Assisi Catholic Church, Lumberton, Rio Arriba County. Around 1915. This adobe church in the California mission style was being used and was undergoing restoration as of 2021. From U.S. Highway 64 turn left on County Road 356. Photograph taken in 2021.

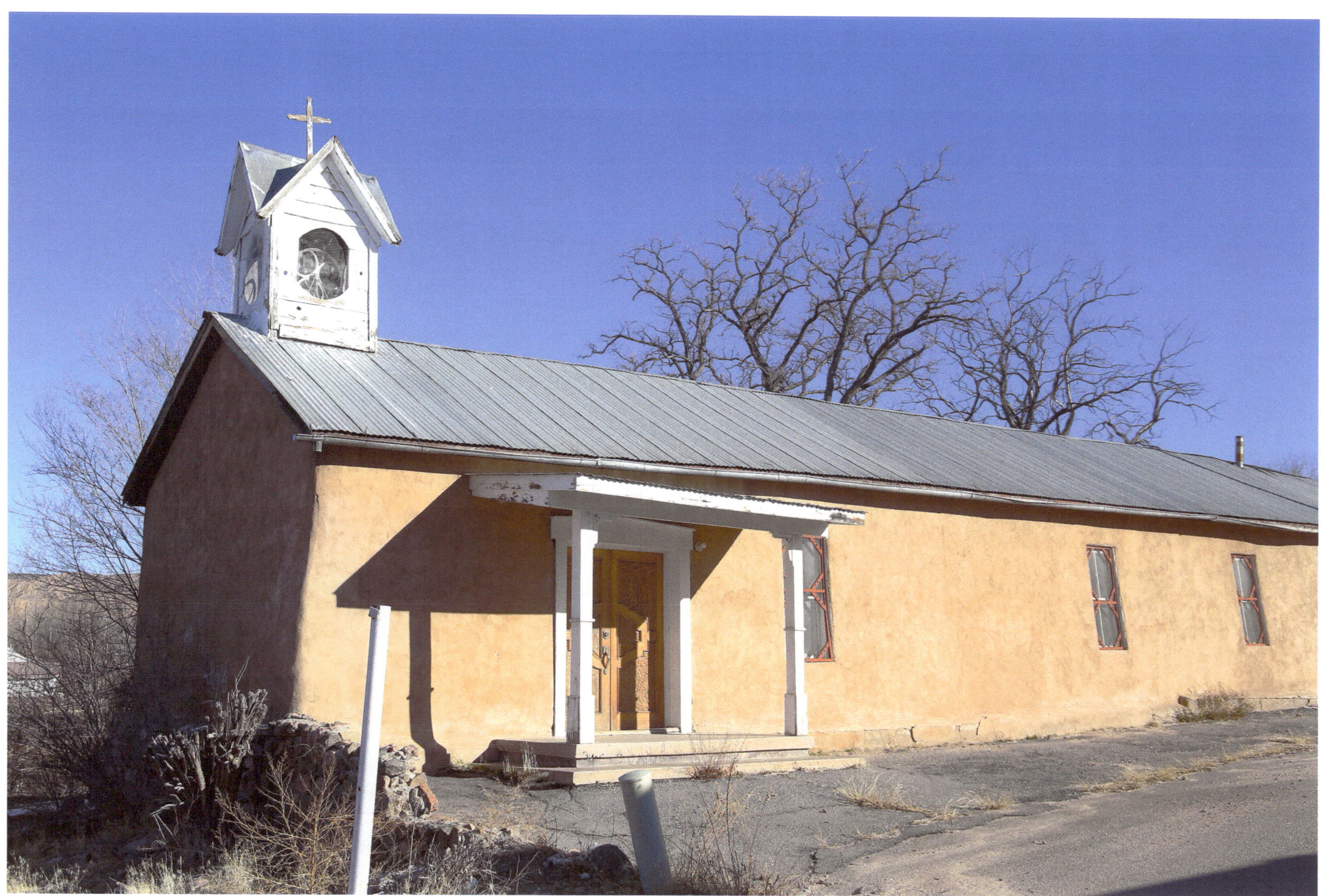

Our Lady of Mt. Carmel Catholic Church, Chimayó, Rio Arriba County. 1840. Chimayó straddles the Rio Arriba-Santa Fe county line, and this adobe church, with the entrance unusually on the side rather than the front, is just on the Rio Arriba County side. On Road 101 off New Mexico Highway 76. Photograph taken in 2020.

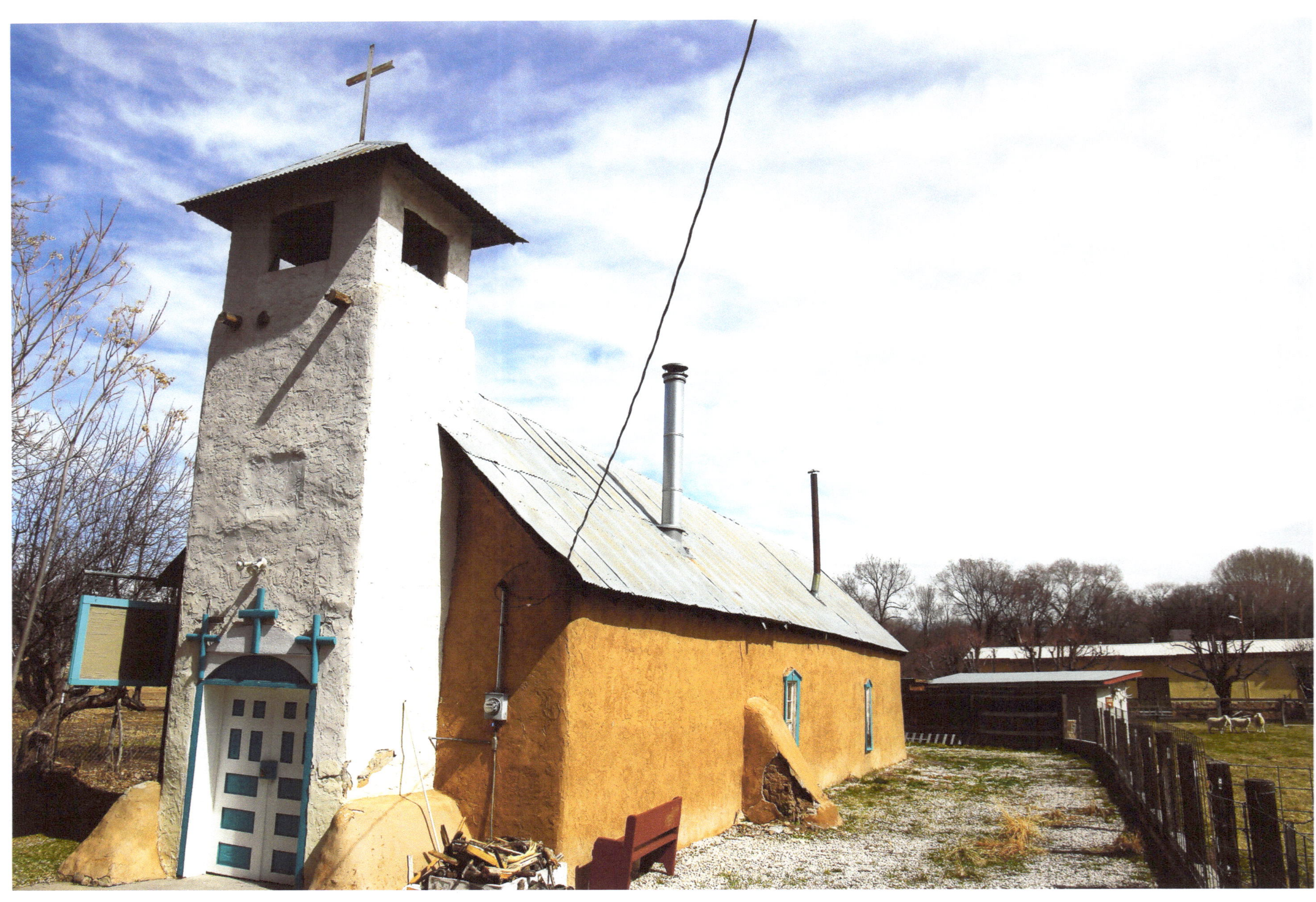

Catholic Chapel of Nuestra Señora de Dolores, Chimayó, Rio Arriba County. Around 1840. This small adobe chapel is just south of New Mexico Highway 76 slightly east of the Holy Family Church (1967, not illustrated), which is on the north side of the highway. Photograph taken in 2019.

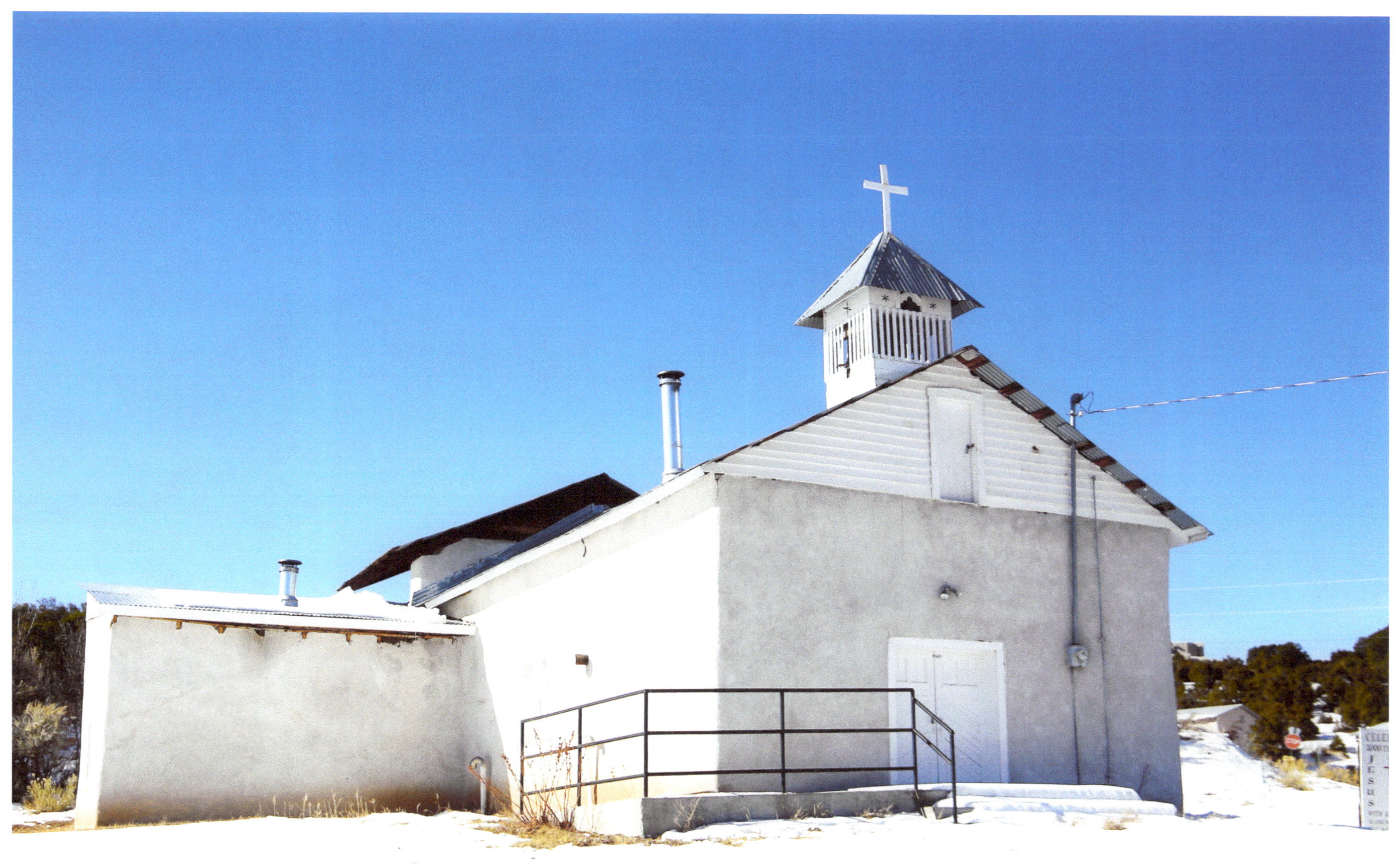

Santo Tomás Catholic Church, Ojo Sarco, Rio Arriba County. 1886. Despite having no windows in the façade, this adobe church is quite attractive. Near the junction of county roads 69 and 73. Photograph taken in 2020.

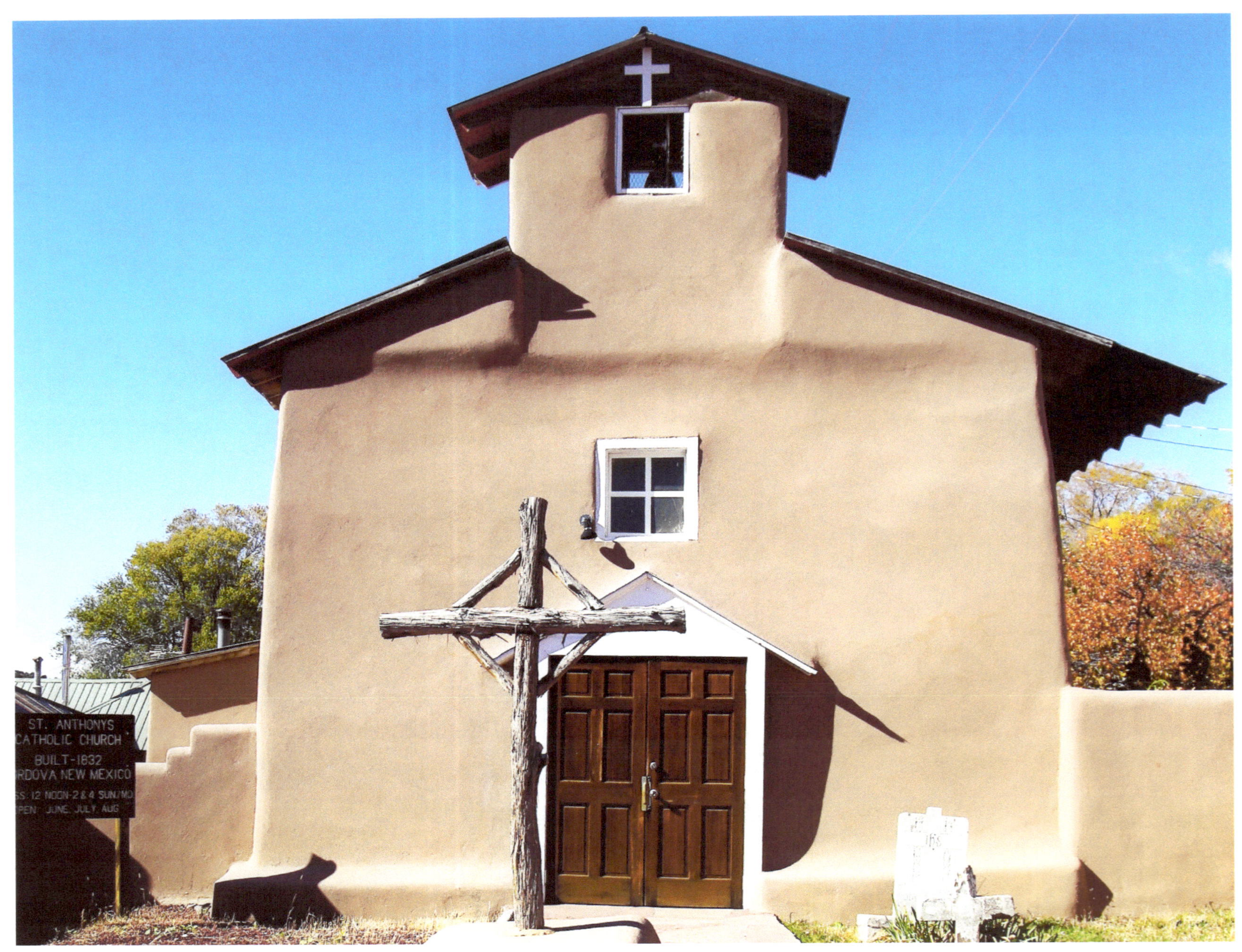

San Antonio de Padua Catholic Church, Córdova, Rio Arriba County. 1832. This iconic adobe church is at 185 County Road 80, off New Mexico Highway 76. Photograph taken in 2022.

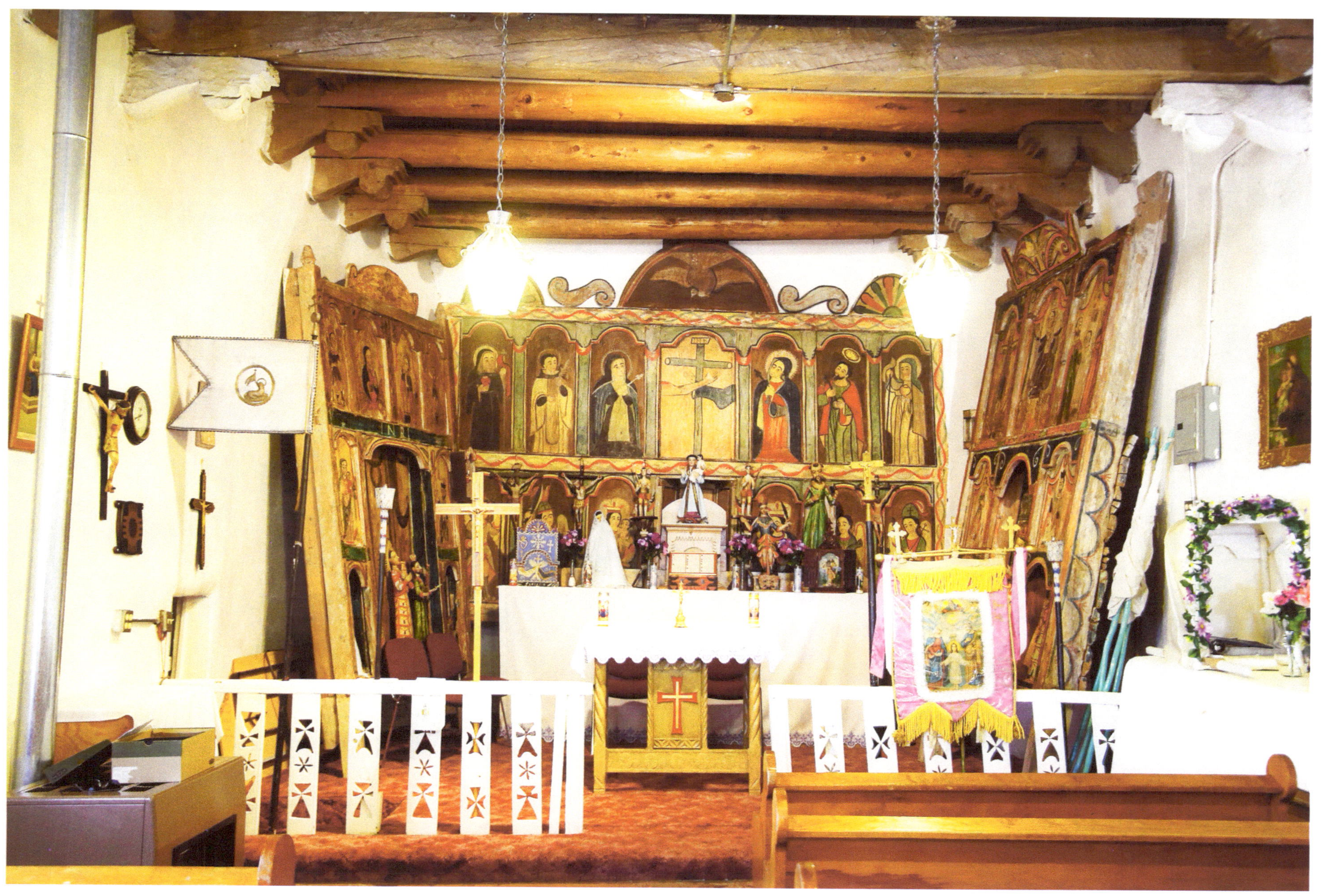

Interior of San Antonio de Padua. The recently restored church contains three altar screens painted in the 1830s by famous *santero* Rafael Aragon (1796–1862). Photograph taken in 2024.

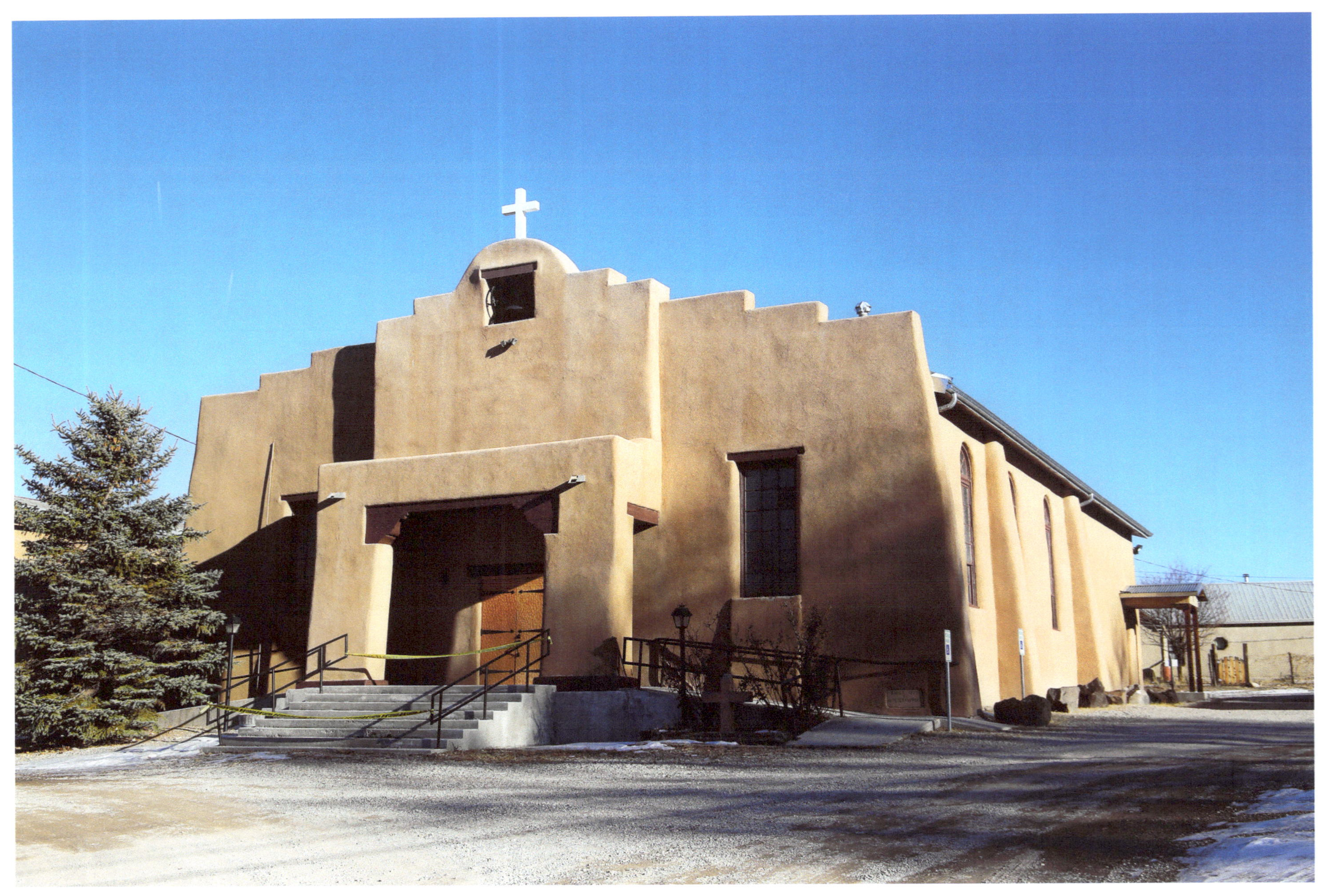

San Antonio de Padua Catholic Church, Dixon, Rio Arriba County. 1929. This large adobe church in the California Mission style is on New Mexico Highway 75 about three miles east of New Mexico Highway 68. Photograph taken in 2021.

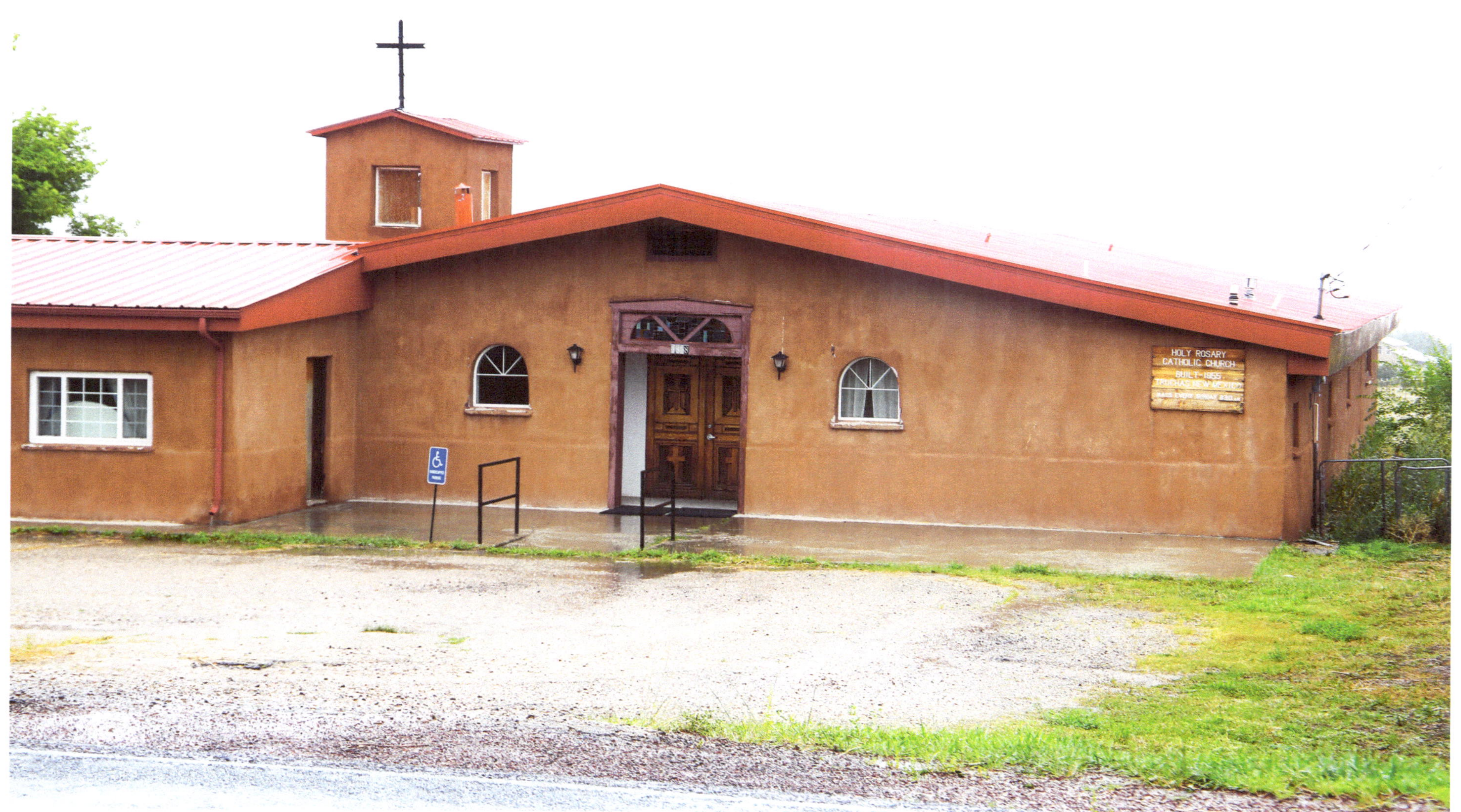

Holy Rosary Catholic Church, Truchas, Rio Arriba County. 1955. The expectation was that this would become the parish church for the historic churches in Truchas and Córdova, but Holy Family Catholic Church in Chimayó, completed in 1967, is now the parish church. On New Mexico Highway 76 less than half a mile north of its ninety-degree turn in Truchas. Photograph taken in 2024.

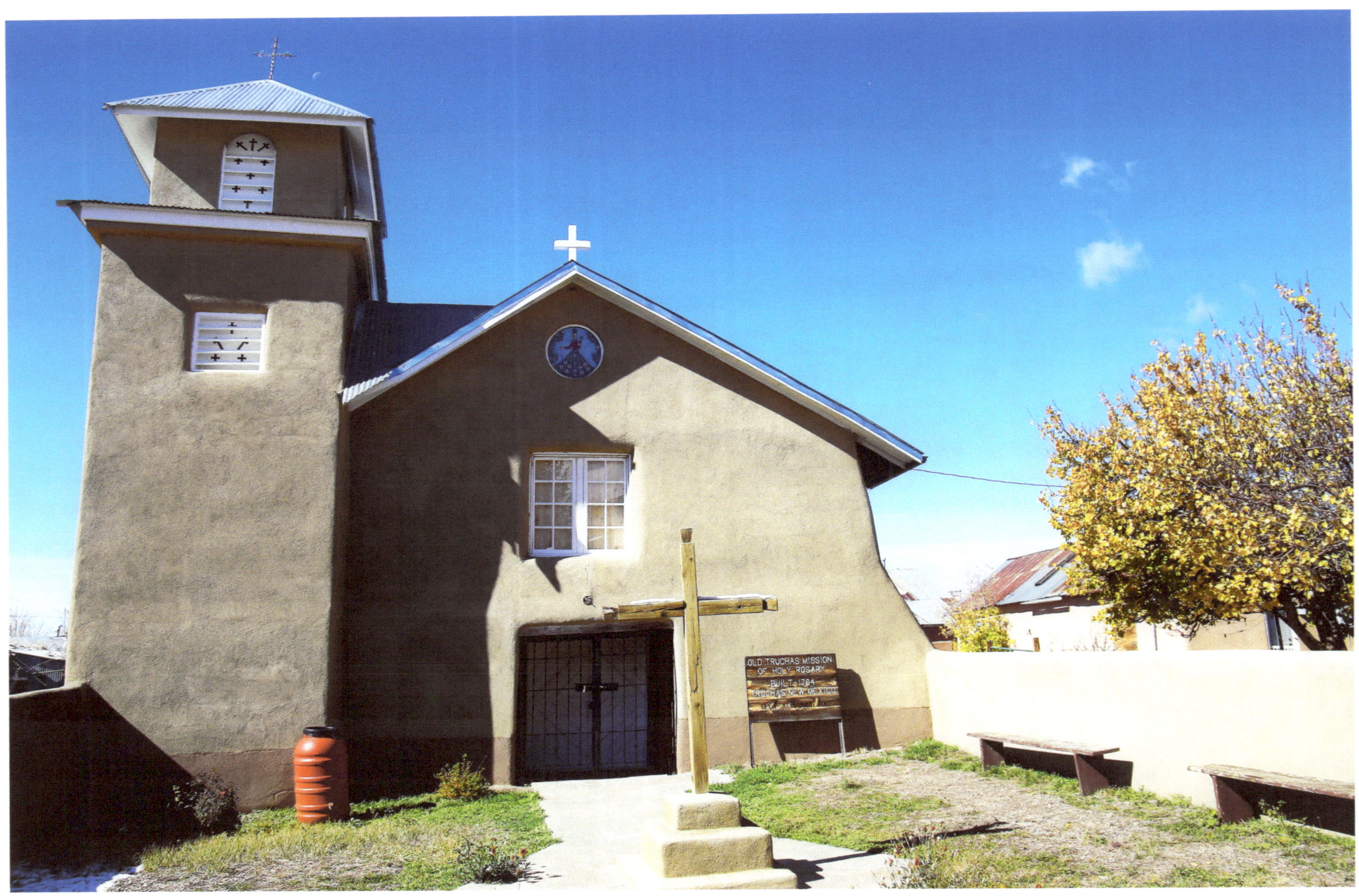

Nuestra Señora del Sagrado Rosario Catholic Church, Truchas, Rio Arriba County. The sign on the adobe church says it was built in 1764, but other sources suggest it was built around 1805. Conversations with the *mayordomo* and *mayordoma* suggest it was built in the late 1700s. Notice that the stucco was removed from the lower two feet of the walls to allow the adobe to breathe. Truchas means trout (plural) in Spanish. At 37 County Road 75. Photograph taken in 2018.

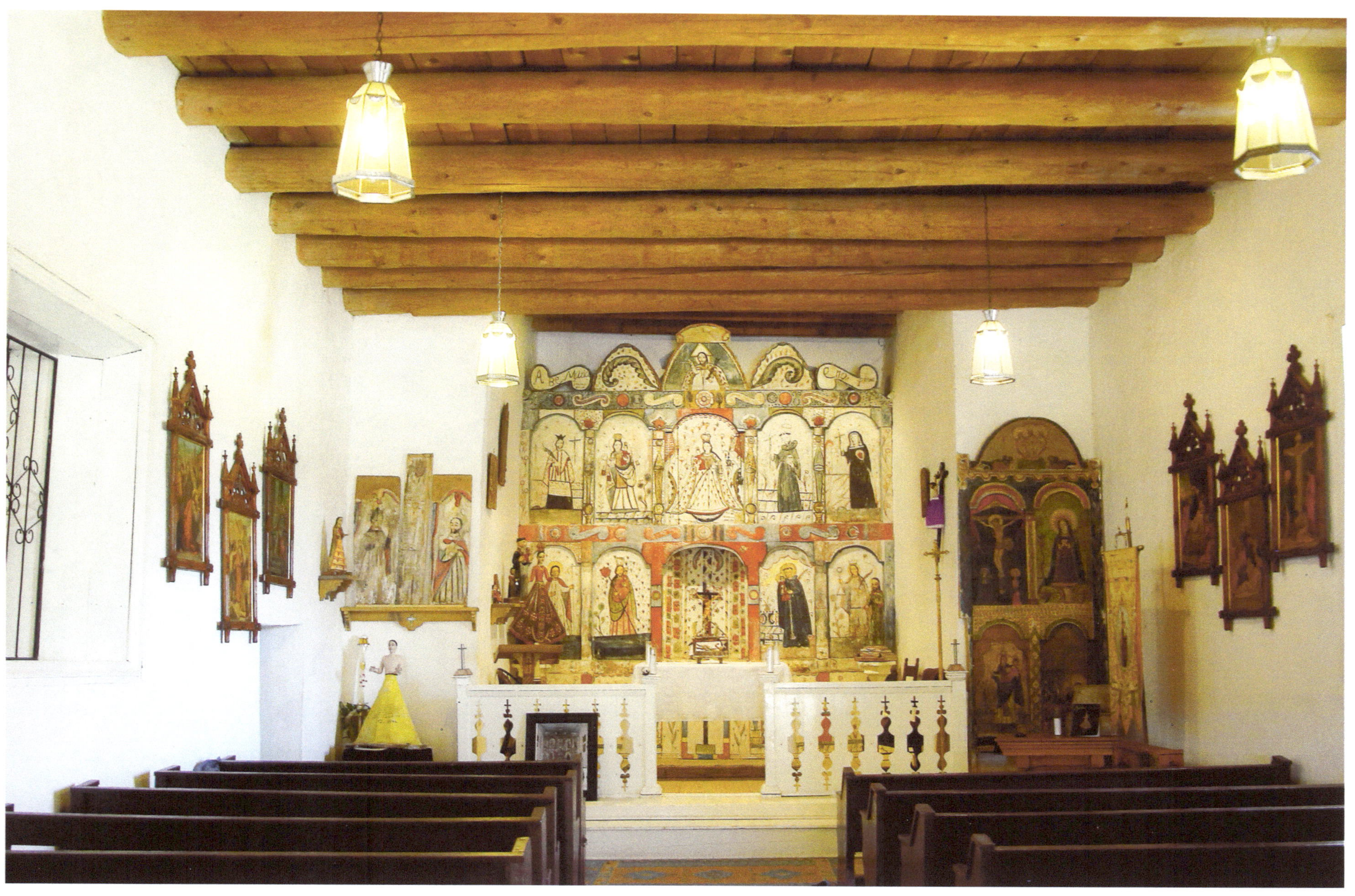

Interior of Nuestra Señora del Sagrado Rosario. Recently restored, the artwork is quite remarkable. The main altar screen was painted by *santero* Pedro Antonio Fresquis (1749–1831) around 1821. Photograph taken in 2024.

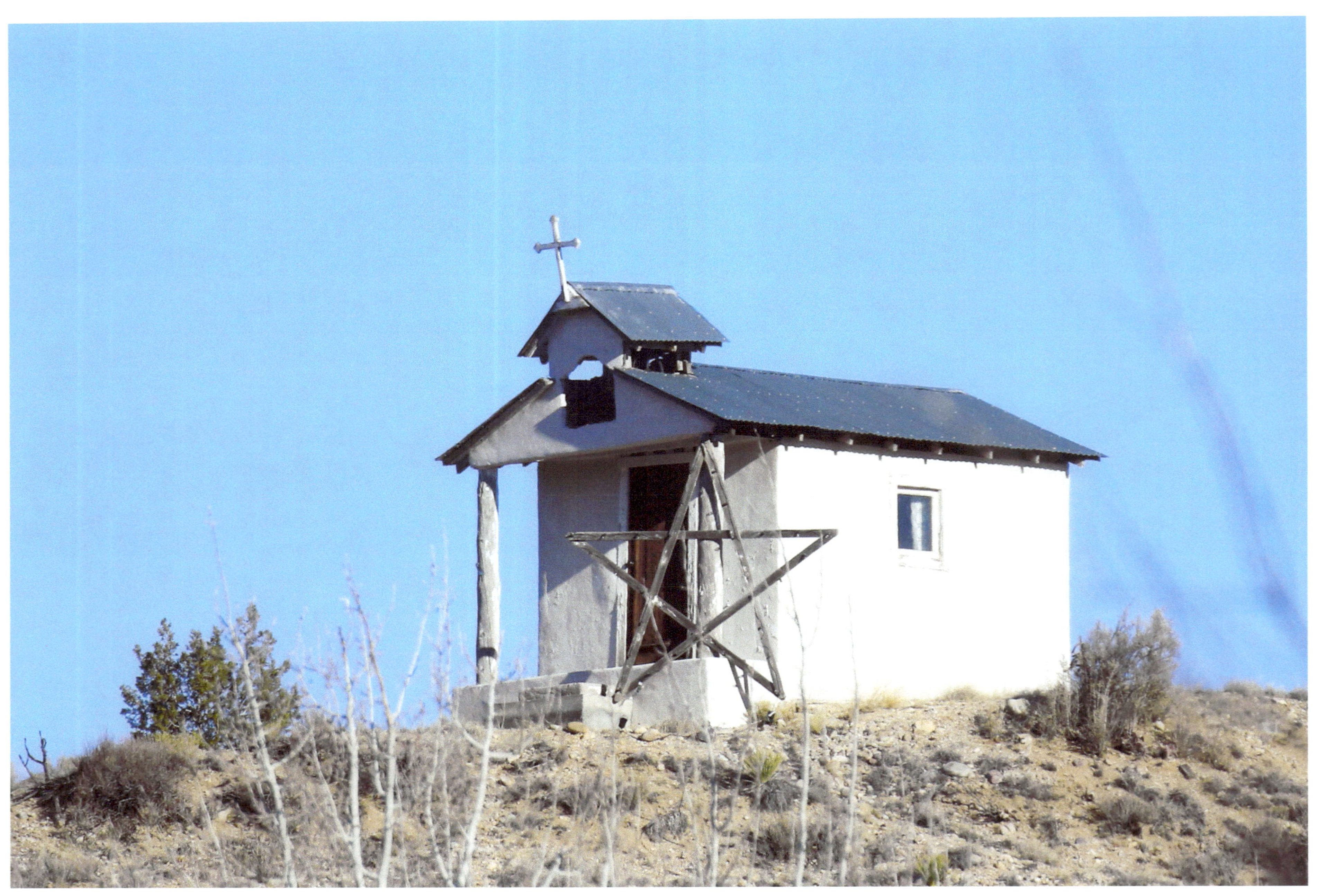

Capilla de Santa Rita, near La Puebla, Rio Arriba County. 1929. The small private chapel is on private property. It can be seen from Road 1431 off New Mexico Highway 76. Photograph taken in 2020.

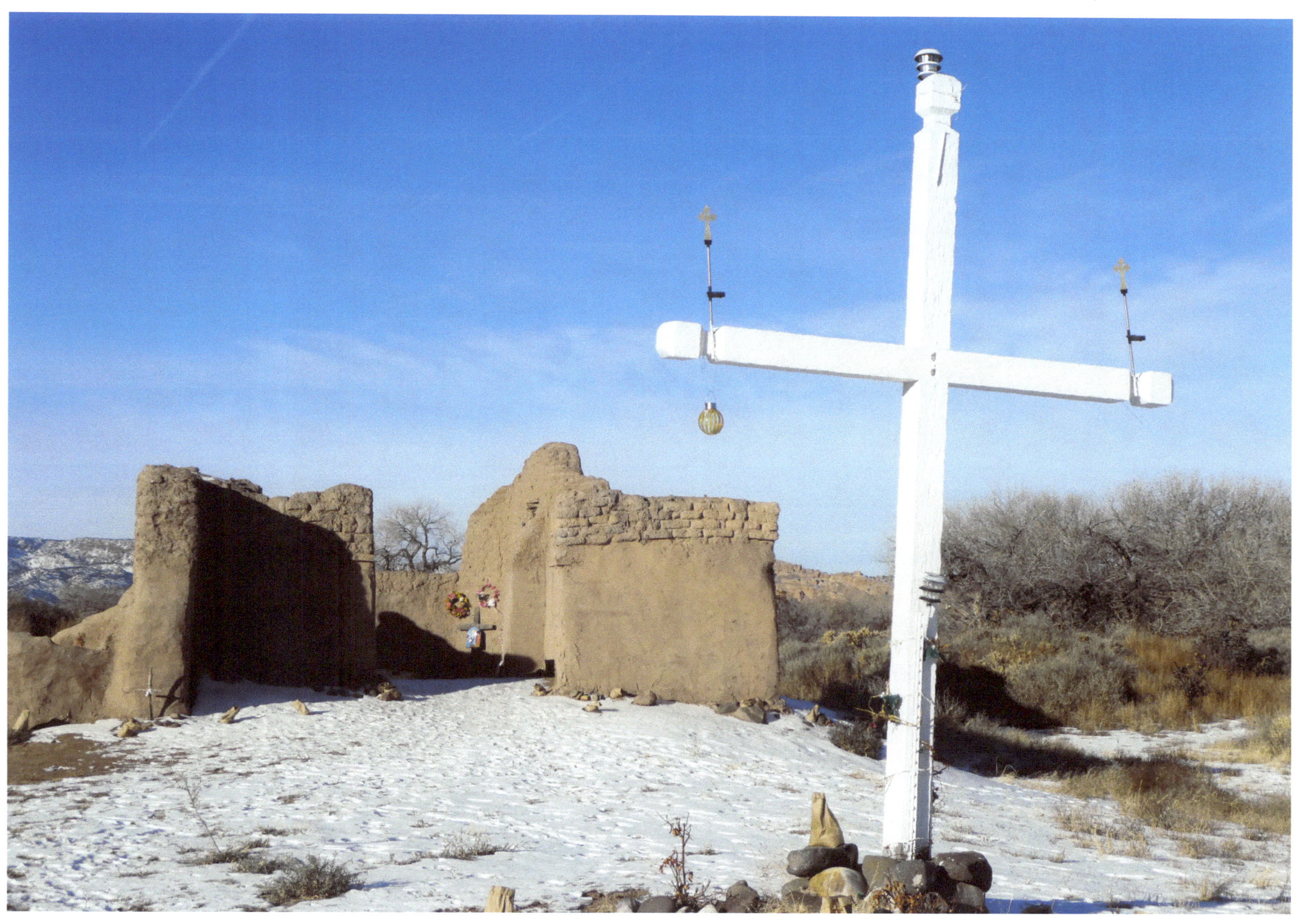

Santa Rosa de Lima Catholic Church (ruin), Abiquiú, Rio Arriba County. 1734. Santa Rosa de Lima de Abiquiú was a name for present-day Abiquiú, a Tewa name of unknown meaning. On the north side of U.S. Highway 84 just east of the village. Photograph taken in 2020.

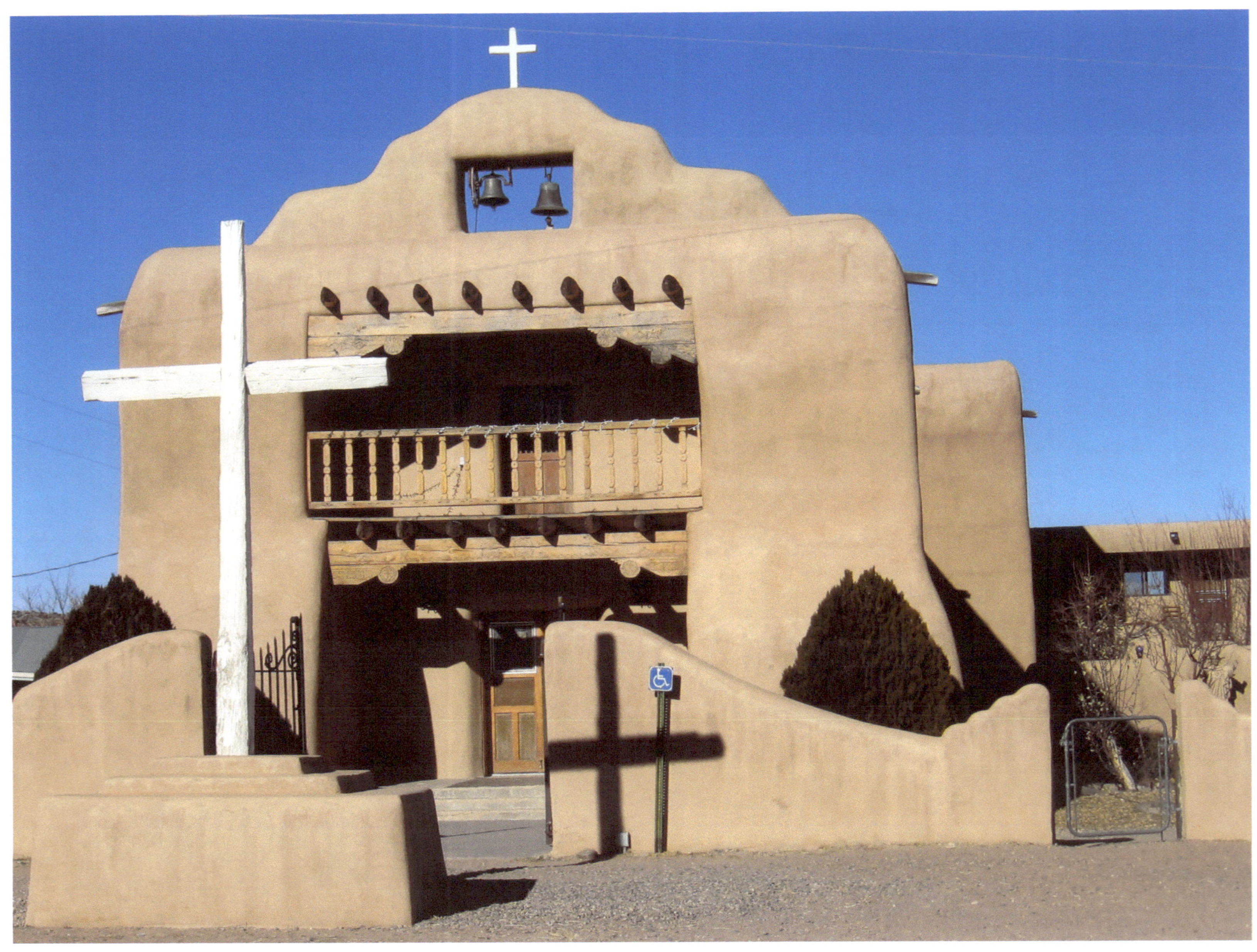

Santo Tomás el Apostól Catholic Church, Abiquiú, Rio Arriba County. Late 1930s. This adobe church was designed by John Gaw Meem. It was originally planned to face east, unlike the previous church on the site, but dissatisfied local residents destroyed the foundation and the church was rebuilt facing south. Just south of U.S. Highway 84 on New Mexico Highway 187. Photograph taken in 2005.

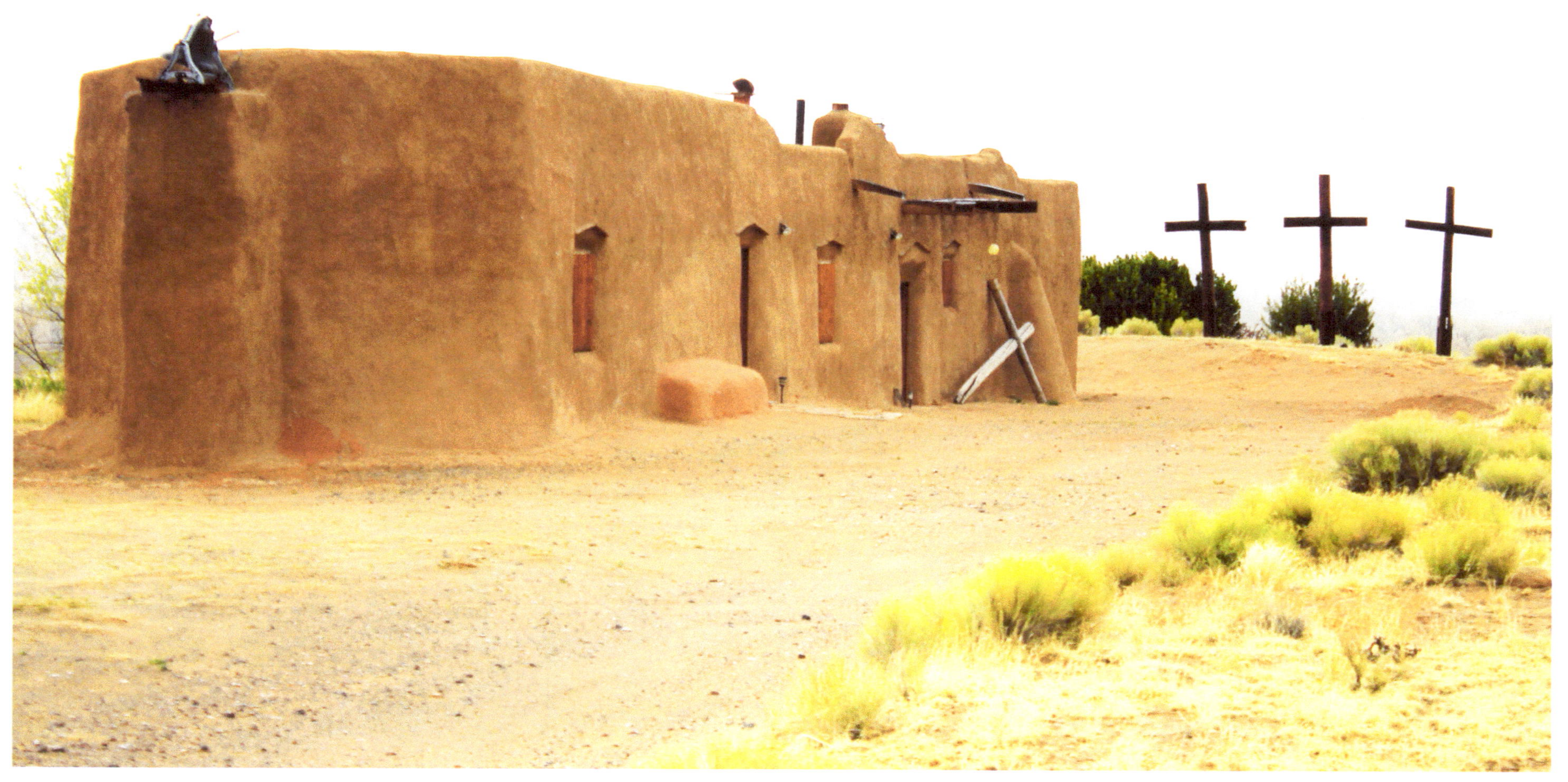

Peninente Brotherhood Morada de Nuestra Señora de Dolores del Alto, Abiquiú, Rio Arriba County. Likely 1830s. The most-famous, most-photographed, most-painted morada in New Mexico. Just west of Santo Tomás Church off Polvadera Road. Photograph taken in 2013.

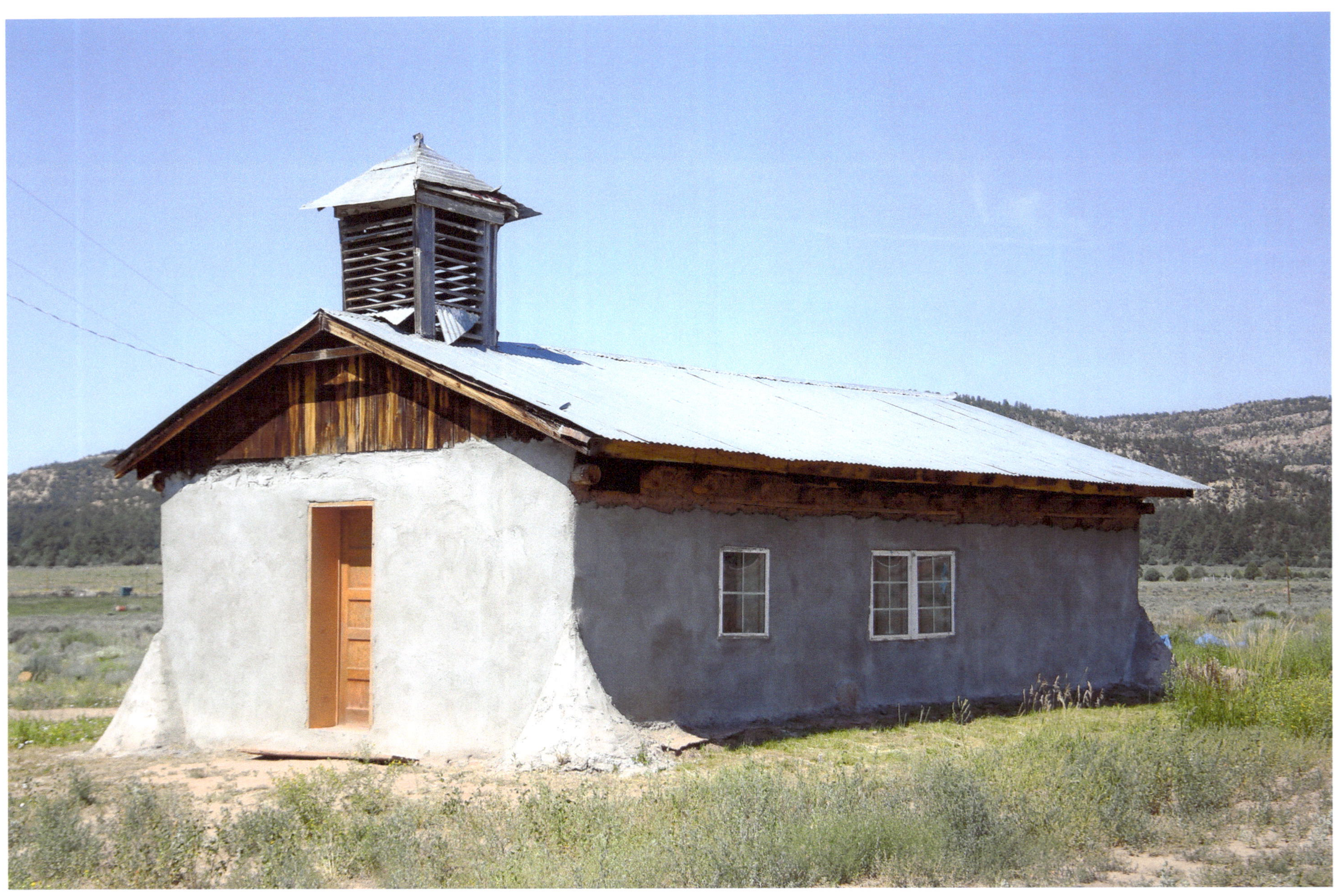

San Ysidro Catholic Church, Llaves, Rio Arriba County. 1938–1940. The remote adobe church was being restored as of mid-2024. Although built on private property, it is served by Santo Tomás Parish in Abiquiú. About 10 miles up New Mexico Highway 112 from its junction with New Mexico 96, the church can be seen less than half a mile east of the highway. Photograph taken in 2024.

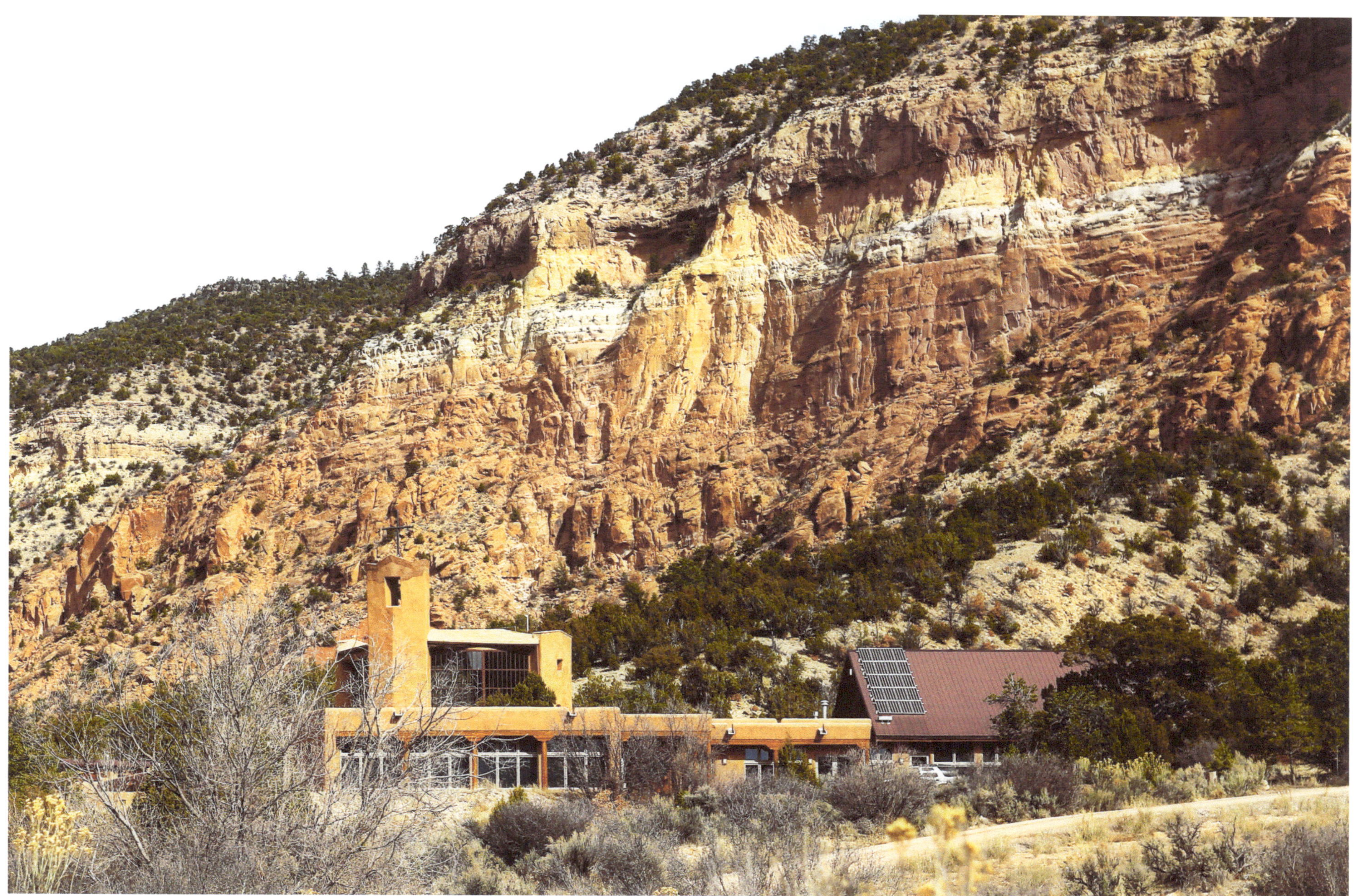

Christ in the Desert Catholic Monastery, on the Chama River, Rio Arriba County. 1964. This striking monastery is open to the public, with some rooms available for overnight stays. Two miles northwest of Ghost Ranch, take Forest Road 151 west from U.S. Highway 84 13 miles along the Chama River. Photograph taken in 2017.

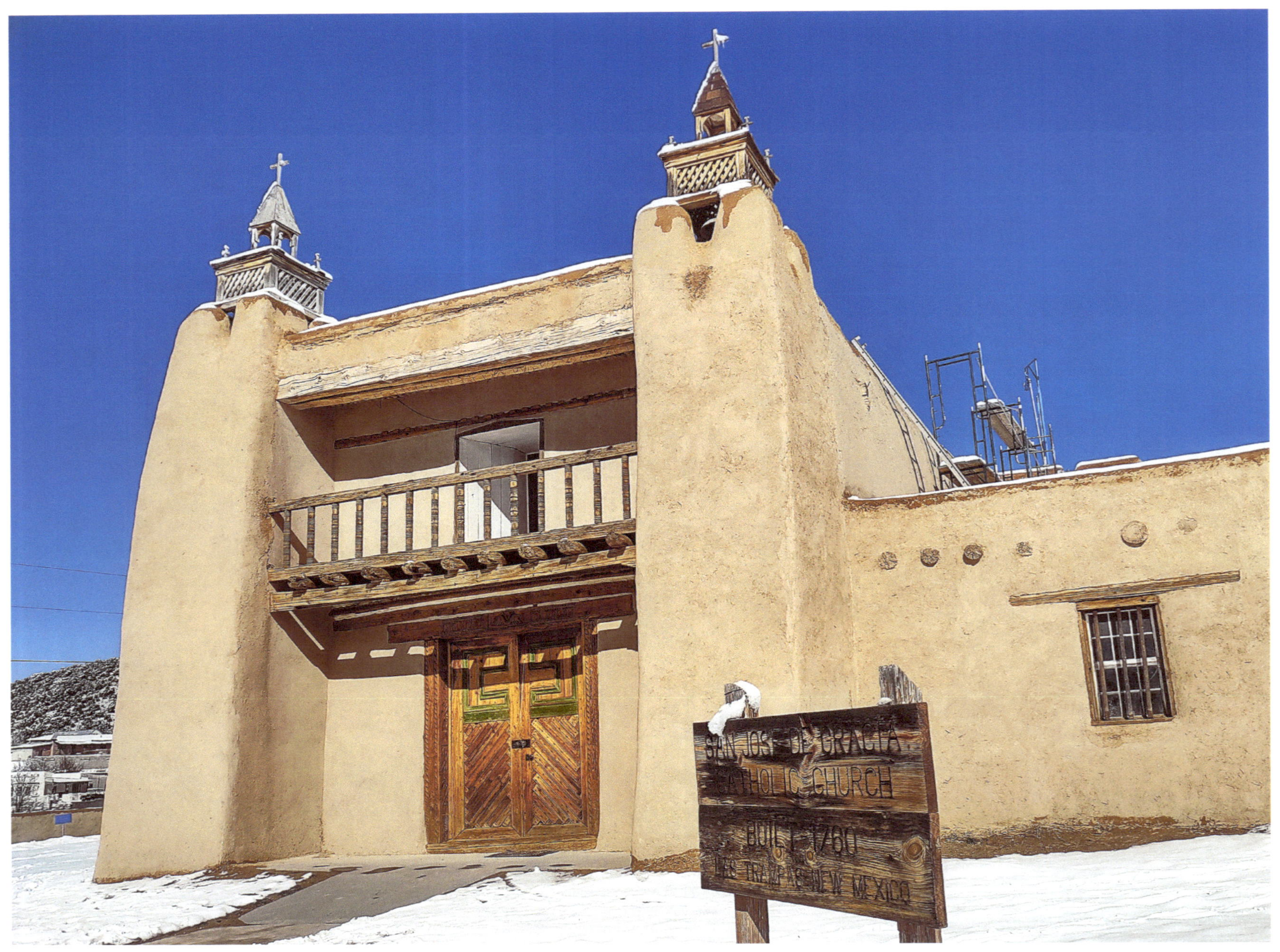

San José de Gracia Catholic Church, Las Trampas, Taos County. 1760–1776. This stunning adobe church is one of the oldest churches in New Mexico, famous and much-photographed. A beautiful restoration of the interior and exterior was completed in July 2024. On New Mexico Highway 76. Photograph taken in 2022.

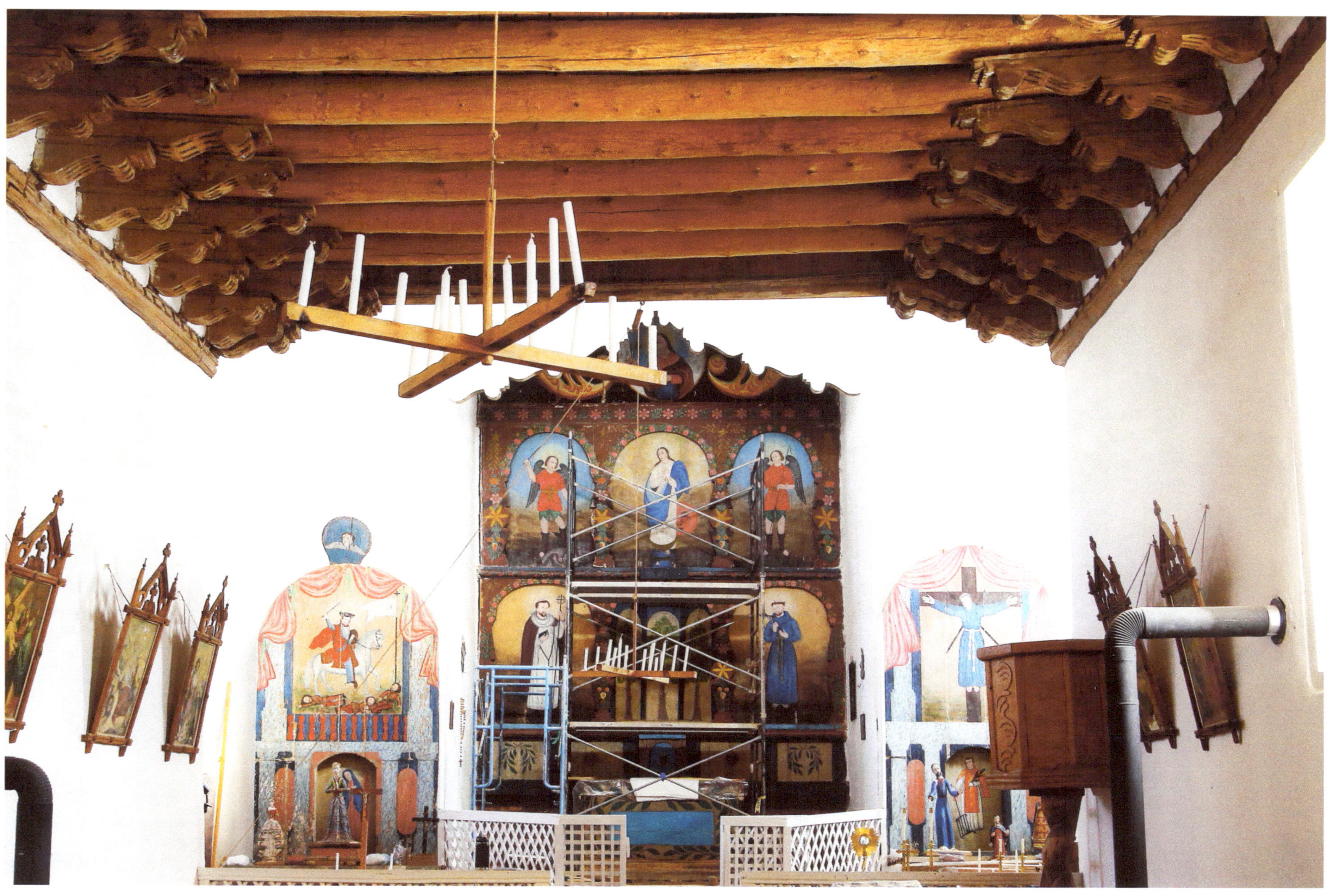

The gorgeous interior of San José de Gracia during the recent renovation of the artwork (see page 21). The artwork, dating from as early as 1776, has been overpainted and modified over the years, but includes work by *santeros* José de Gracia Gonzales and Bernardo Miera y Pacheco. Photograph taken in 2022.

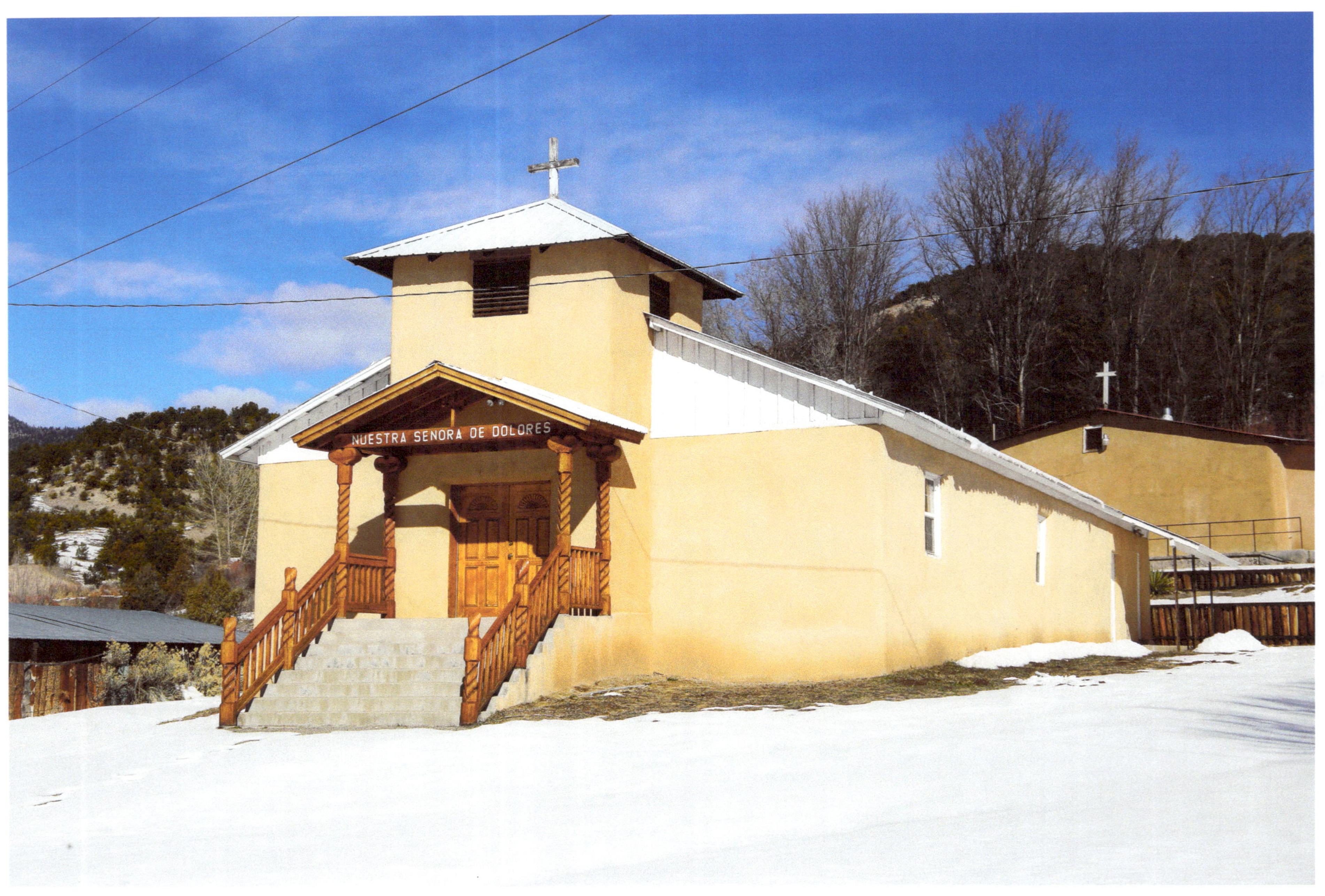

Nuestra Señora de Dolores Catholic Church, Vadito, Taos County. 1961. This attractive, traditional, adobe church is included for its pleasing design, including the carved balustrades and their supports. On New Mexico Highway 75. Photograph taken in 2020.

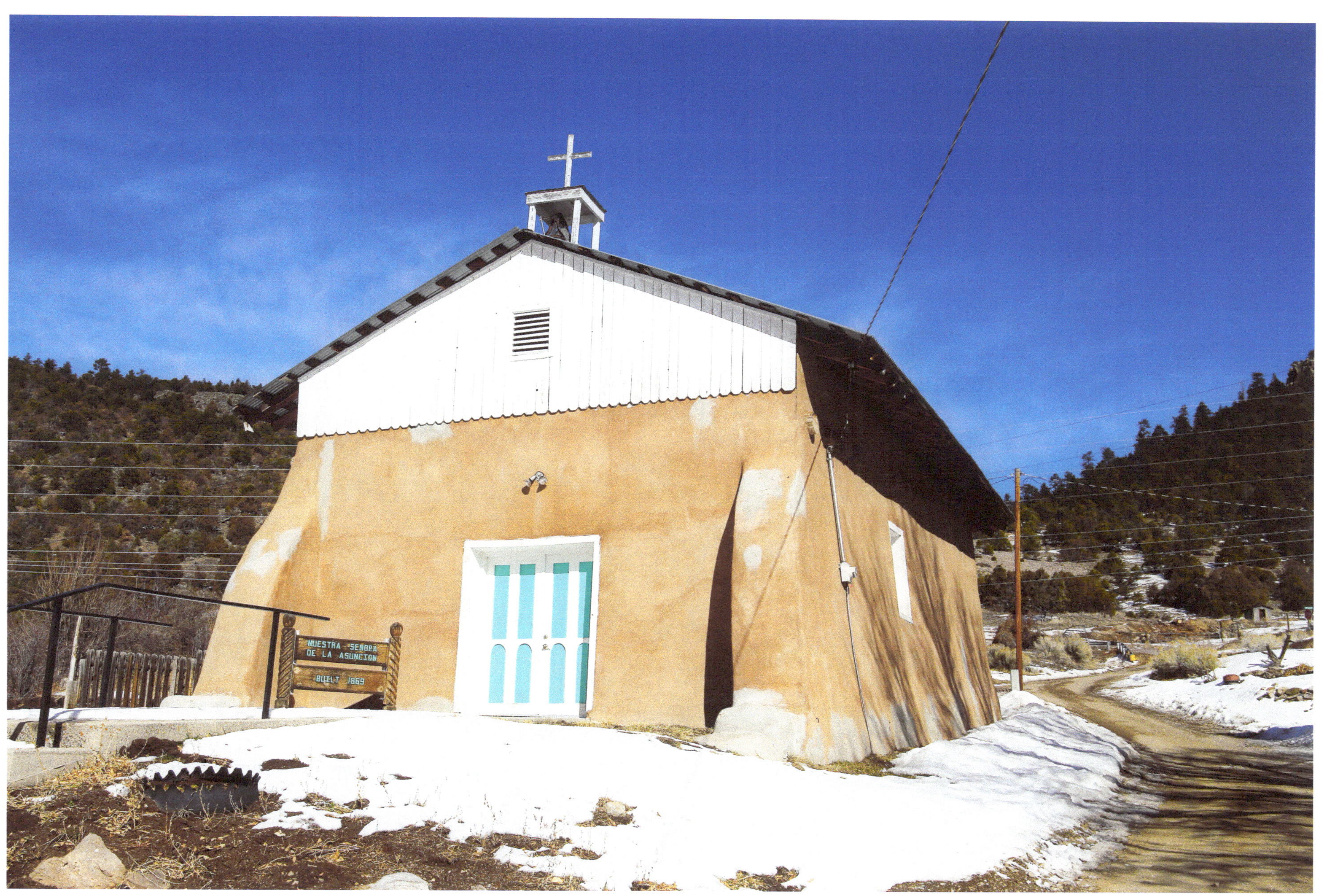

Nuestra Señora de Asunción Catholic Church, Placita, Taos County. 1869. This colorful adobe church is used and well maintained. It is just west of Vadito, a hundred yards south of New Mexico Highway 75, from which it can be seen. Photograph taken in 2020.

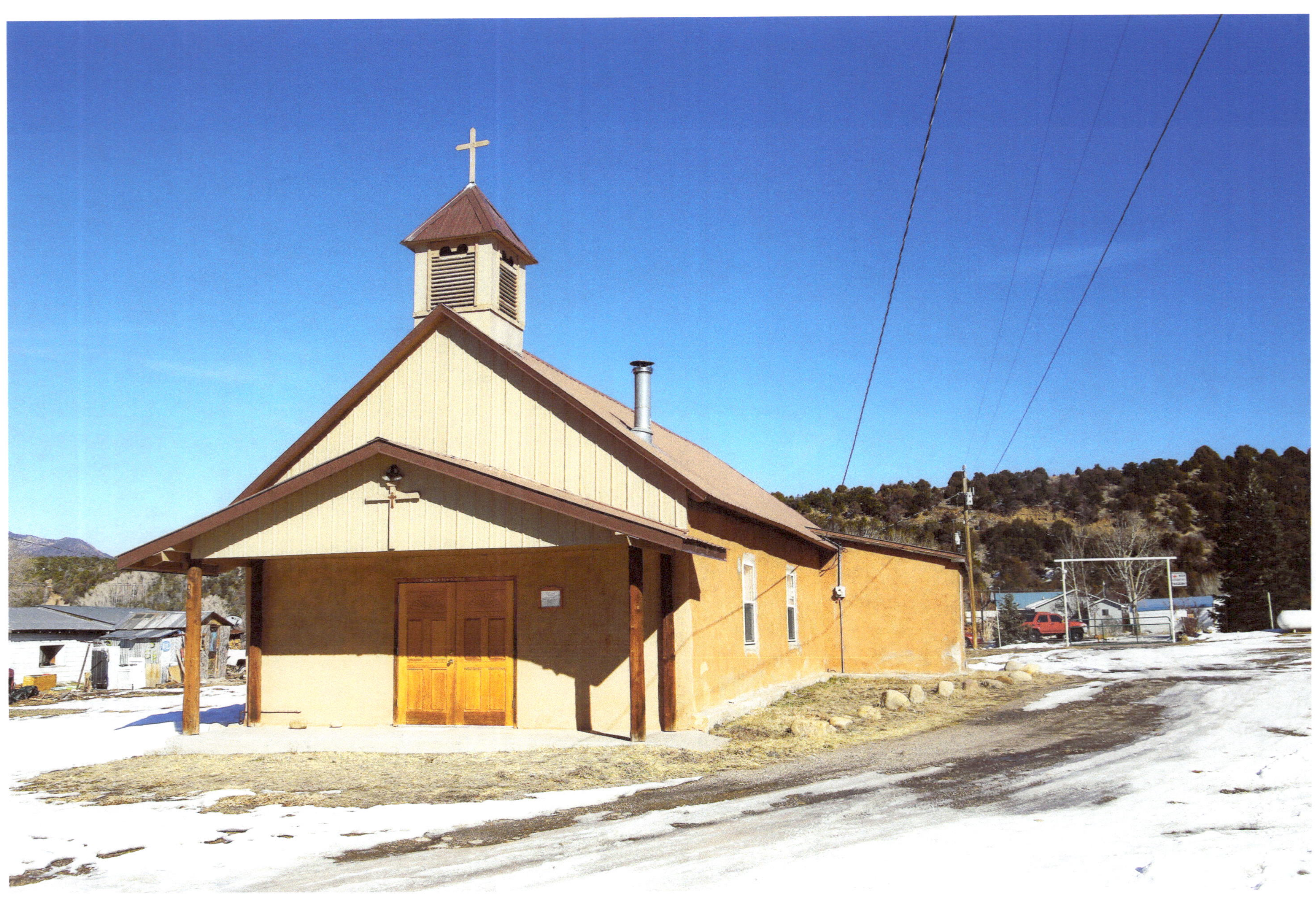

Santa Bárbara Catholic Church, Rodarte, Taos County. 1922. This attractive adobe church is just off New Mexico Highway 73 southeast of Peñasco, on Capilla Road. Photograph taken in 2020.

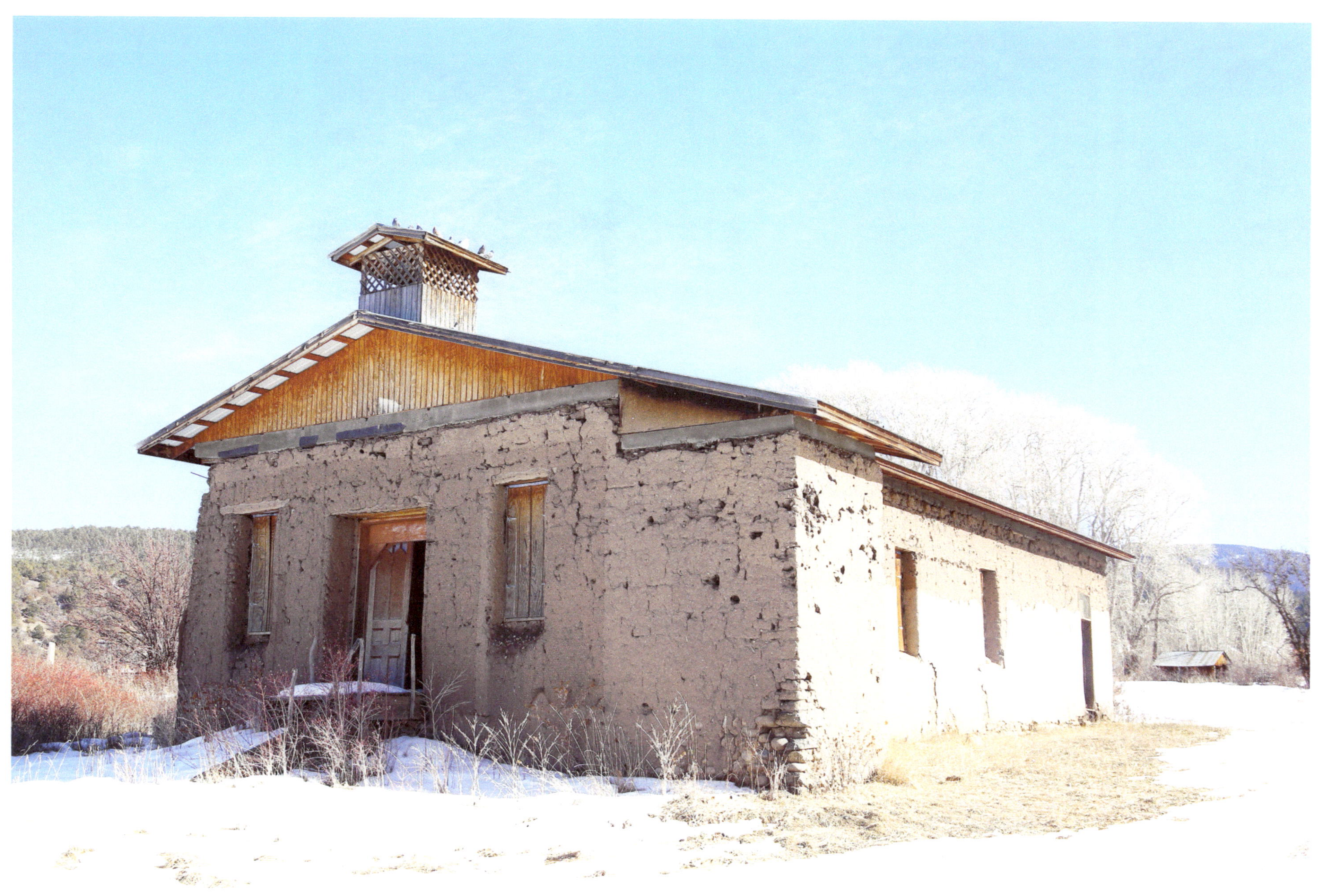

San Acacio Catholic Church, Llano Largo, Taos County. 1936. The adobe church is sadly abandoned and deteriorating. Take Santa Bárbara Road off New Mexico Highway 73 about 2.5 miles, then right on Camino Abajo Road to the church. Photograph taken in 2021.

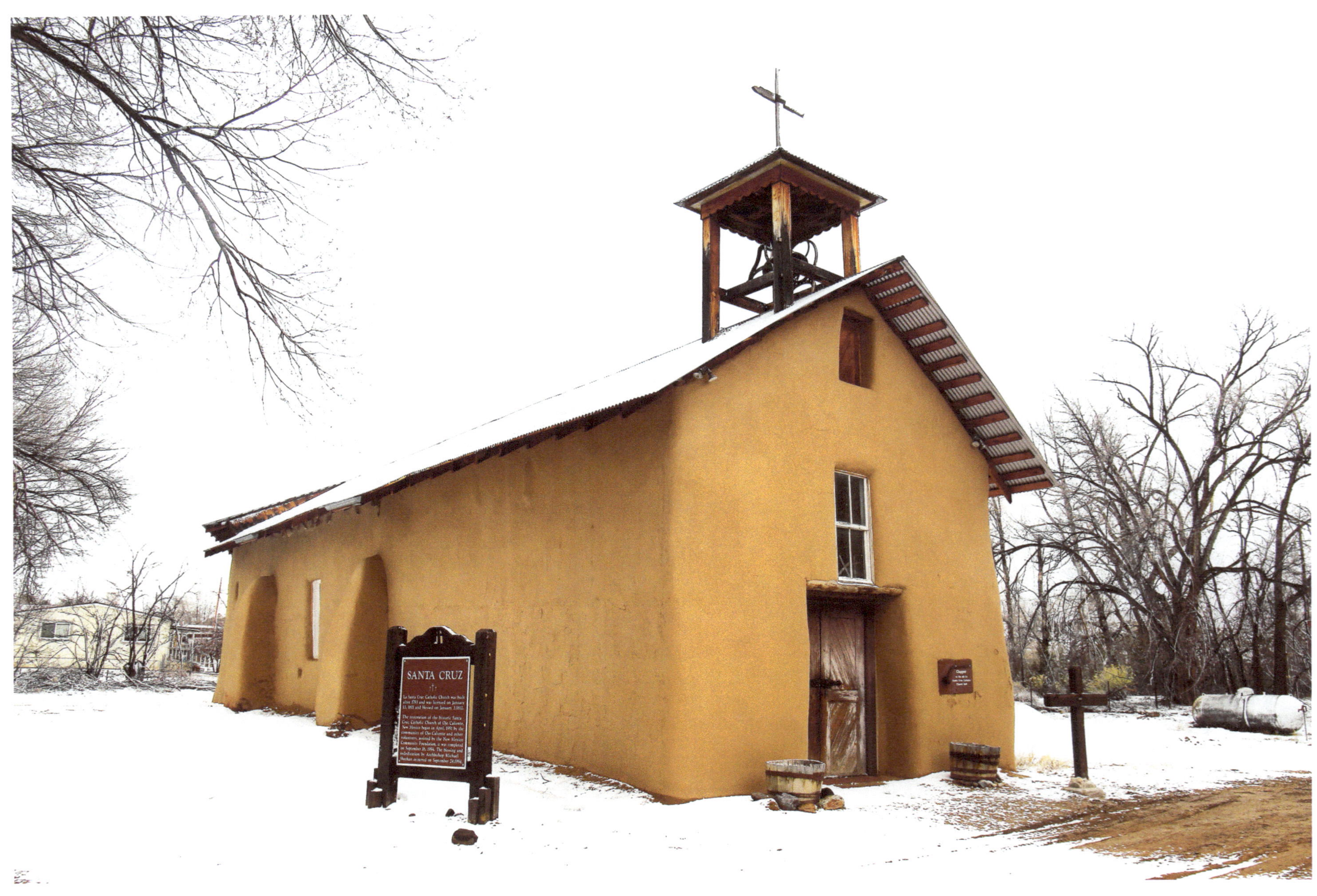

Santa Cruz Catholic Church, Ojo Caliente, Taos and Rio Arriba counties. Around 1800. This historic adobe church is just off New Mexico Highway 414, a short distance west of U.S. Highway 285. Photograph taken in 2019.

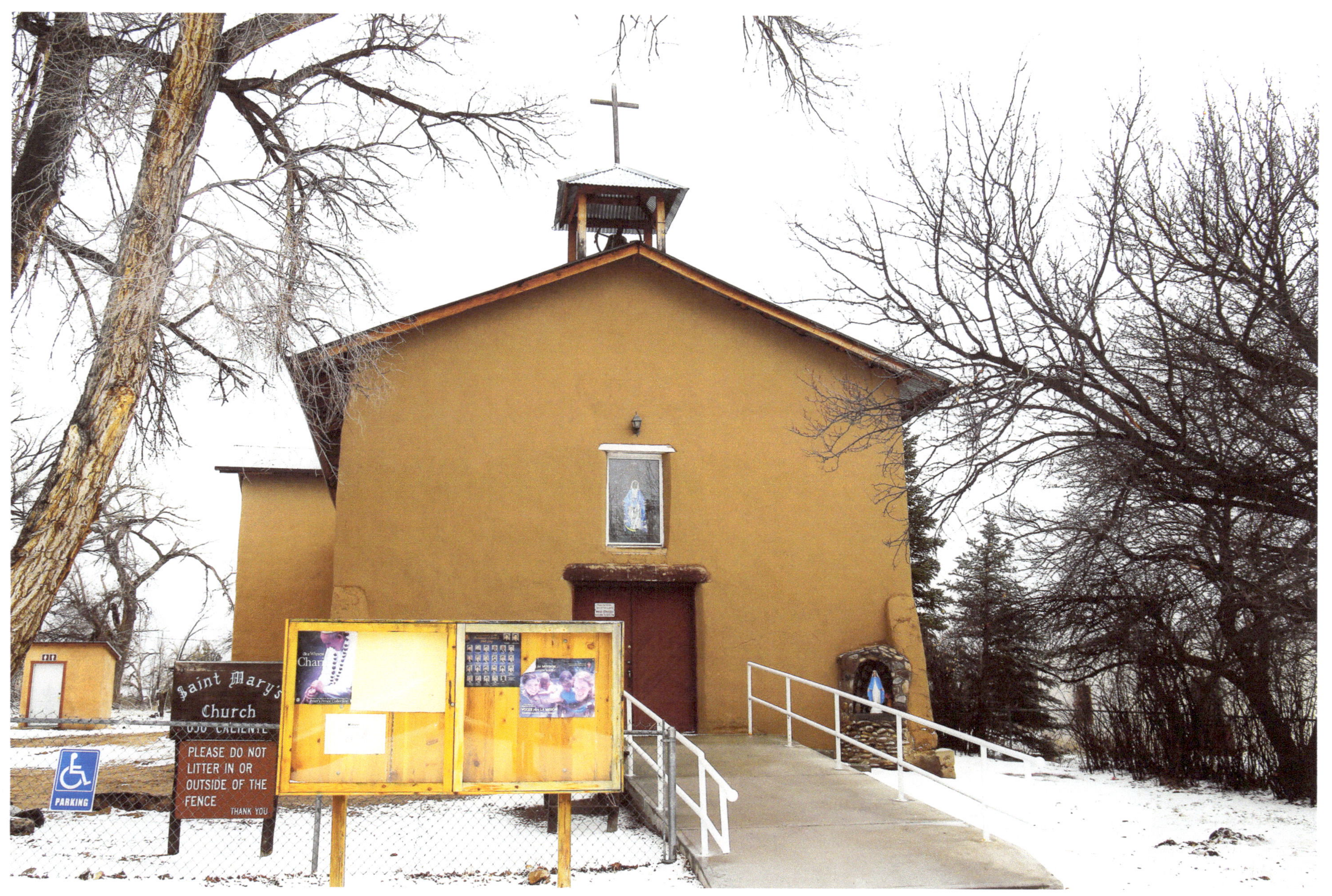

St. Mary's Catholic Church, Ojo Caliente, Taos and Rio Arriba counties. 1939. The adobe church is next door to Santa Cruz Church. Photograph taken in 2019.

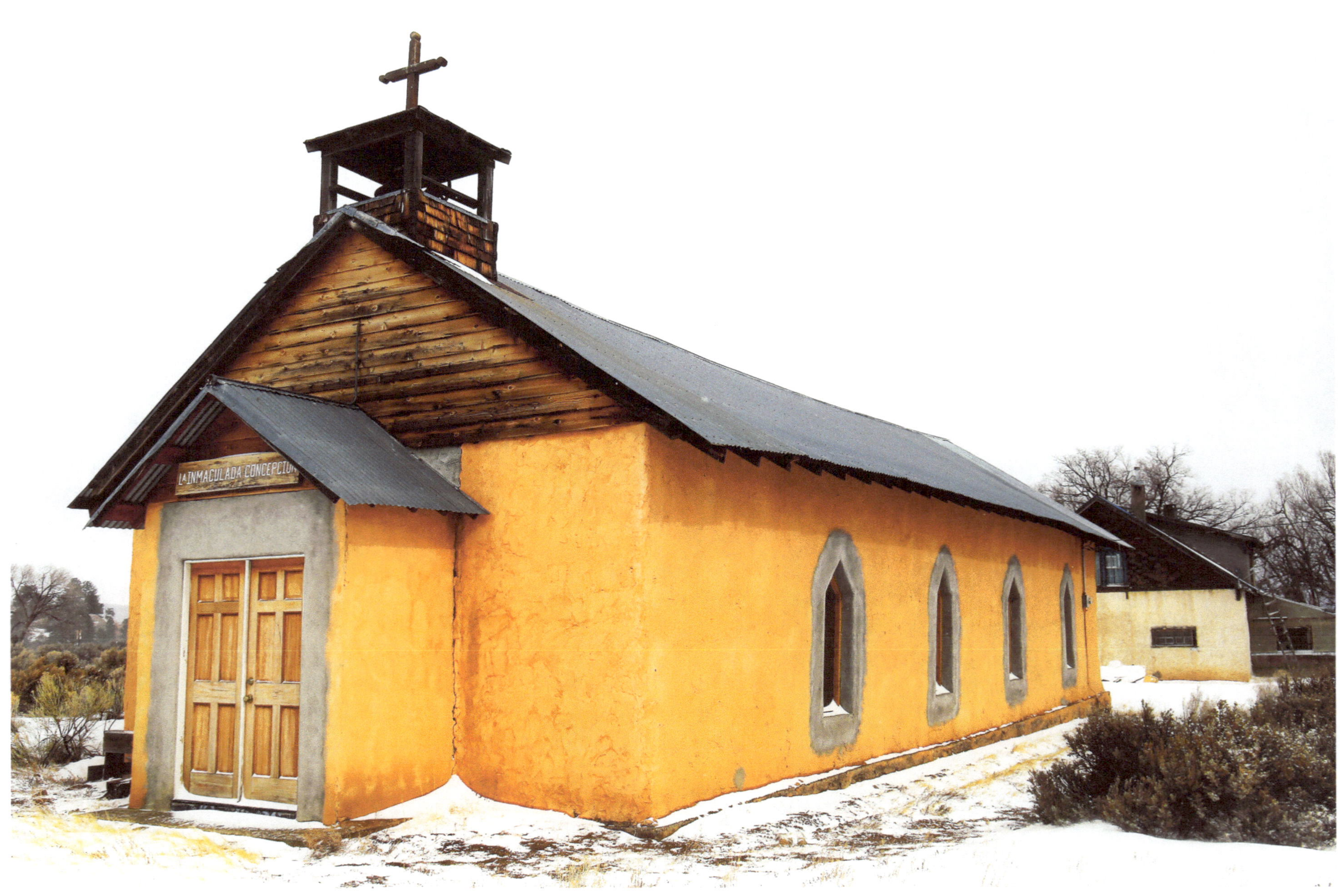

La Immaculada Concepción Catholic Church, Tres Piedras, Taos County. 1900. This adobe church with its neo-Gothic windows was colorful and attractive on a cold, snowy day. West several hundred yards from U.S. Highway 285 on Escudero Road. Photograph taken in 2019.

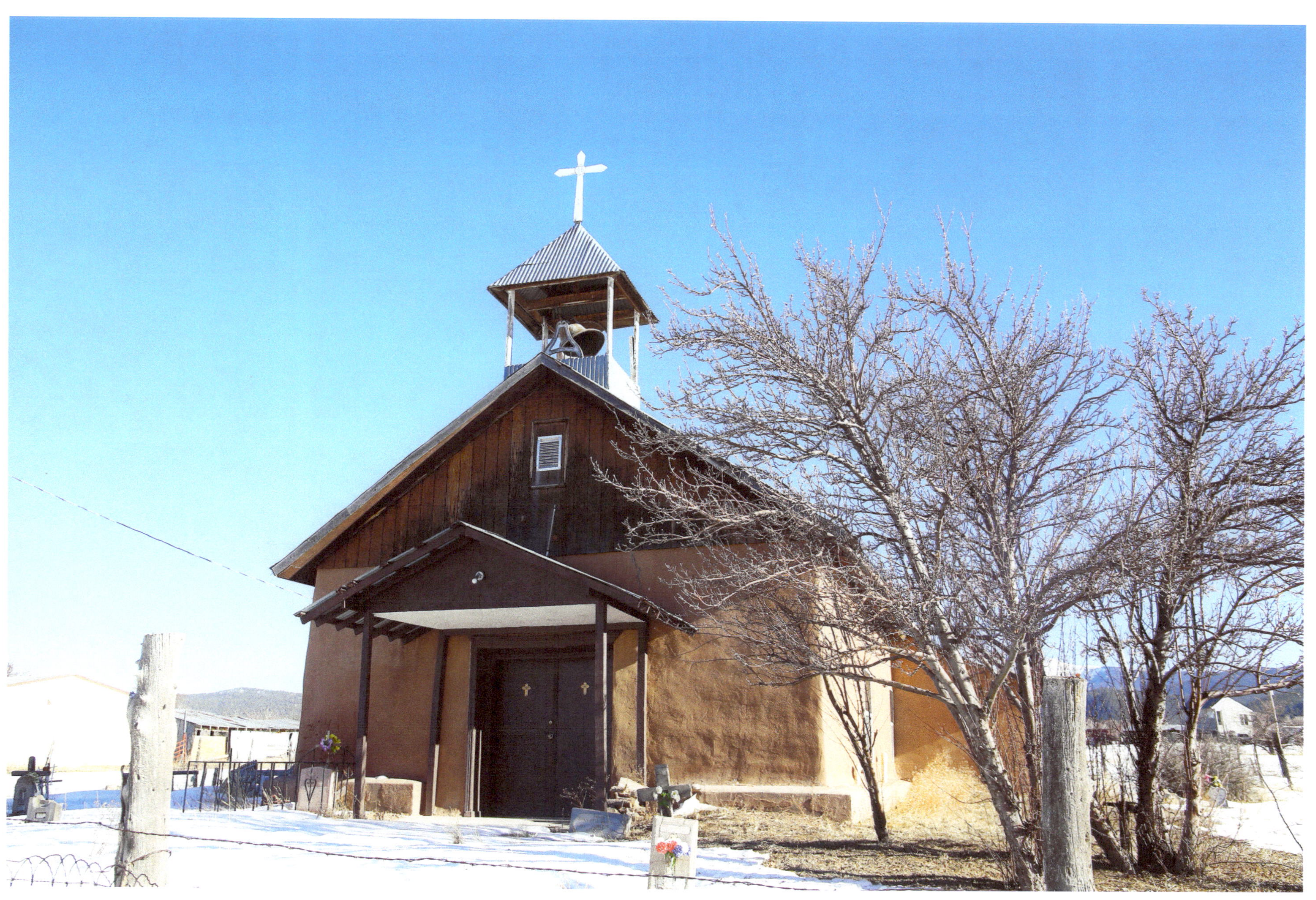

San Juan Nepomucemo Catholic Church, Llano, Taos County. 1832. A traditional adobe church, about 2.5 miles southeast of Peñasco. Take New Mexico Highway 73 to Plaza Road. Photograph taken in 2021.

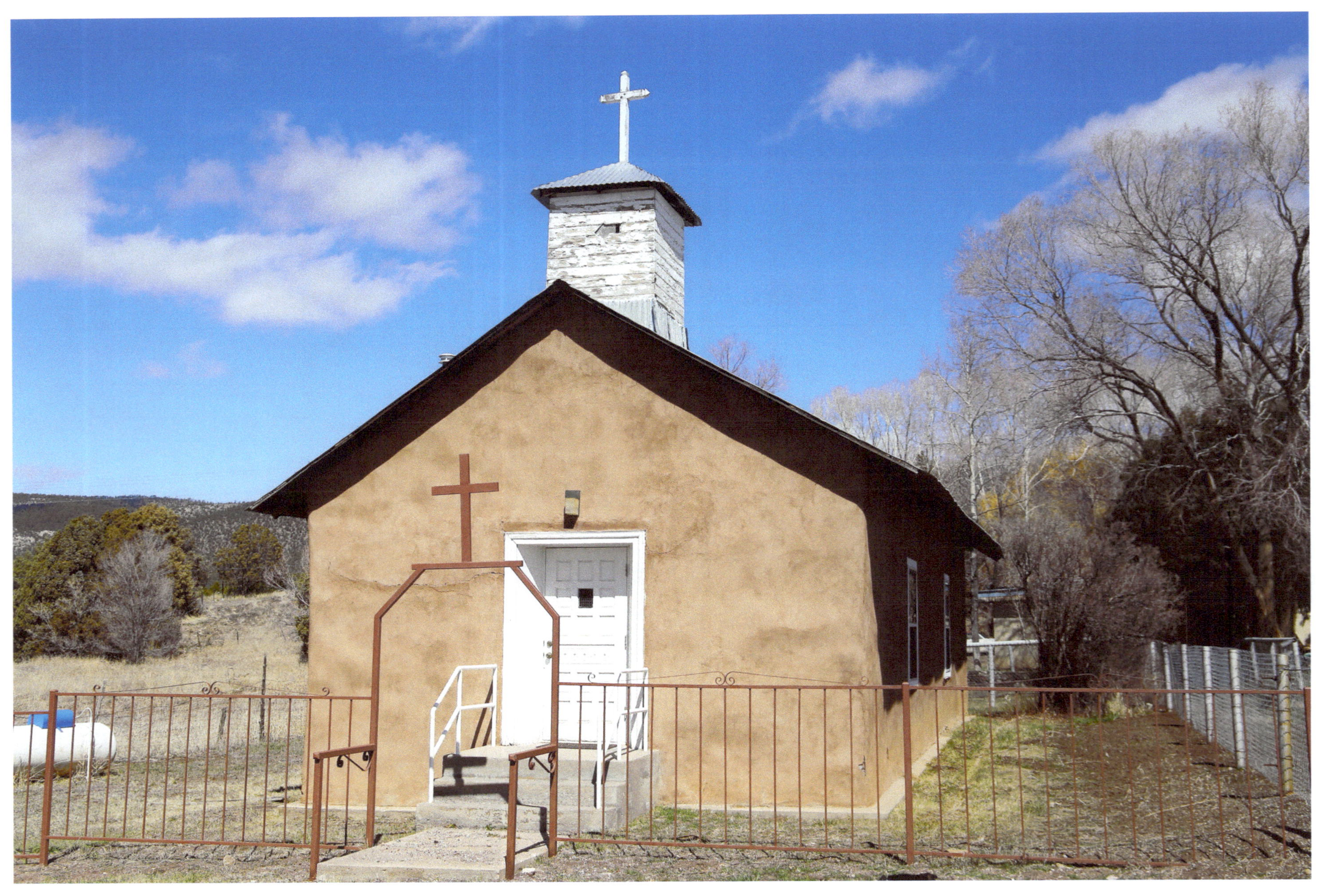

Sagrado Corazón Catholic Church, Rio Lucio, Taos County. 1920. The adobe church is on the north side of New Mexico Highway 75 about a mile west of its junction with New Mexico Highway 76. Photograph taken in 2020.

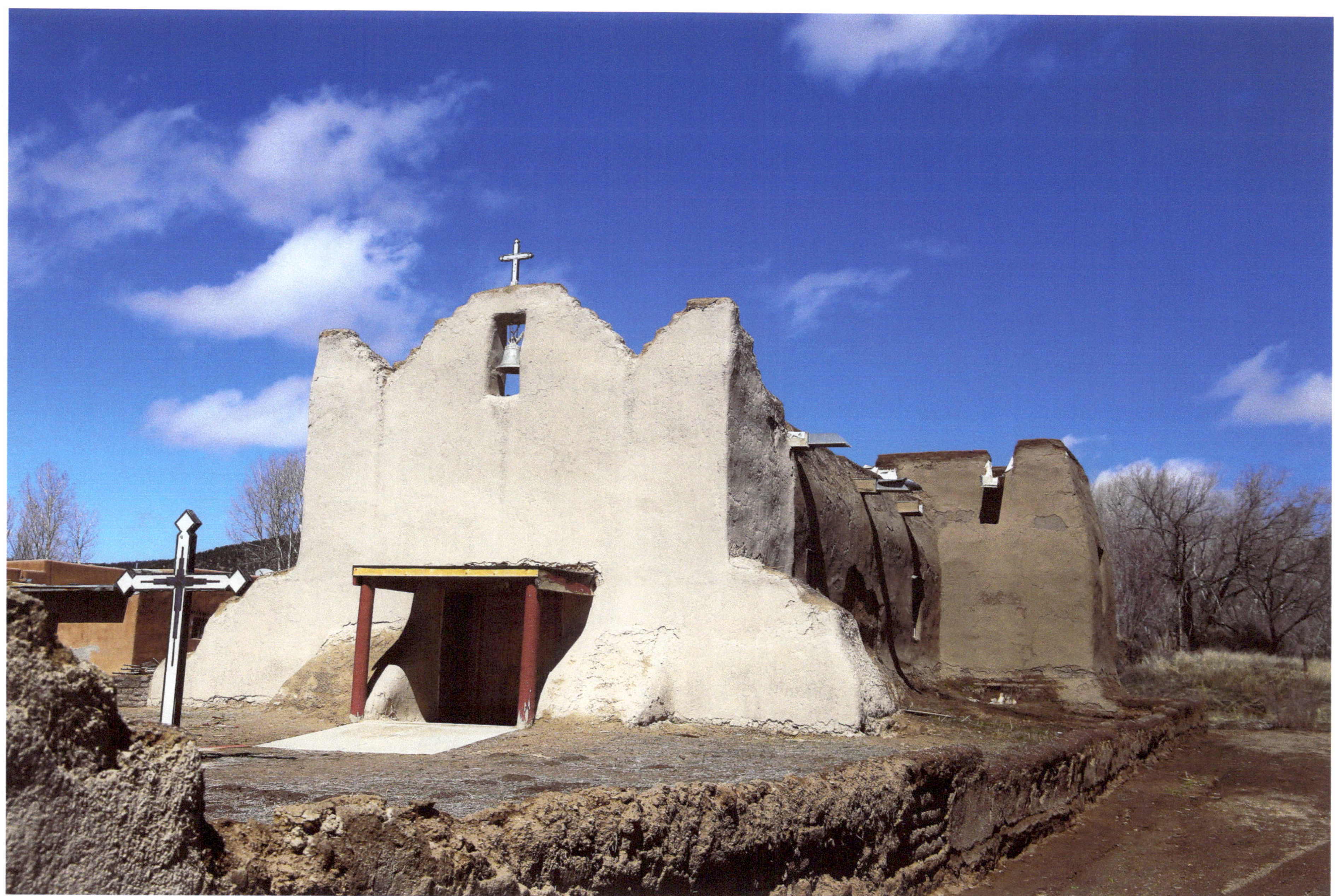

San Lorenzo de Picurís Catholic Church, Picurís Pueblo, Taos County. 1786/1990. The adobe church was rebuilt to the original plans in 1990 after several rebuilds and a collapse in the 1980s. From New Mexico Highway 75 take Indian Service Road 201 to Buffalo Trail. Photograph with required permit taken in 2020.

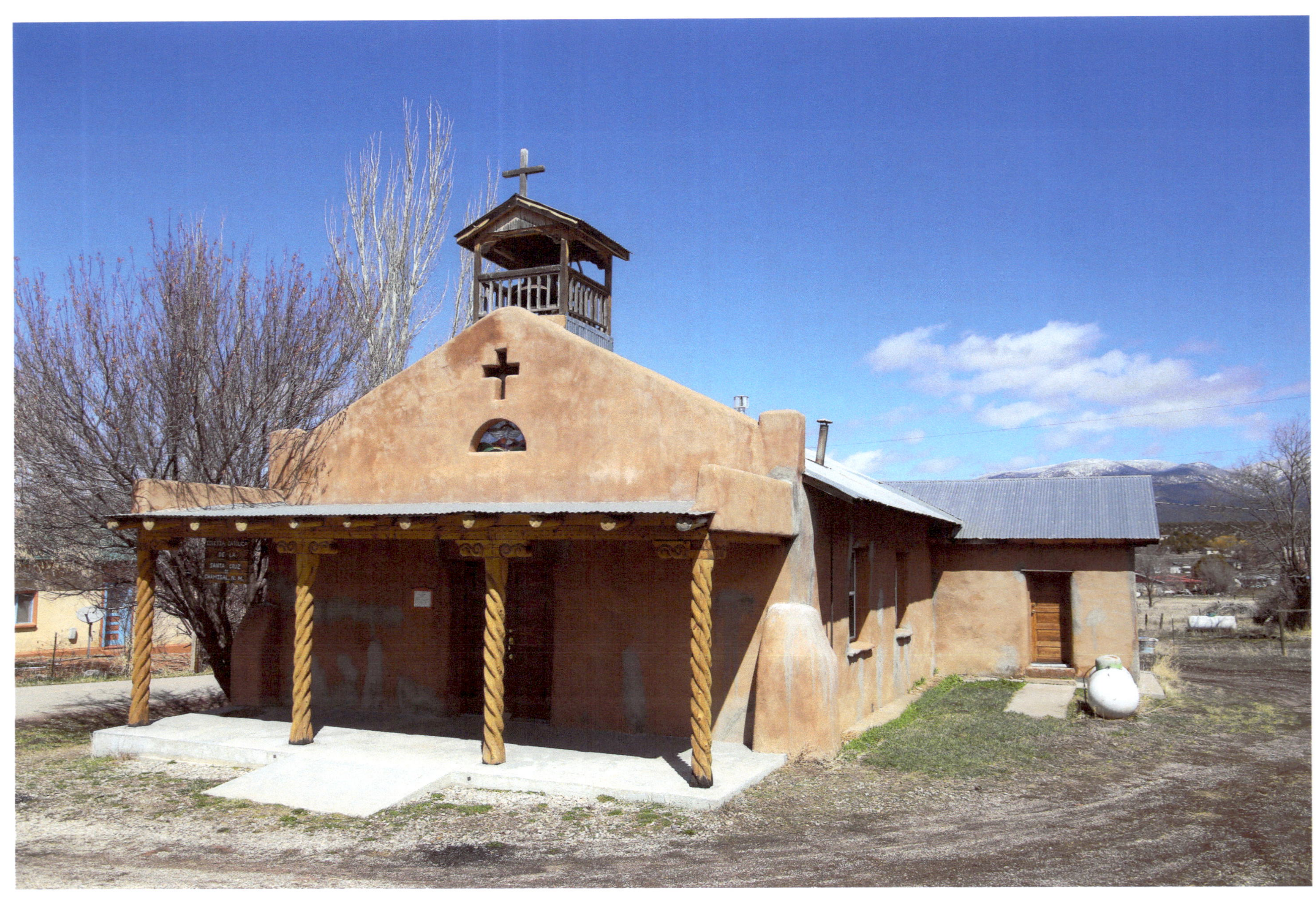

Iglesia Catolica (Catholic Church) de Santa Cruz, Chamisal, Taos County. 1930. This adobe church, with its carved portico supports, is on La Plaza Road off New Mexico Highway 76. Photograph taken in 2020.

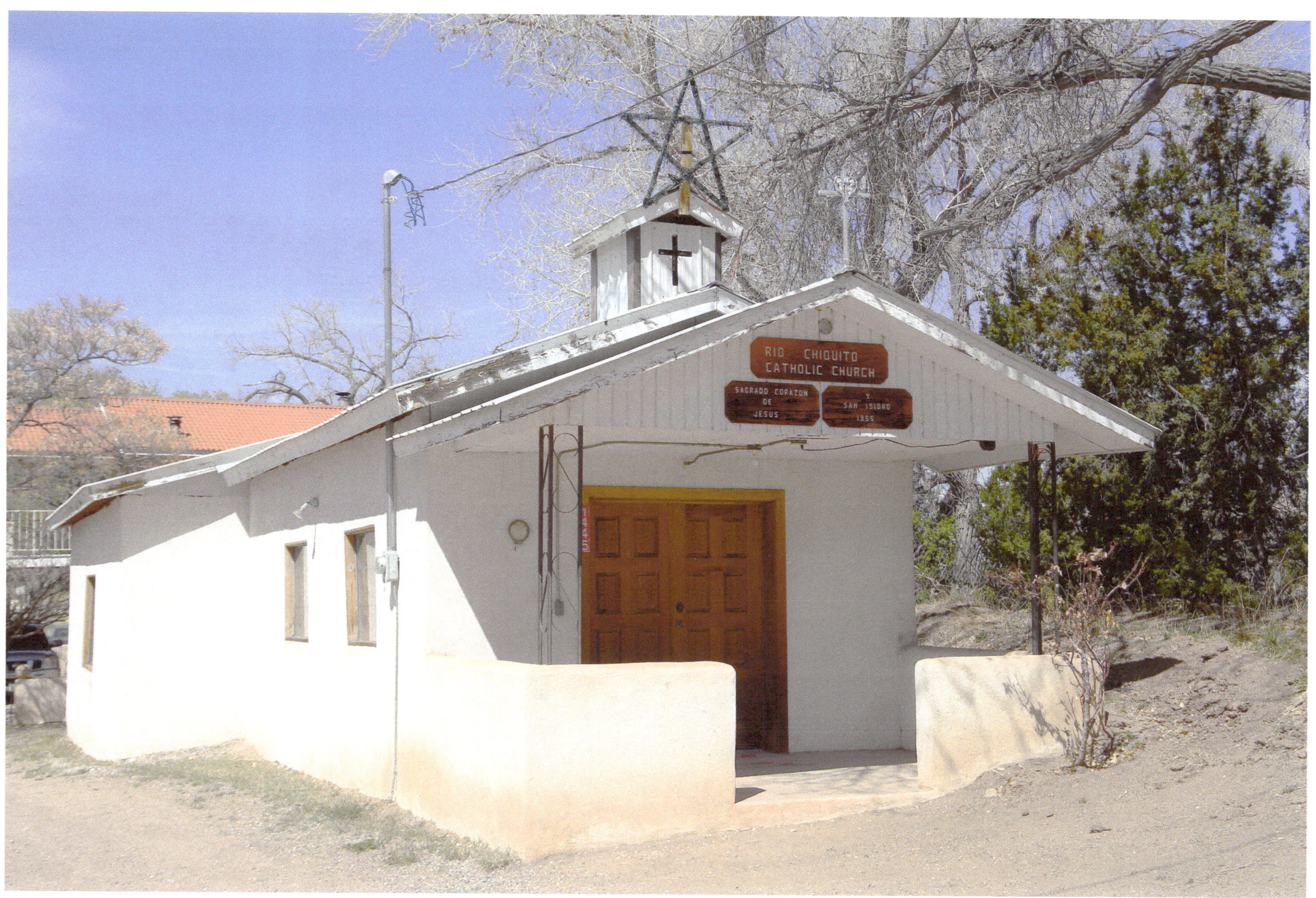

Rio Chiquito Catholic Church (Sagrado Corazón de Jesus y San Isidro), Rio Chiquito, Santa Fe County. 1955. Unusual in having two names, this small, traditional church is on New Mexico Highway 503 about one-quarter mile from its junction with New Mexico Highway 76. Photograph taken in 2022.

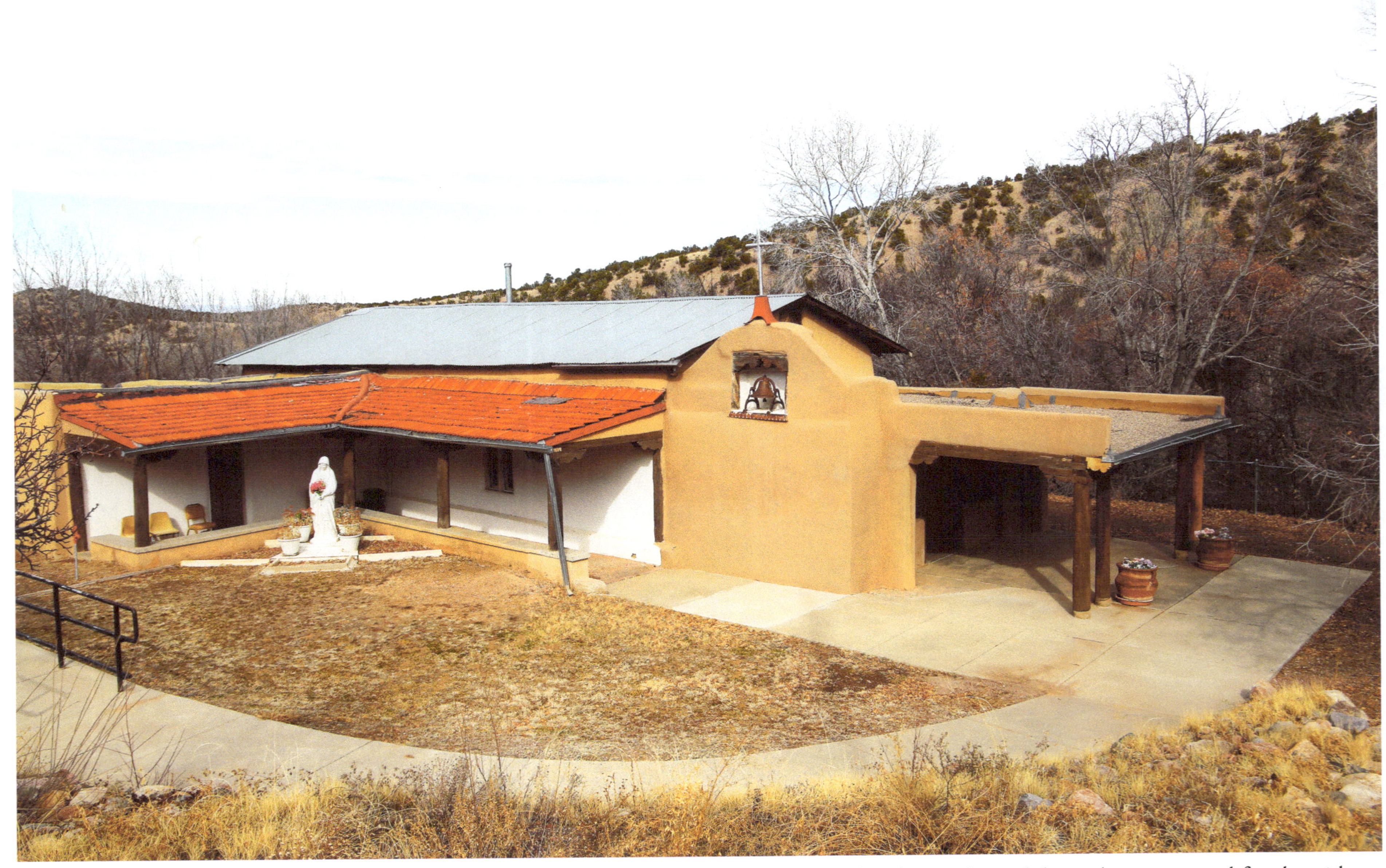

Our Lady of Sorrows, Rio en Medio, Santa Fe County. 1883. The main body of the adobe church is traditional, but it has an unusual façade, with no door, and a covered structure on the left. At the end of New Mexico Highway 592, about 5.3 miles from its junction with New Mexico Highway 591, Tesuque Village Road. Photograph taken in 2023.

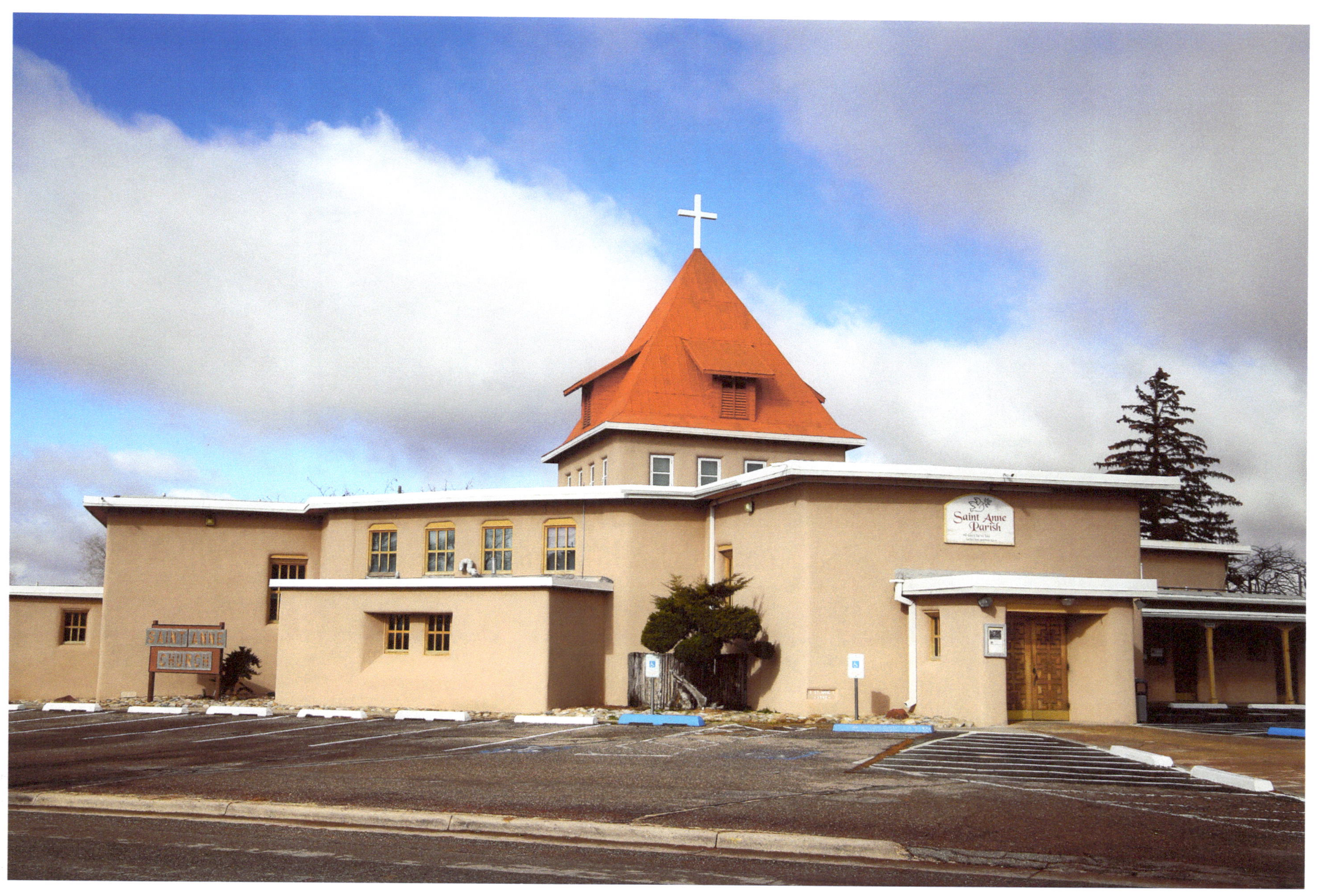

St. Anne Parish Church, Santa Fe, Santa Fe County. 1942. Not quite traditional and yet not quite modern, the church is at 511 Alicia Street. Photograph taken in 2019.

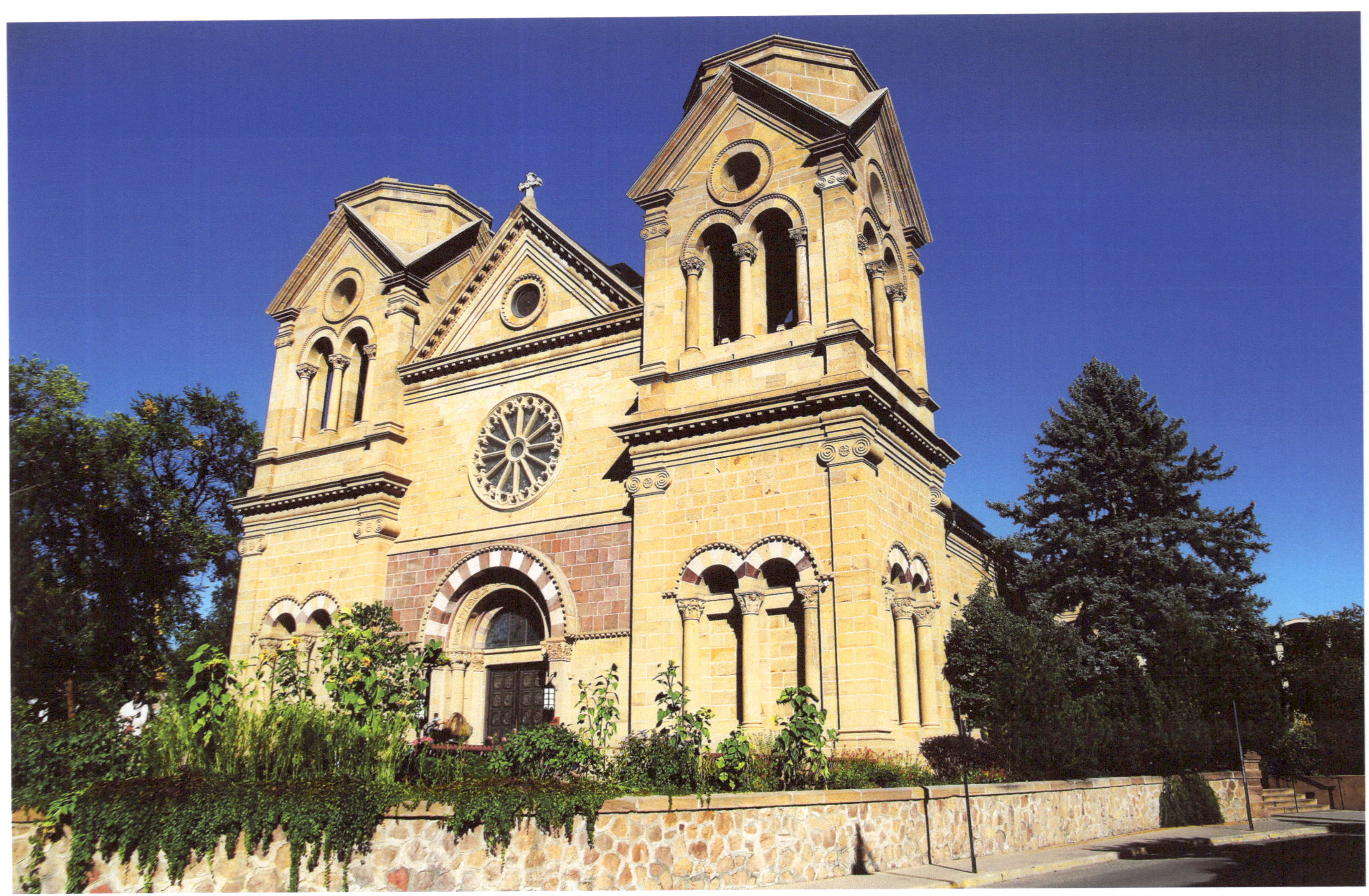

Cathedral Basilica of St. Francis of Assisi, Santa Fe, Santa Fe County. 1869–1886. This imposing, Romanesque cathedral was built over an adobe parish church (*parroquia)*, later removed, dating to 1717. Santa Fe's first bishop and archbishop, Jean-Baptiste Lamy (1853–1885), preferred the styles of his native France to New Mexican styles, although recent archbishops have favored *santero*-style artwork inside the church. At 131 Cathedral Place. Photograph taken in 2024.

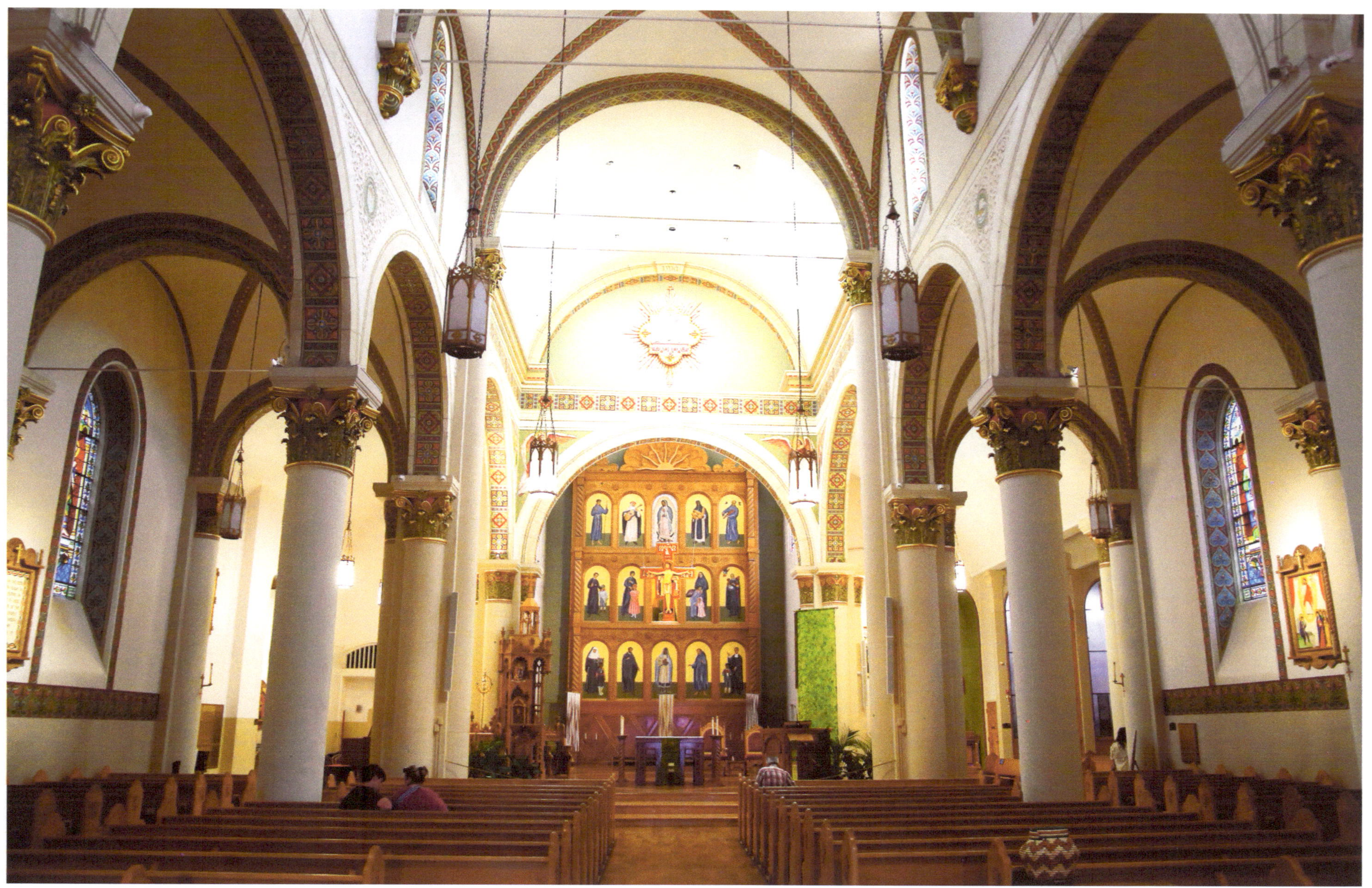

The impressive interior of the cathedral. The altar screen was created in the 1980s by Franciscan artist Robert Lentz, who painted the Apache Christ in St. Joseph's Apache Mission Church in Mescalero. The stations of the cross, one of which is visible on the right, were painted by contemporary *santera* Marie Romero Cash. Photograph taken in 2024.

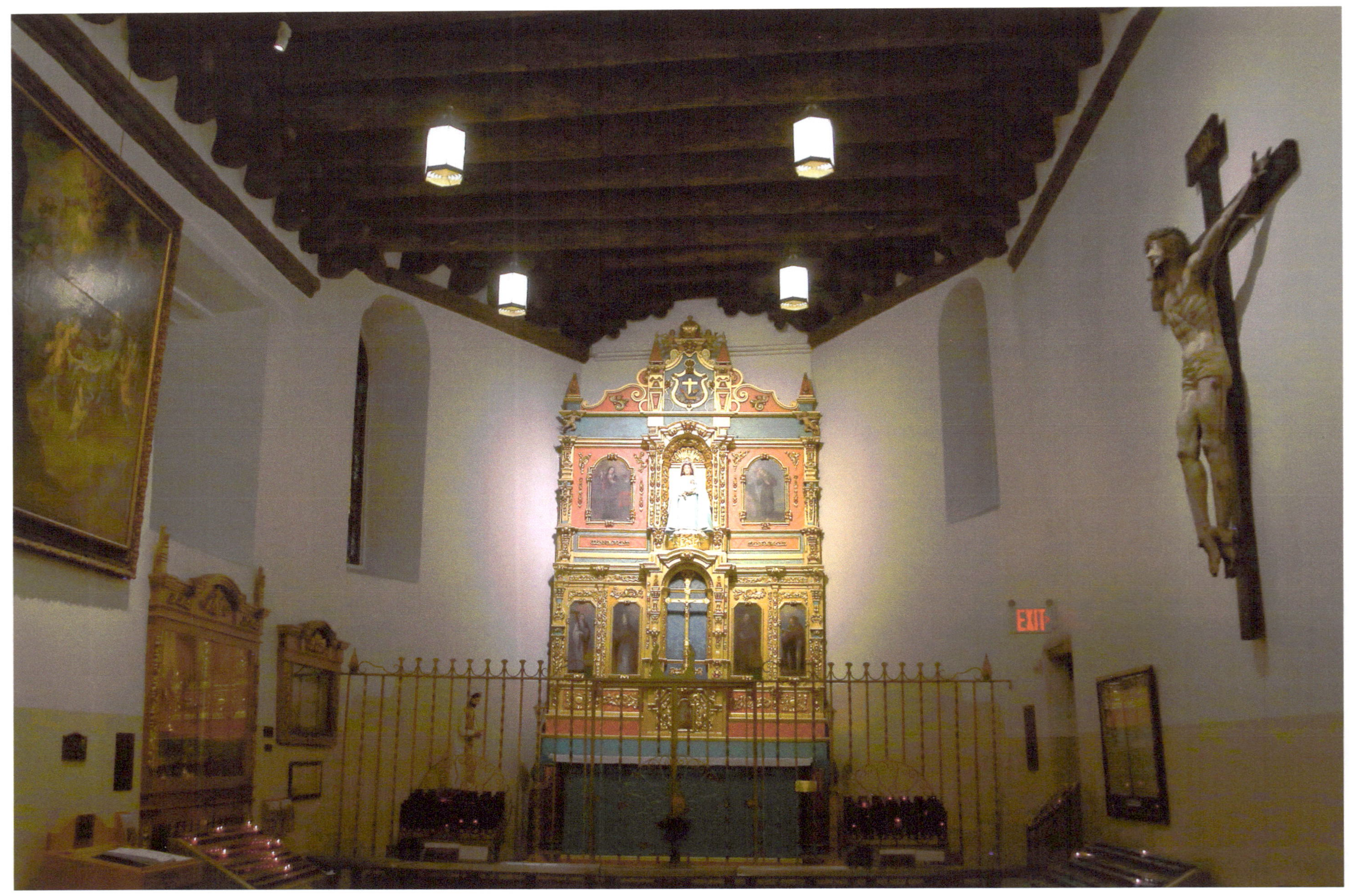

La Conquistadora Chapel in the Cathedral Basilica of St. Francis, Santa Fe, Stanta Fe County. 1717. This chapel is all that remains of the *parroquia* that the cathedral replaced. The altar screen is made of two sections from the old church, dating to the 1700s. The Madonna statue ("La Conquistadora") was brought to New Mexico via Mexico from Spain in 1625 or 1626. She has hundreds of sets of hand-sewn clothes. Photograph taken in 2024.

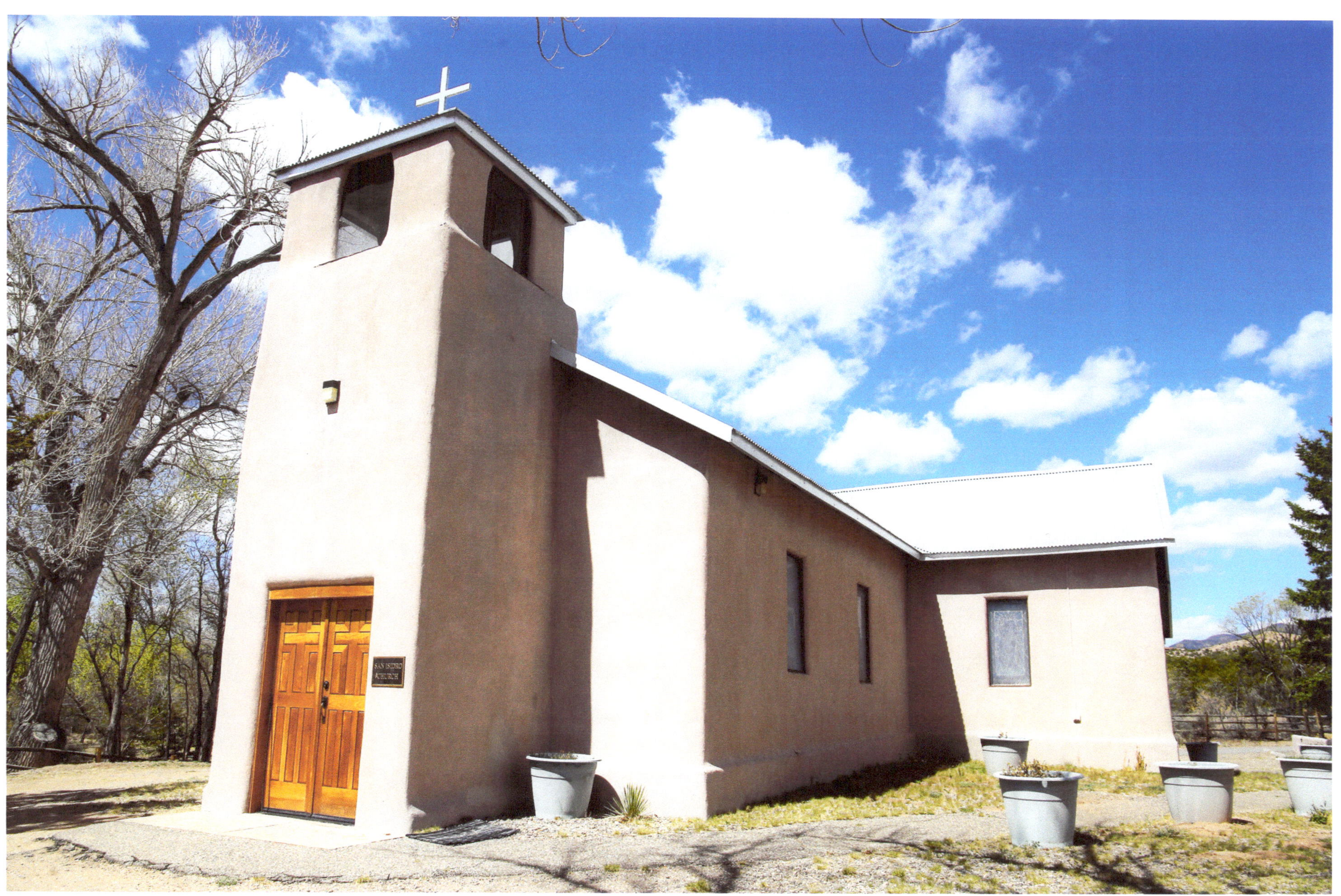

San Isidro Catholic Church, Santa Fe, Santa Fe County. Around 1900. This adobe church is more like a rural church than most others in Santa Fe. It has an adjacent cemetery. On Camino Miguel off Bishop's Lodge Road. A (usually) locked gate prevents vehicular, but not pedestrian, access. Photograph taken in 2021.

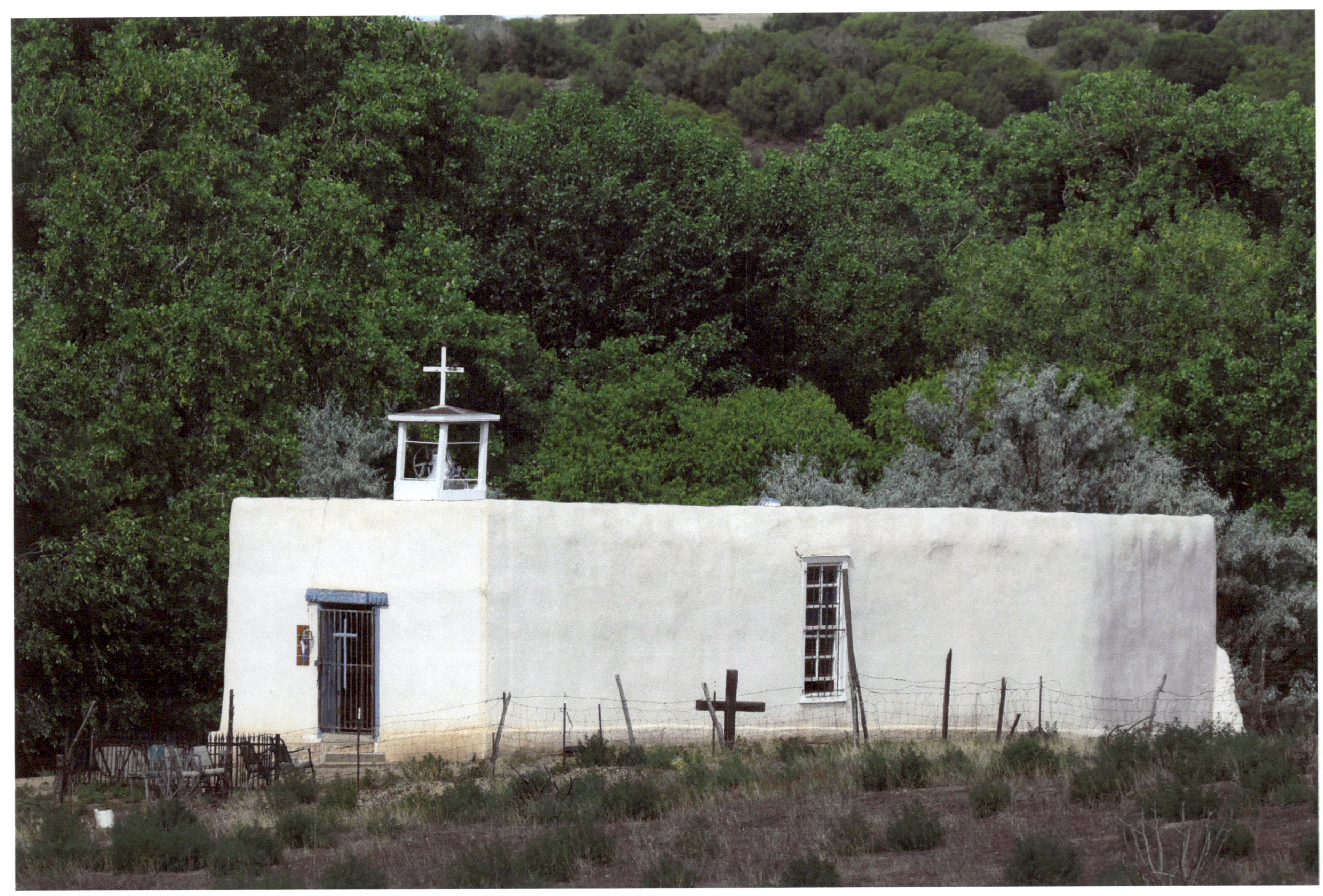

La Capilla de San Antonio, Cieneguilla (Santa Fe), Santa Fe County. 1818–1820. This lovely adobe chapel, on private property but visible from a public road, was built by the Mora family and remains in the family today. Take Airport Road to Paseo Real to Paseo de San Antonio. Photograph taken in 2024.

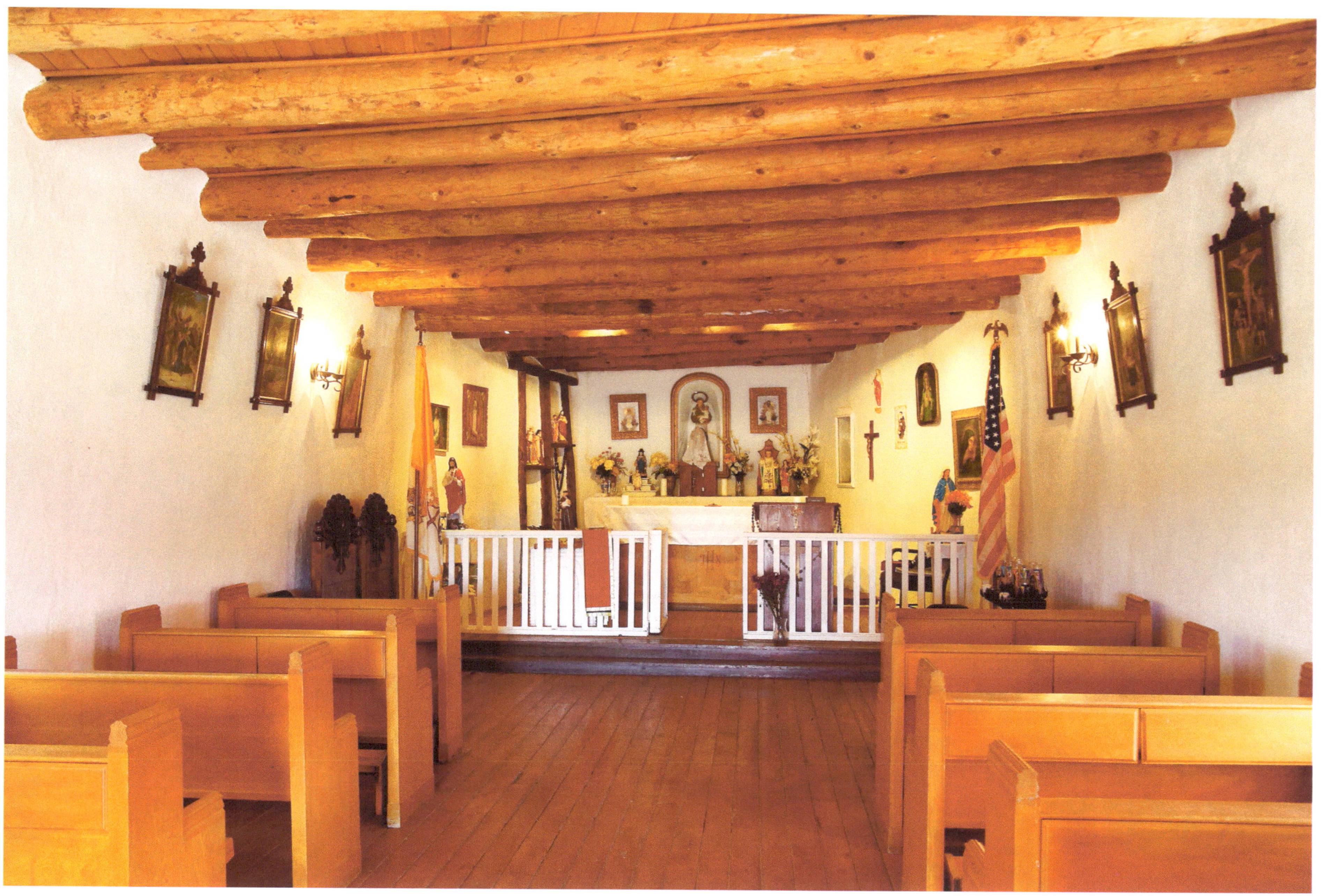

The beautifully maintained interior of La Capilla de San Antonio. The history of the artwork is lost to time, but some is from the 20th century. Sadly, even this capilla has not escaped burglary. Photograph taken in 2024.

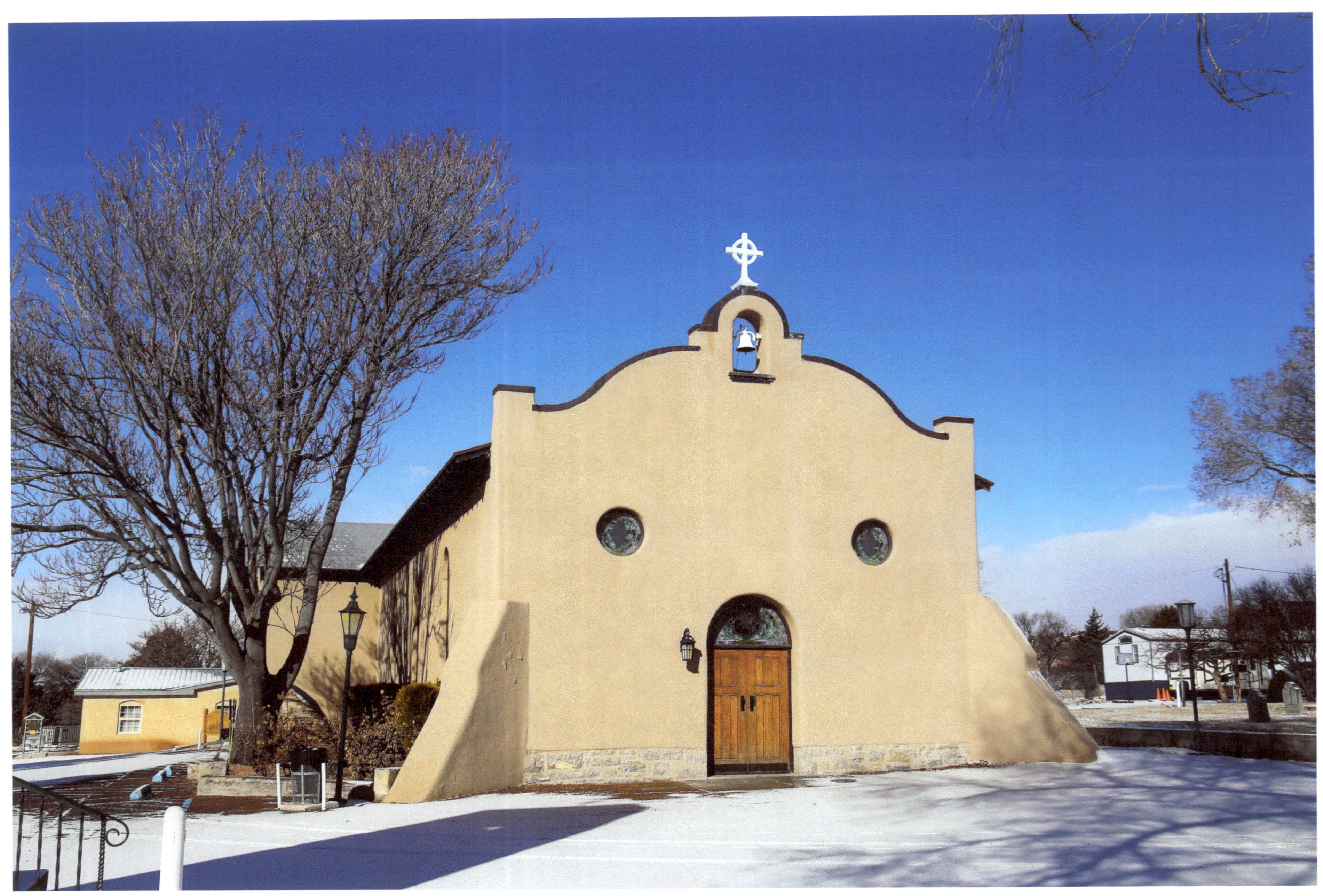

Rosario Chapel, Santa Fe, Santa Fe County. 1807. The front of the adobe chapel looks like a face expressing mild surprise. It is behind the large Rosario Cemetery, across the street from the DeVargas Center on Guadalupe Street. Photograph taken in 2019.

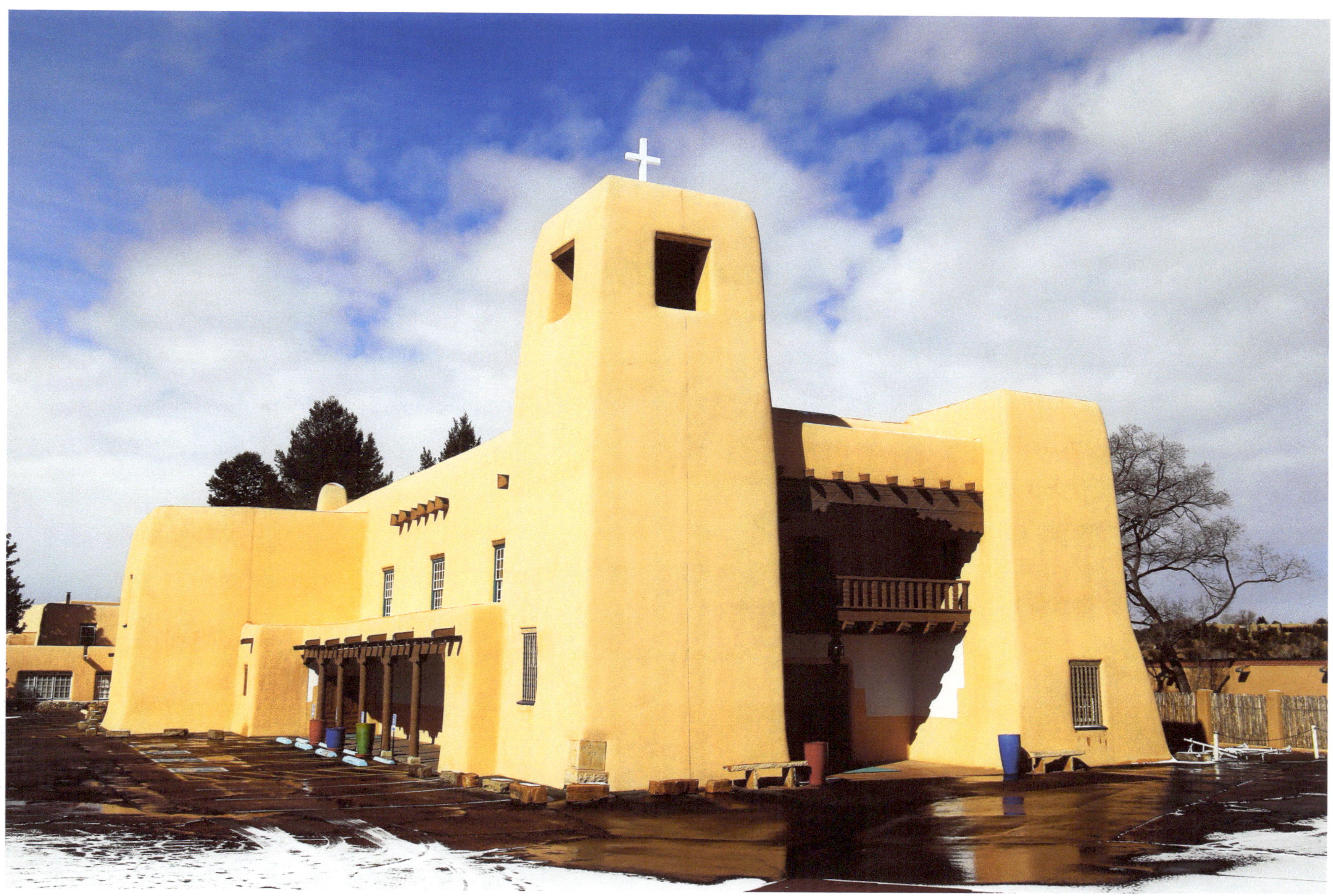

Cristo Rey Catholic Church, Santa Fe, Santa Fe County. 1939. Designed by architect John Gaw Meem, this large, striking adobe church has a hidden steel frame and has the stone altar screen that used to be in Nuestra Señora de la Luz Church ("La Castrense") on the plaza before it was demolished around 1860. At 1120 Canyon Road. Photograph taken in 2019.

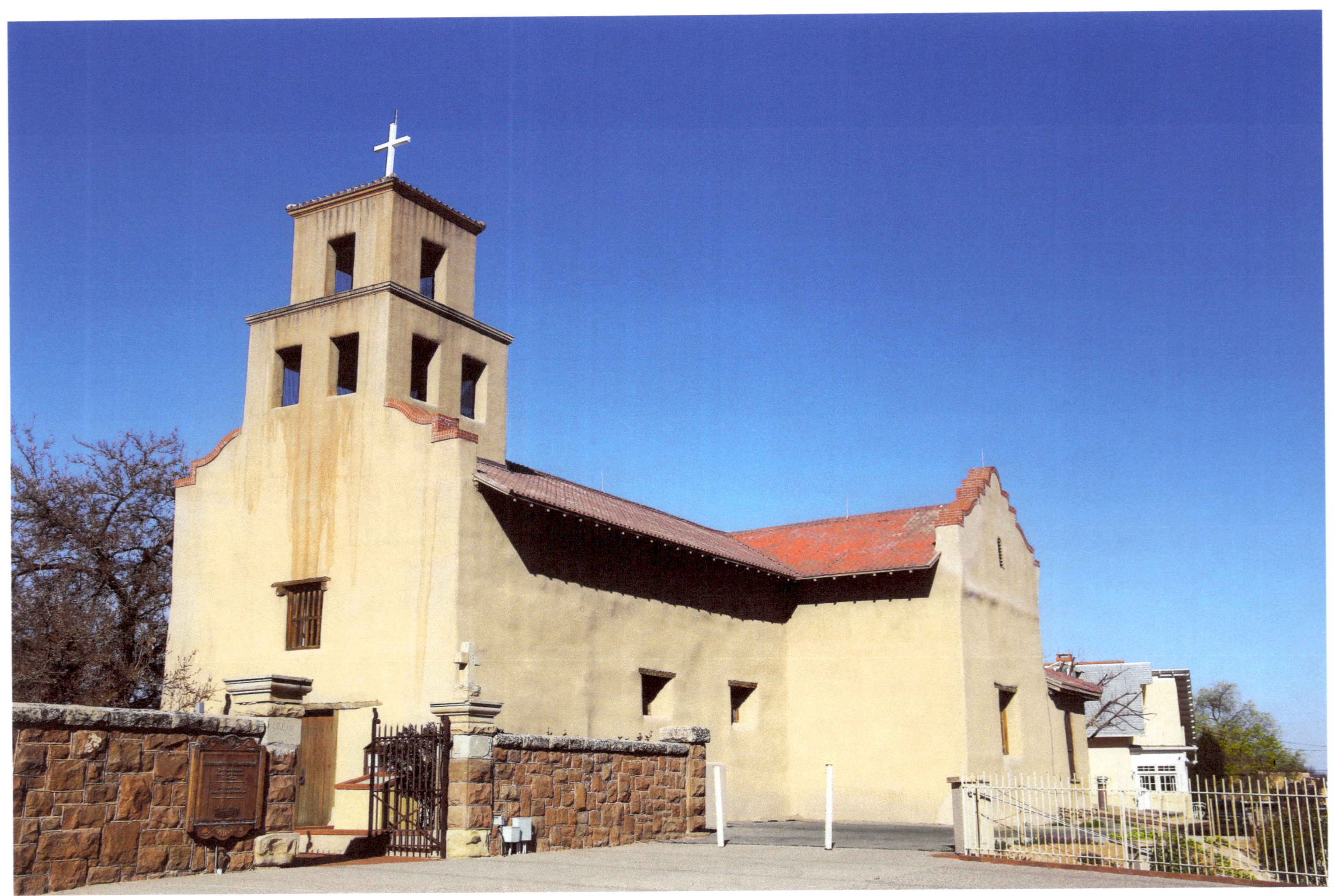

Santuario de Guadalupe, Santa Fe, Santa Fe County. Likely around or just before 1800. This famous adobe church, one of the oldest in New Mexico, has been remodeled several times. Most services are held at the new (1961) church next door (not pictured). At 100 South Guadalupe Street. Photograph taken in 2019.

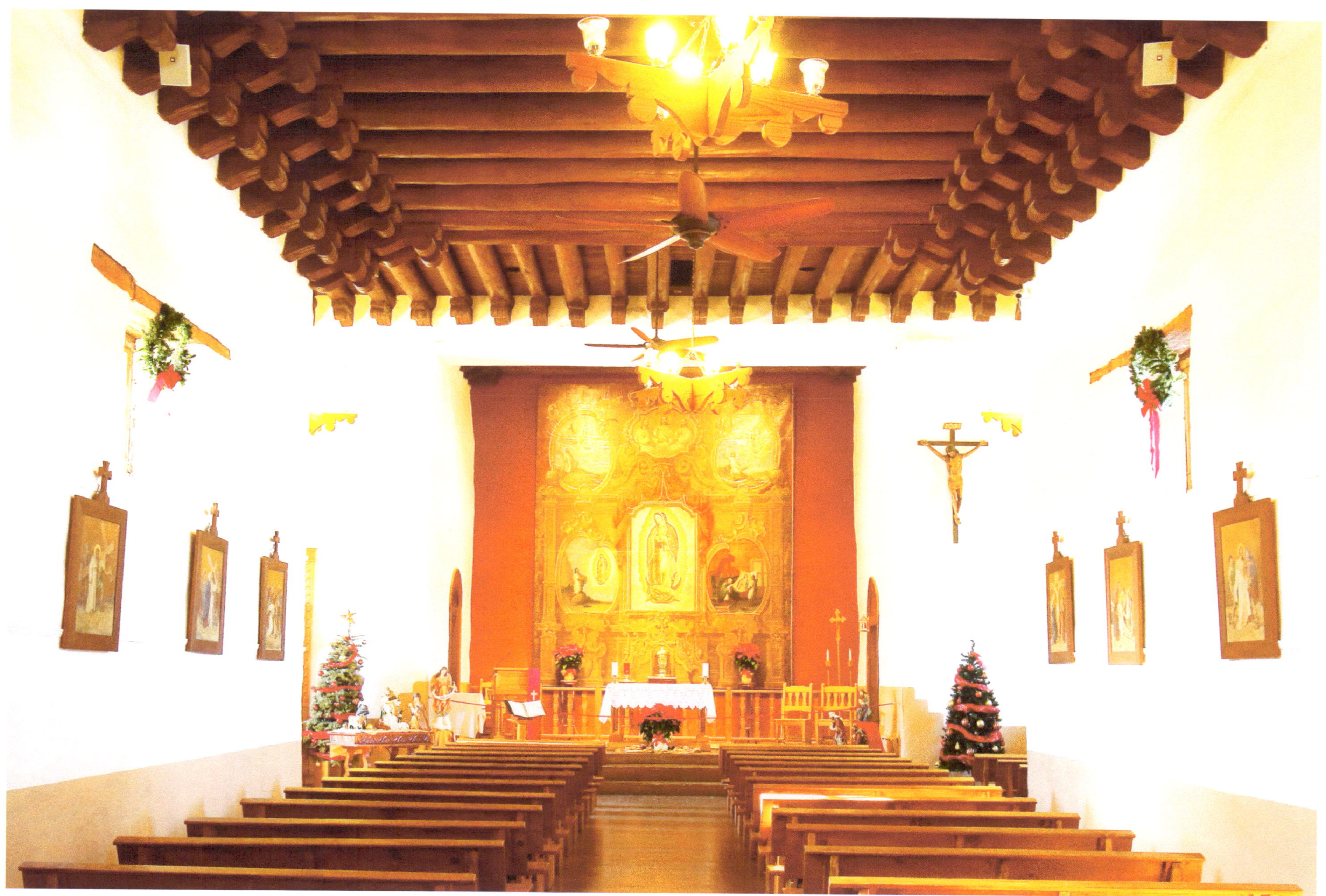

The lovely interior of the Santuario de Guadalupe is graced with an altar screen predating the church, painted by Mexican artist José de Alcibar in 1783, and hand-carved corbels. Photograph taken in 2021.

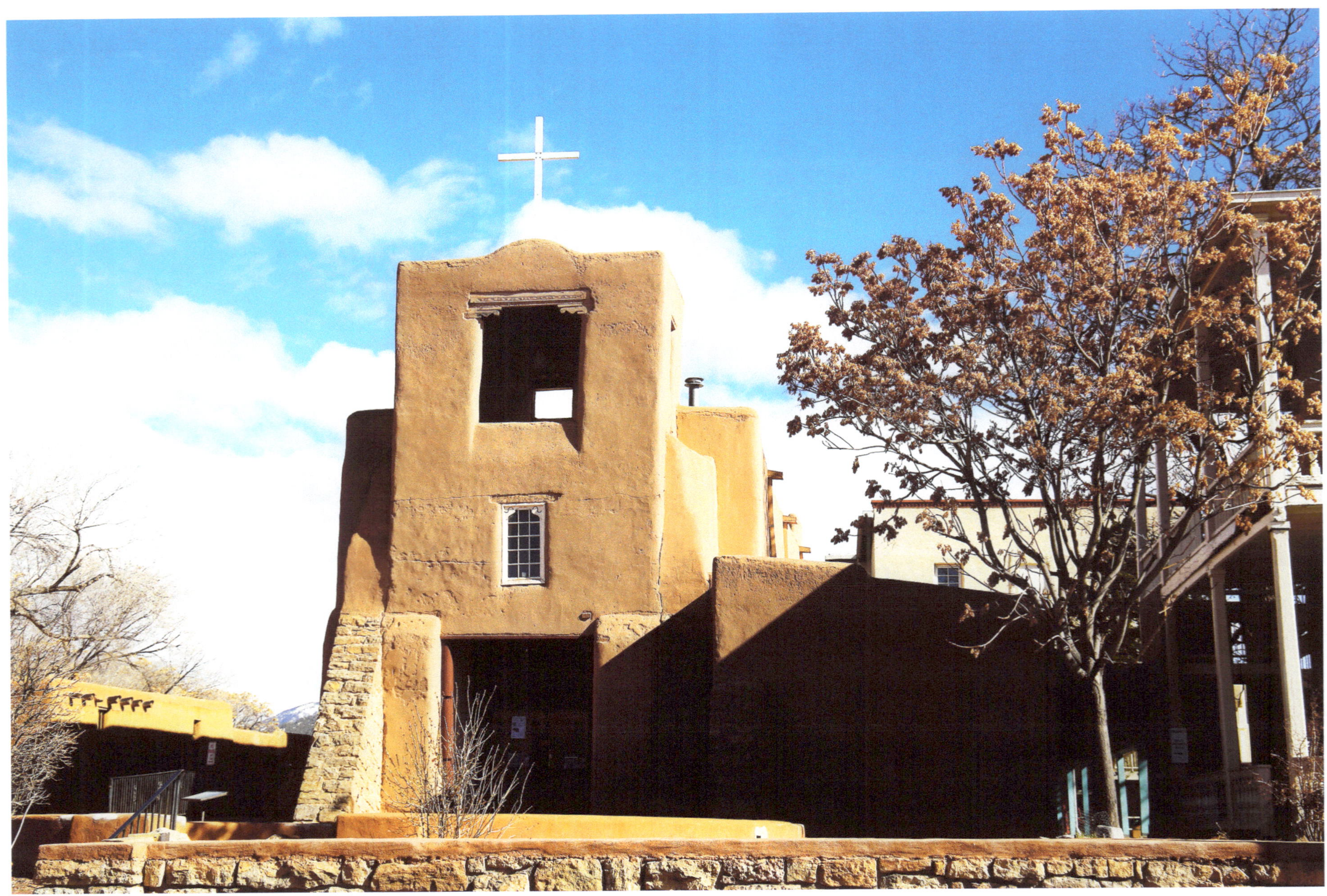

Old San Miguel Mission (San Miguel Catholic Chapel), Santa Fe, Santa Fe County. 1710. An earlier church on the site, almost entirely destroyed in the Pueblo Revolt of 1680, dated from around 1640.This famous adobe church has been remodeled and renovated many times since 1710. At Old Santa Fe Trail and East De Vargas Street. Photograph taken in 2019.

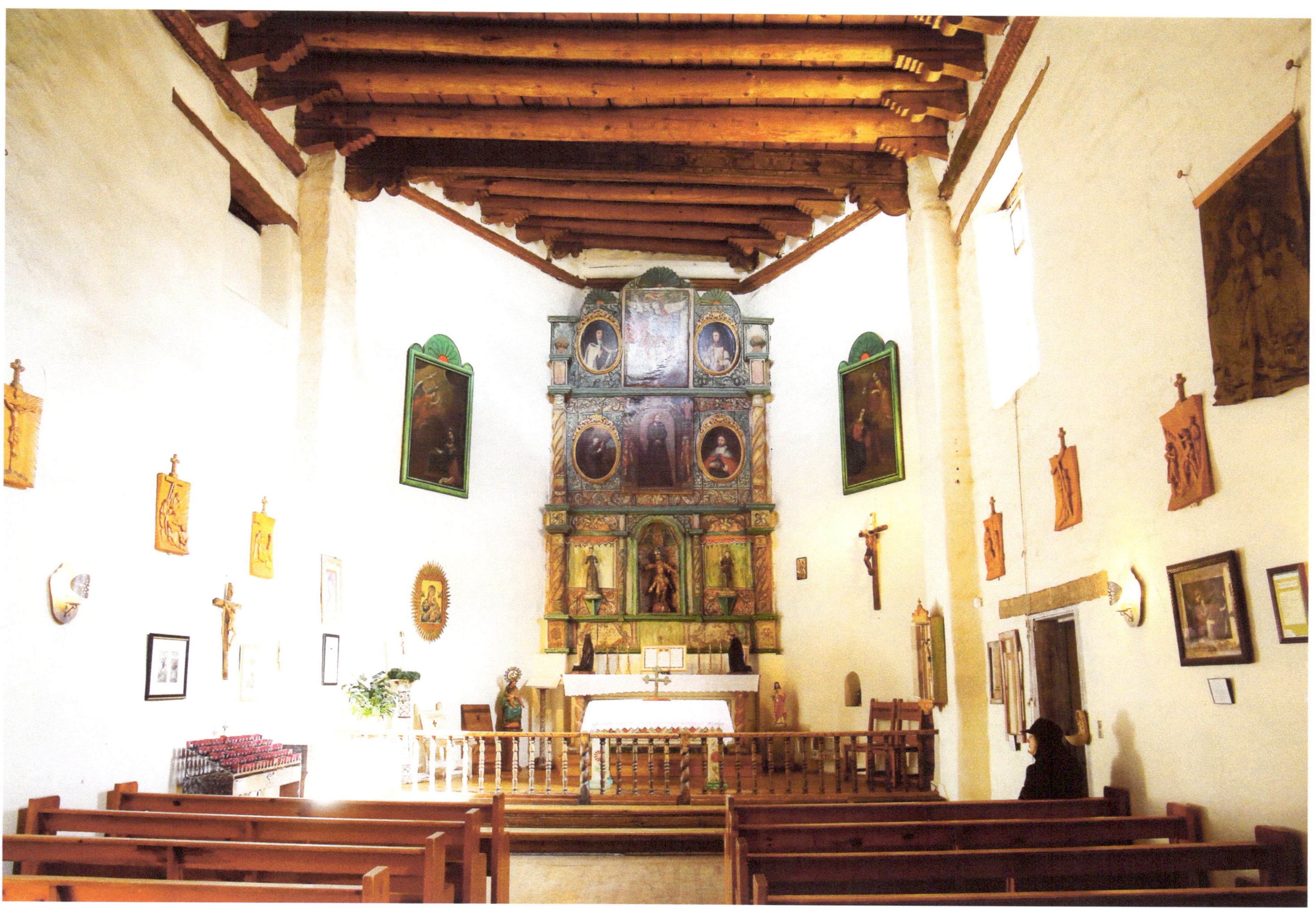

The interior of Old San Miguel Mission, now a museum, filled with wonderful art, mainly from the 18th century. The altar screen, by the Laguna Santero, was painted in 1798. Photograph taken in 2019.

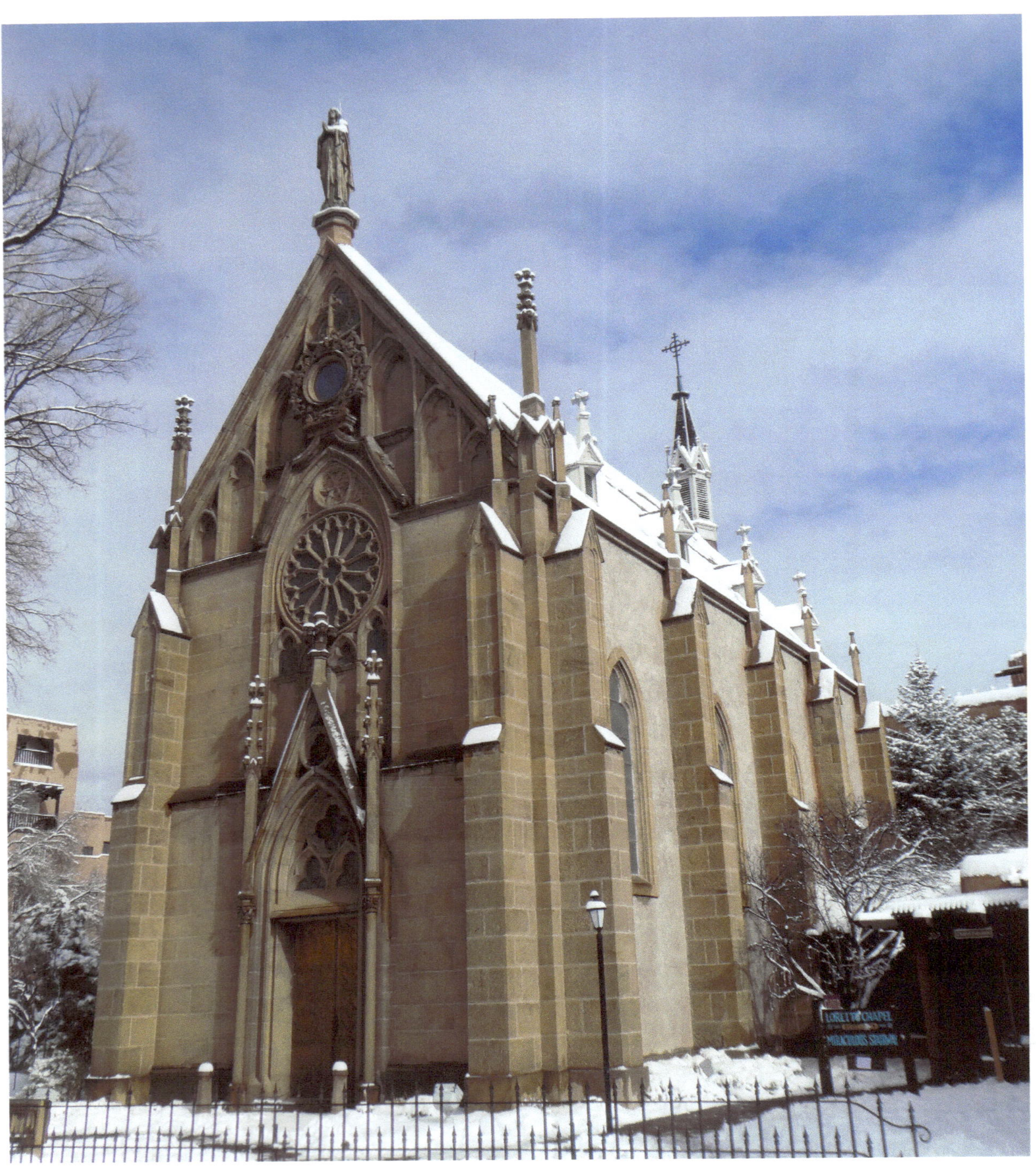

Loretto Chapel, Santa Fe, Santa Fe County. 1878. Built for the Sisters of Loretto, this neo-Gothic church, like the Cathedral Basilica of St. Francis, was commissioned by Archbishop Lamy. At 207 Old Santa Fe Trail. Photograph taken in 2019.

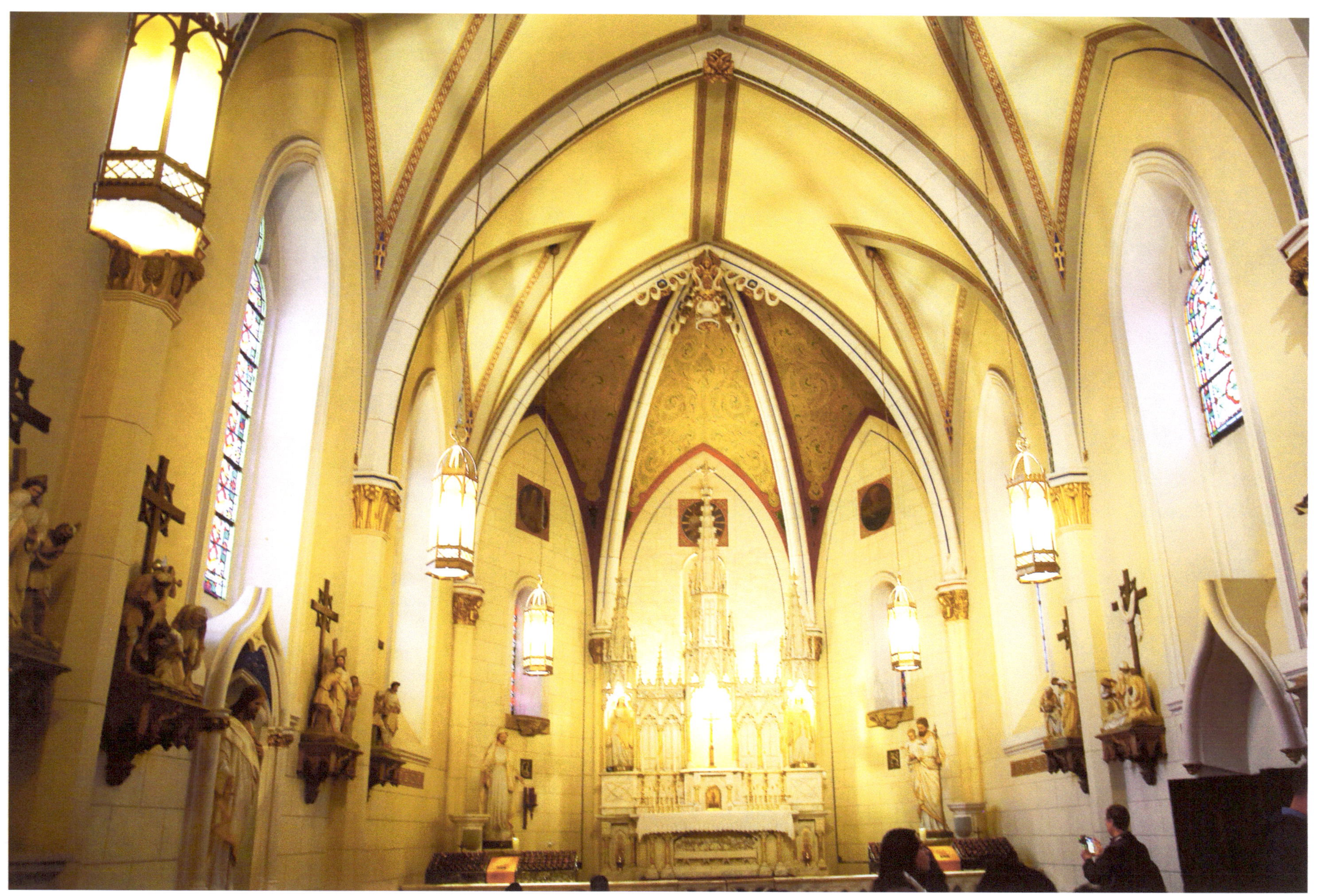

The interior of the Loretto Chapel, now a museum. The famous spiral staircase is toward the rear of the chapel. Photograph taken in 2019.

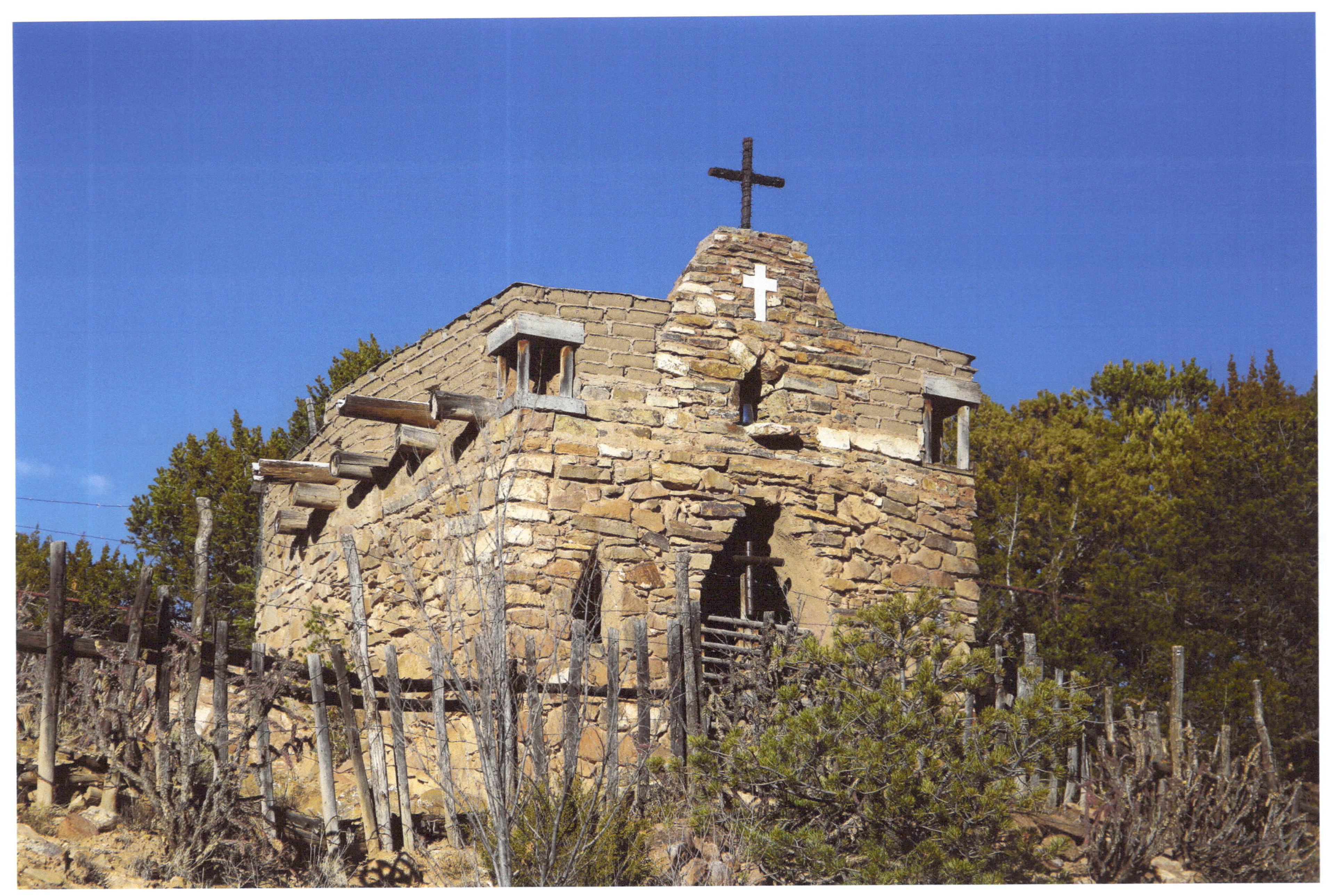

La Capilla de San Ysidro, Santa Fe, Santa Fe County. 1930s. This private, stone chapel is maintained and used for some services. It is on private property fronting Cerro Gordo Road. Photograph taken in 2020.

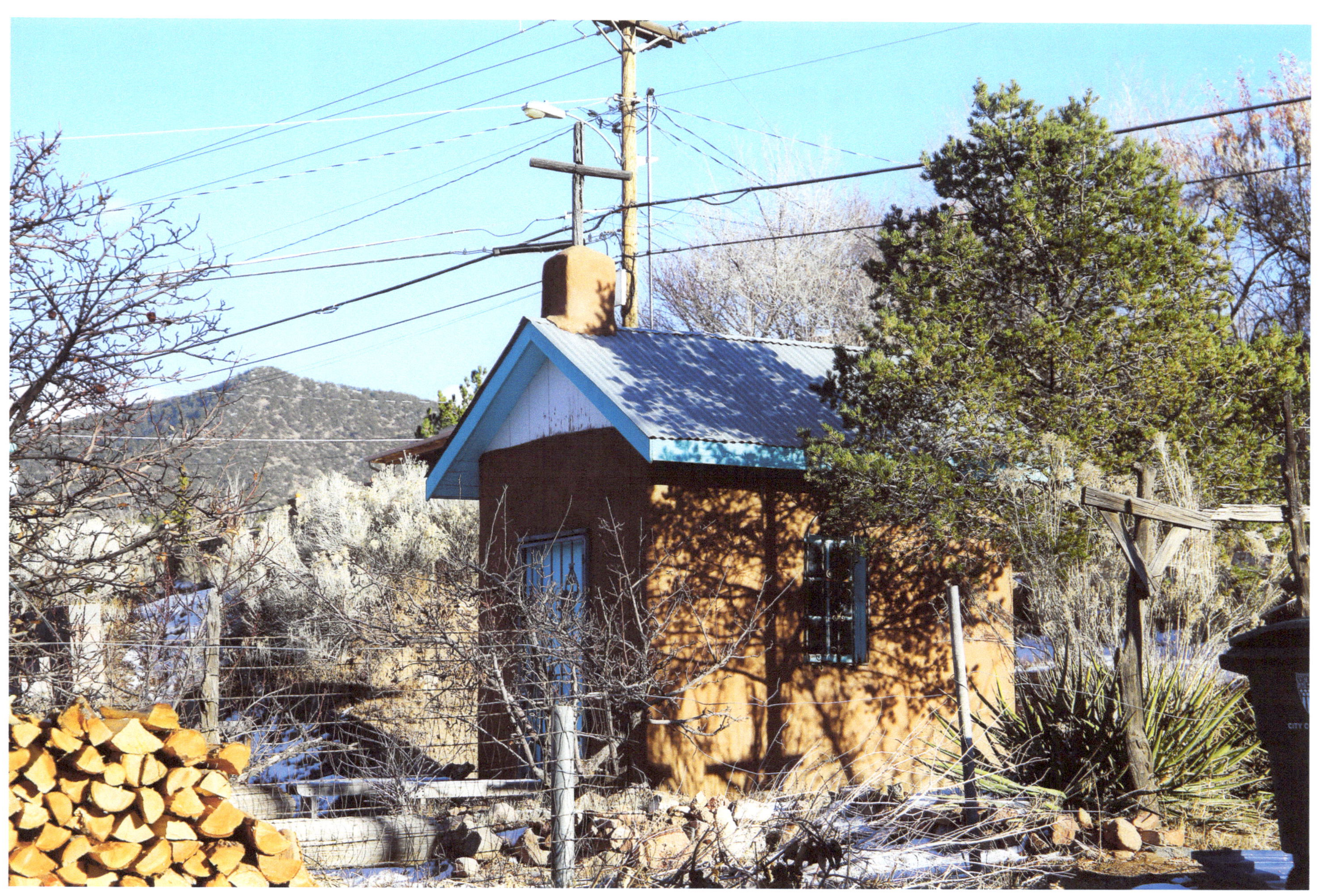

La Capilla de Santa Ines del Campo, Santa Fe, Santa Fe County. 1930s. This tiny, private, stone chapel is off Acequia Madre Road. Photograph taken in 2020.

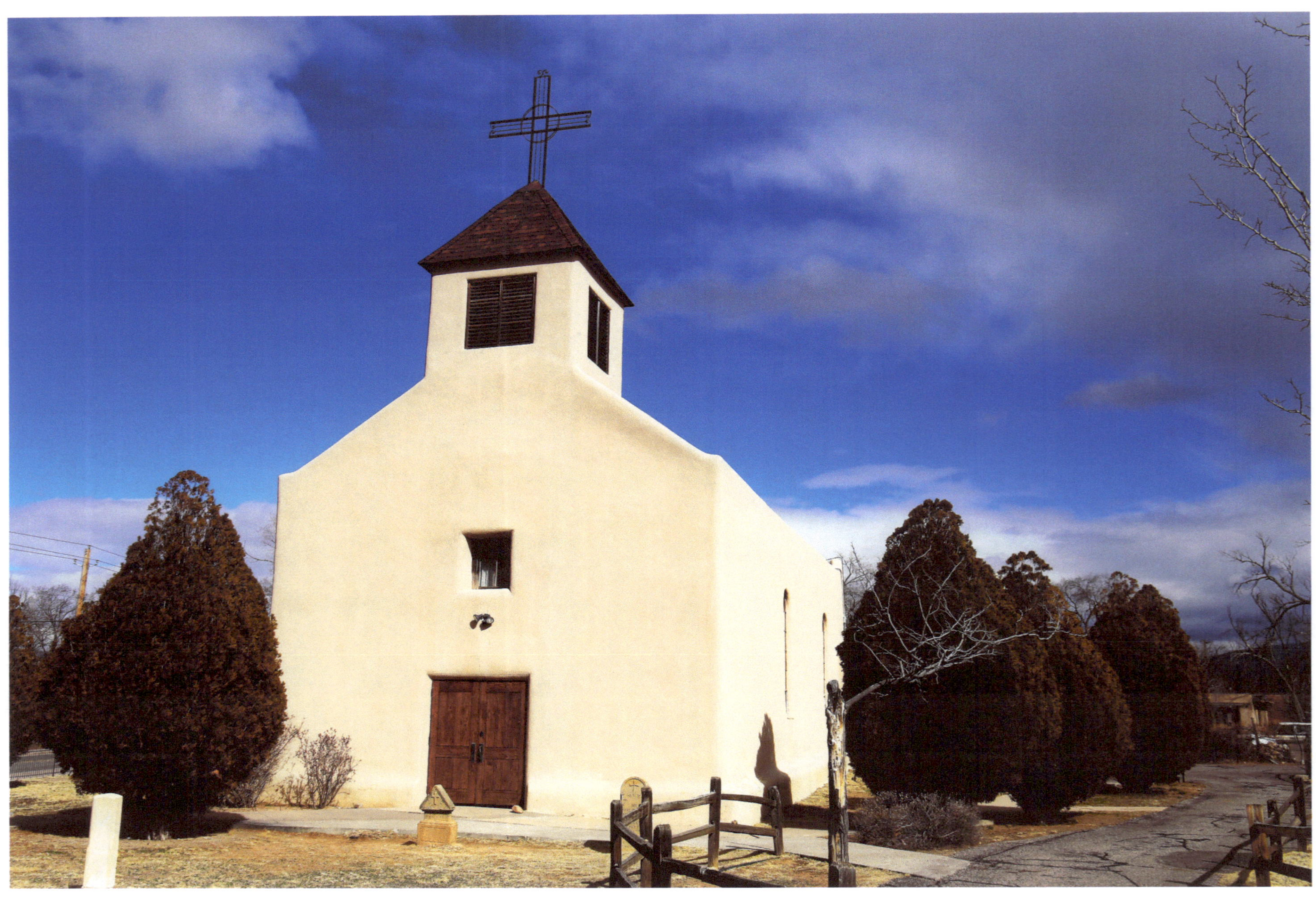

San Isidro Catholic Church, Agua Fria (Santa Fe), Santa Fe County. 1835. A classic, adobe church. As of 2024, a new, larger church is being planned for a nearby site, but the old one will be maintained and used for some services. At 3552 Agua Fria Street. Photograph taken in 2019.

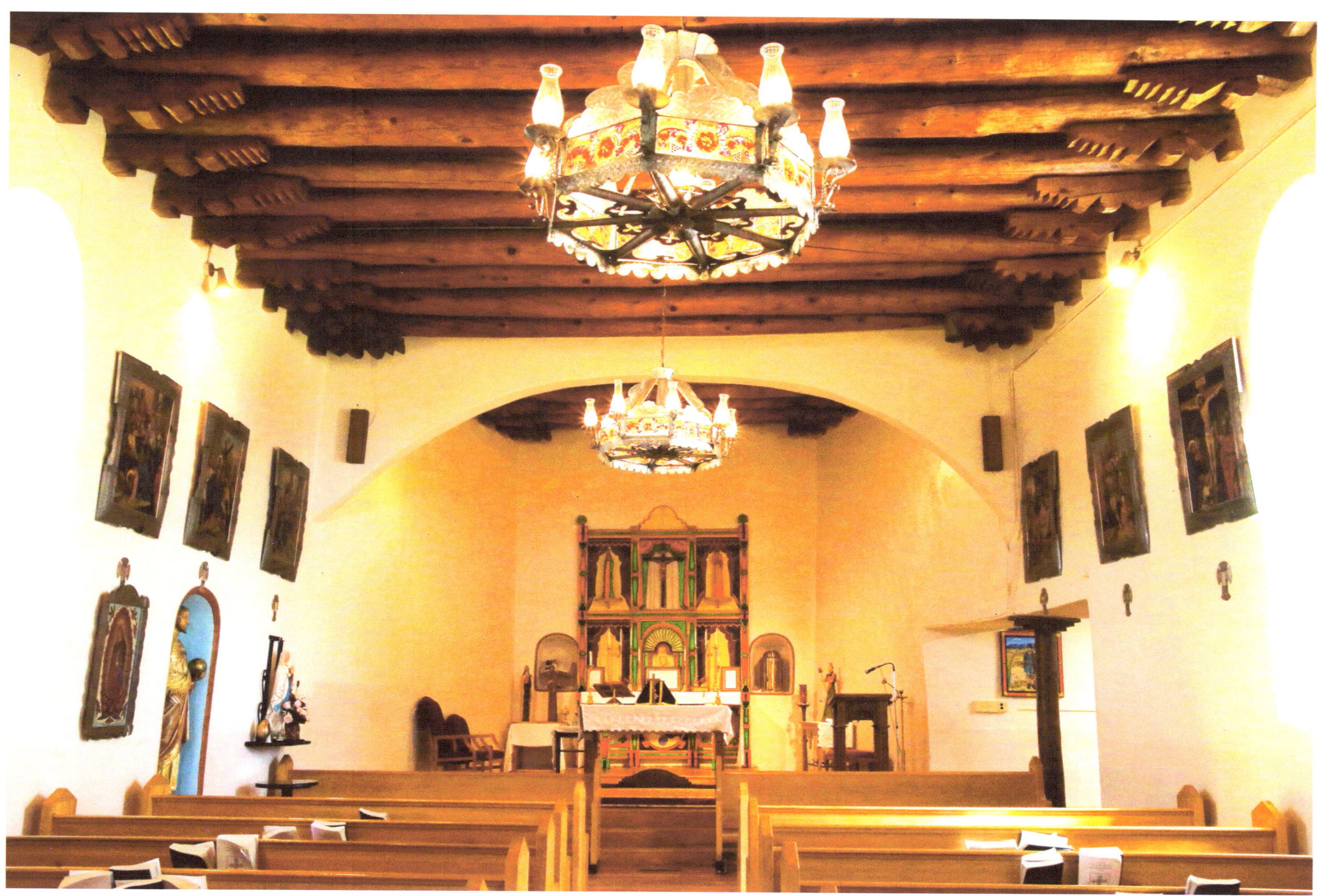

The interior of San Isidro. Notice the carved corbels. The artwork is of varying ages; the lovely altar screen was painted by Luis Capia in 1986. Photograph taken in 2024.

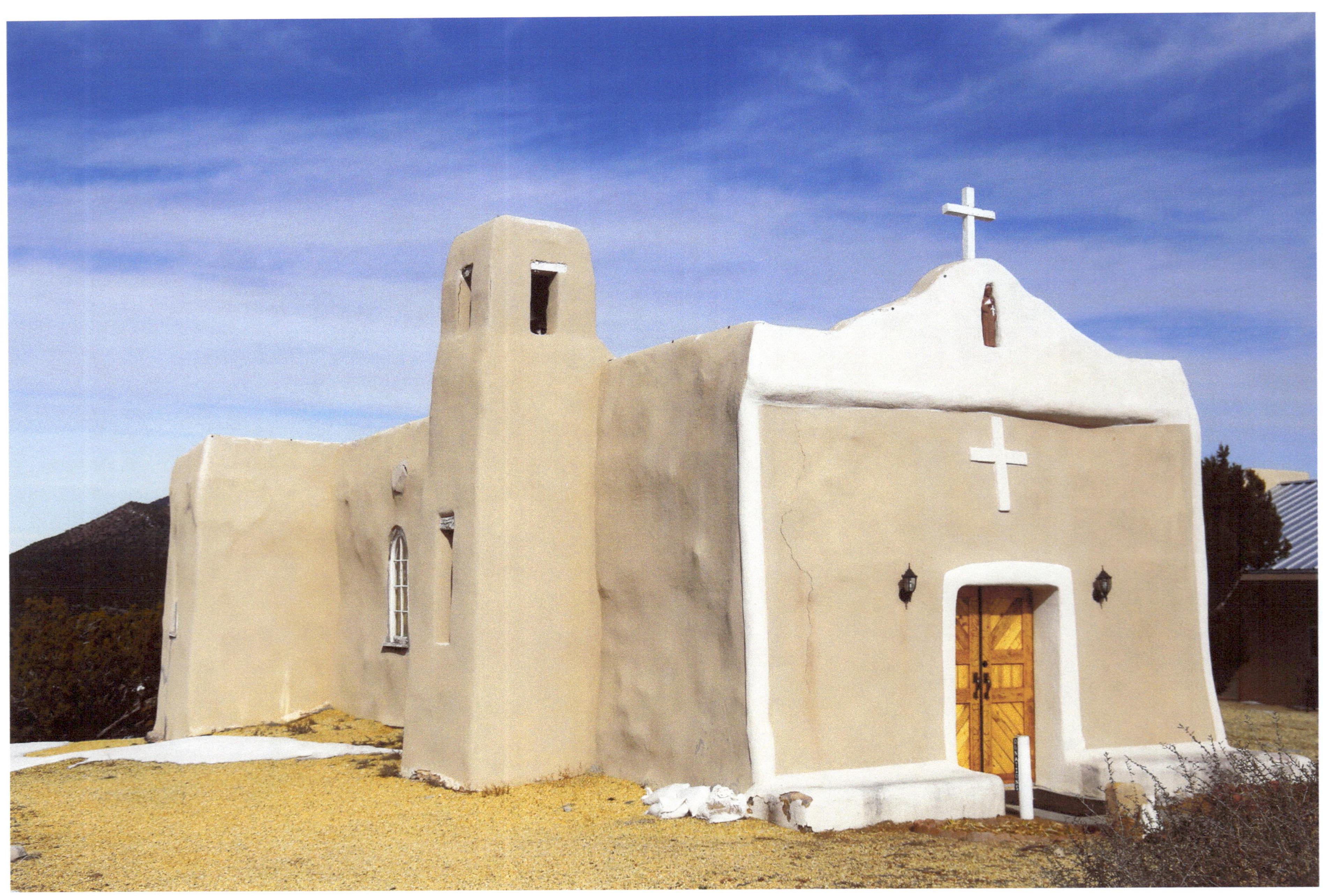

San Francisco de Asís Catholic Church, Golden, Santa Fe County. 1839. This adobe church is the subject of many photographs and paintings, perhaps second only to San Francisco de Asís Catholic Church in Ranchos de Taos. On New Mexico Highway 14. Photograph taken in 2019.

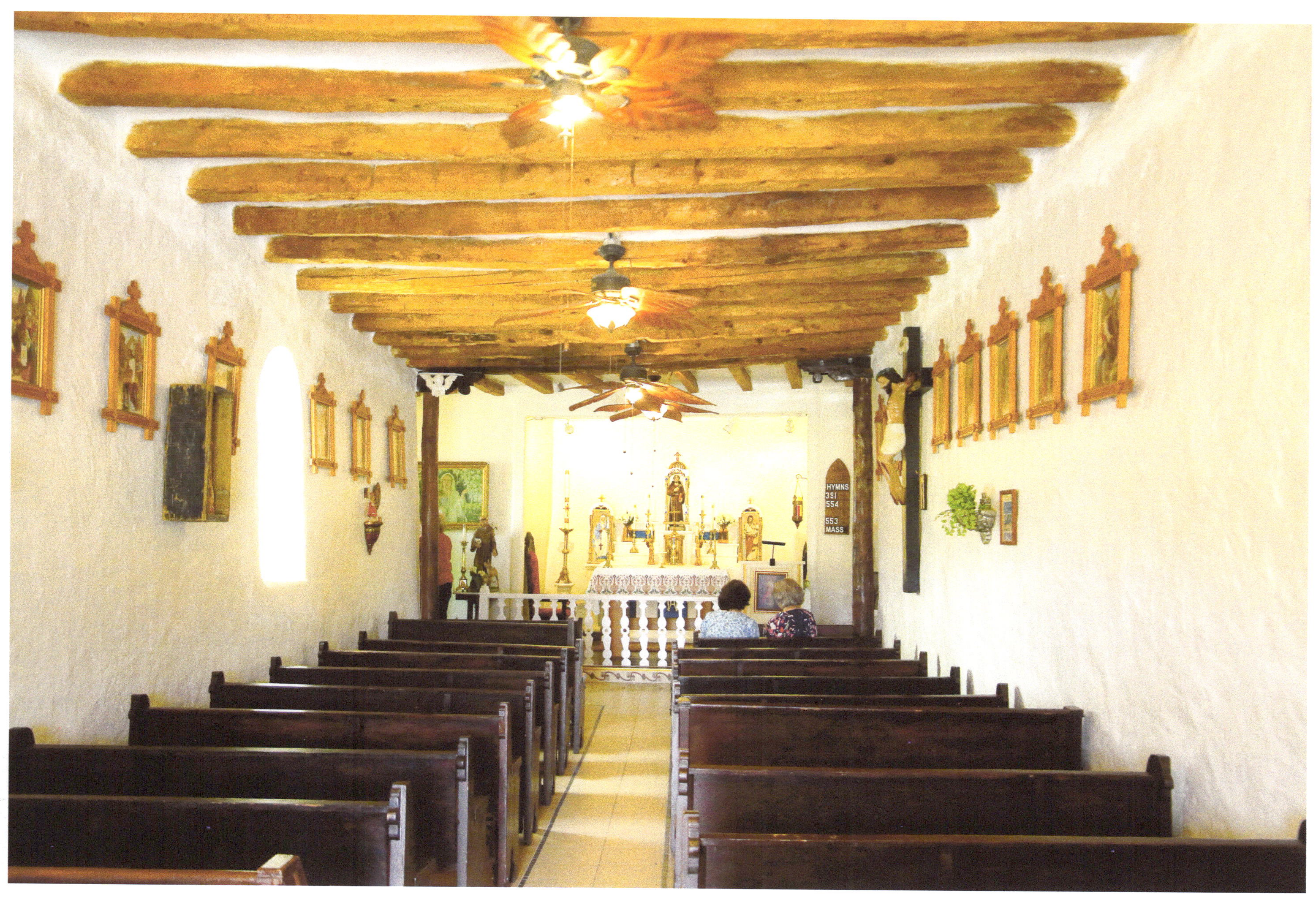

The recently restored interior of San Francisco de Asís. Photograph taken in 2024.

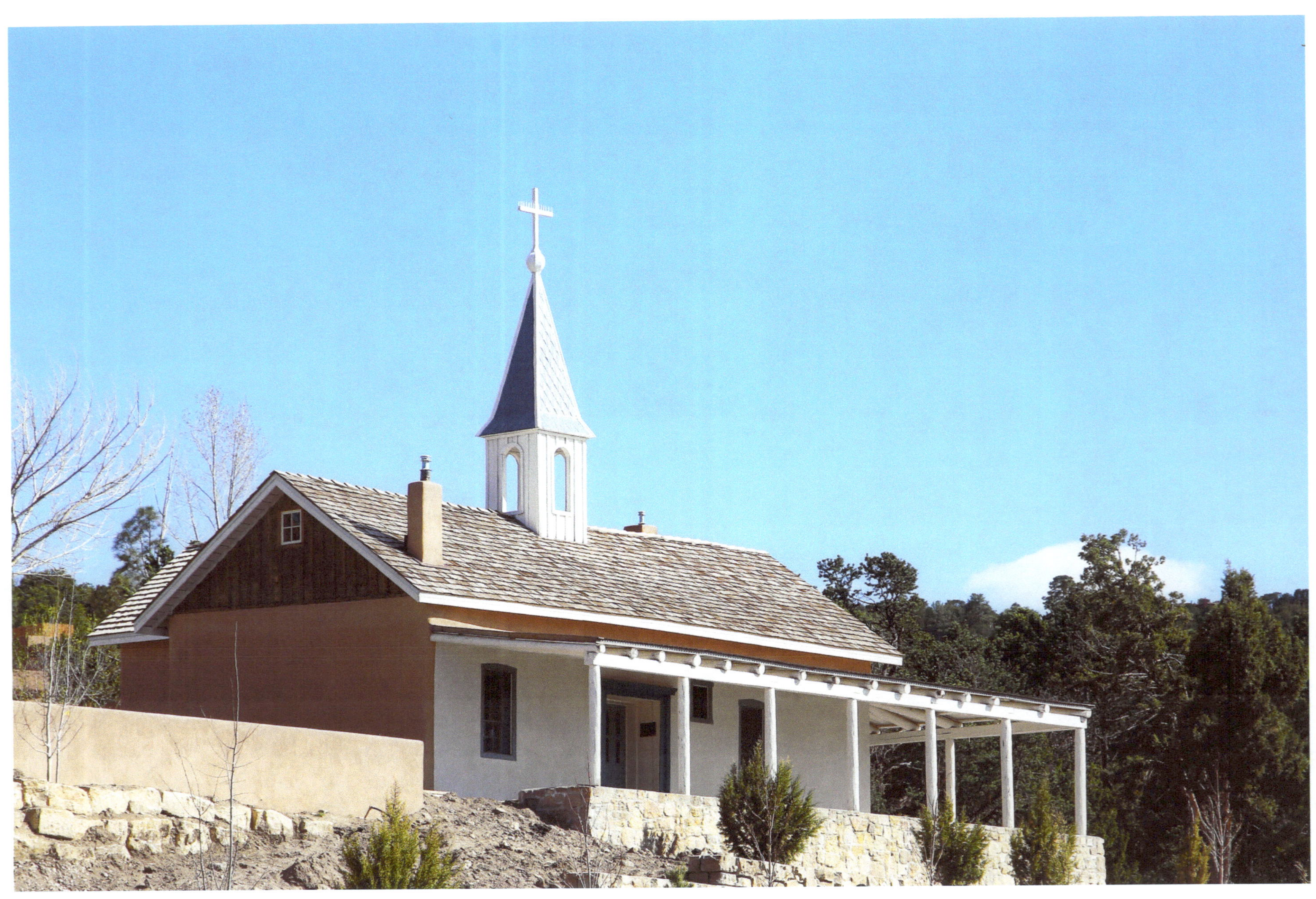

Archbishop Lamy's Chapel, Santa Fe, Santa Fe County. 1874/2020. Lamy had the chapel built as a retreat. It has adobe walls and a major renovation was completed in 2020. On the Bishop's Lodge Resort property at 1297 Bishop's Lodge Road. Photograph taken in 2021.

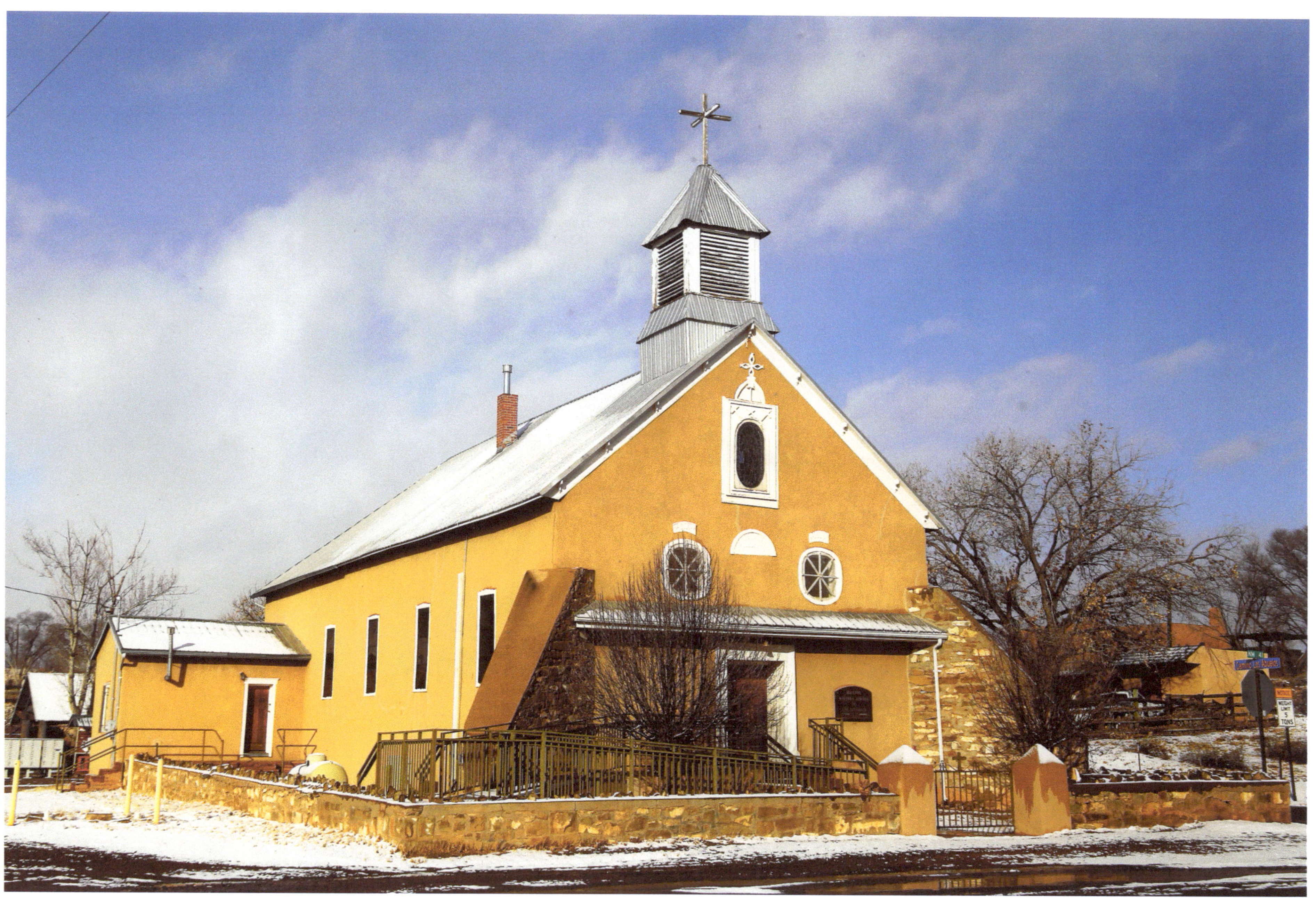

Nuestra Señora de los Remedios Catholic Church, Galisteo, Santa Fe County. 1884. This attractive adobe church with stone buttresses and a four-way cross is a mission of St. Joseph Parish in Cerillos and has mass every Sunday. On New Mexico Highway 41. Photograph taken in 2021.

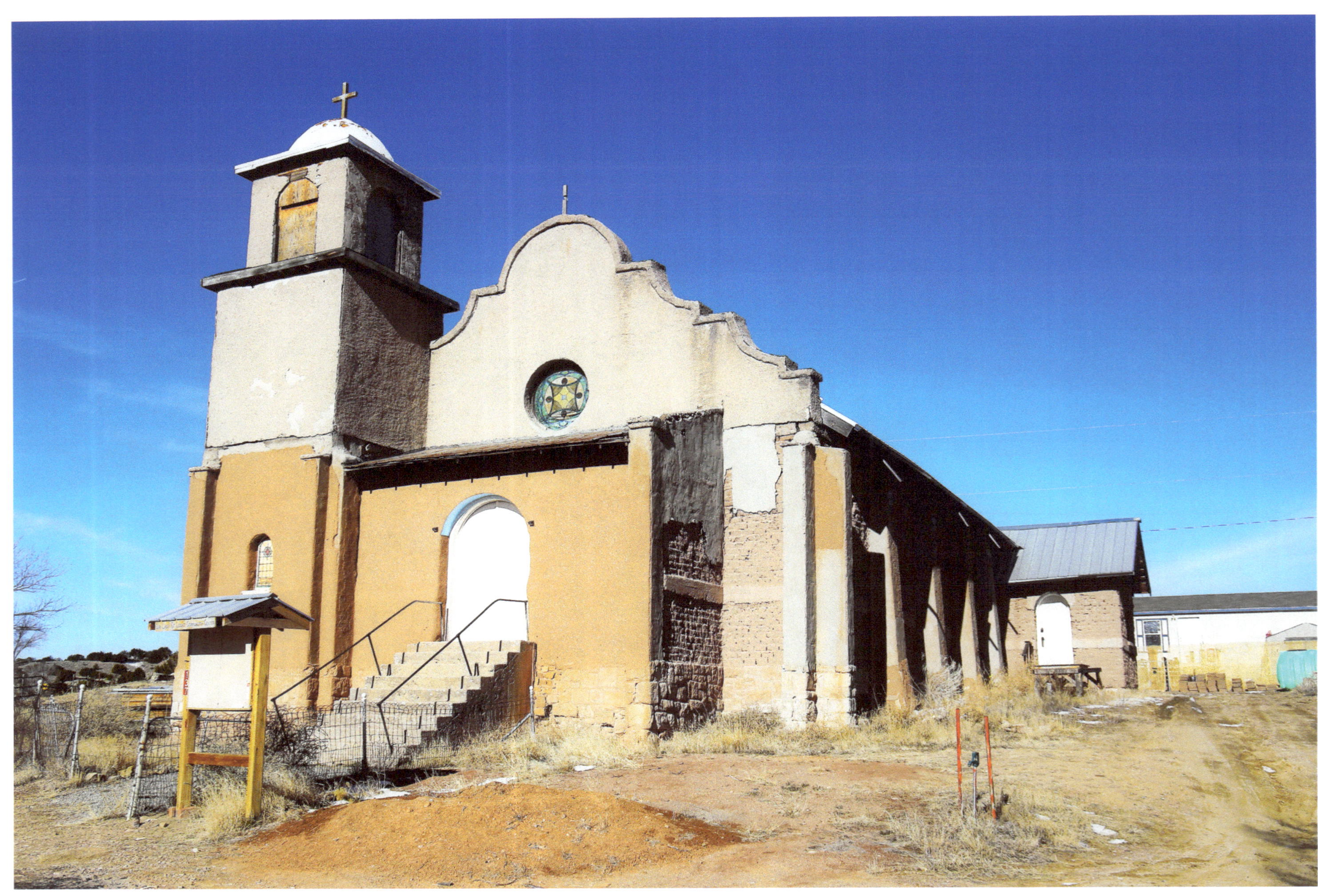

Nuestra Señora de la Luz, Lamy, Santa Fe County. 1926. This mission-revival church was deconsecrated in 1994. Some restoration and renovation have occurred, but not every church is beautiful. On New Mexico Highway 33, Old Lamy Trail. Photograph taken in 2019.

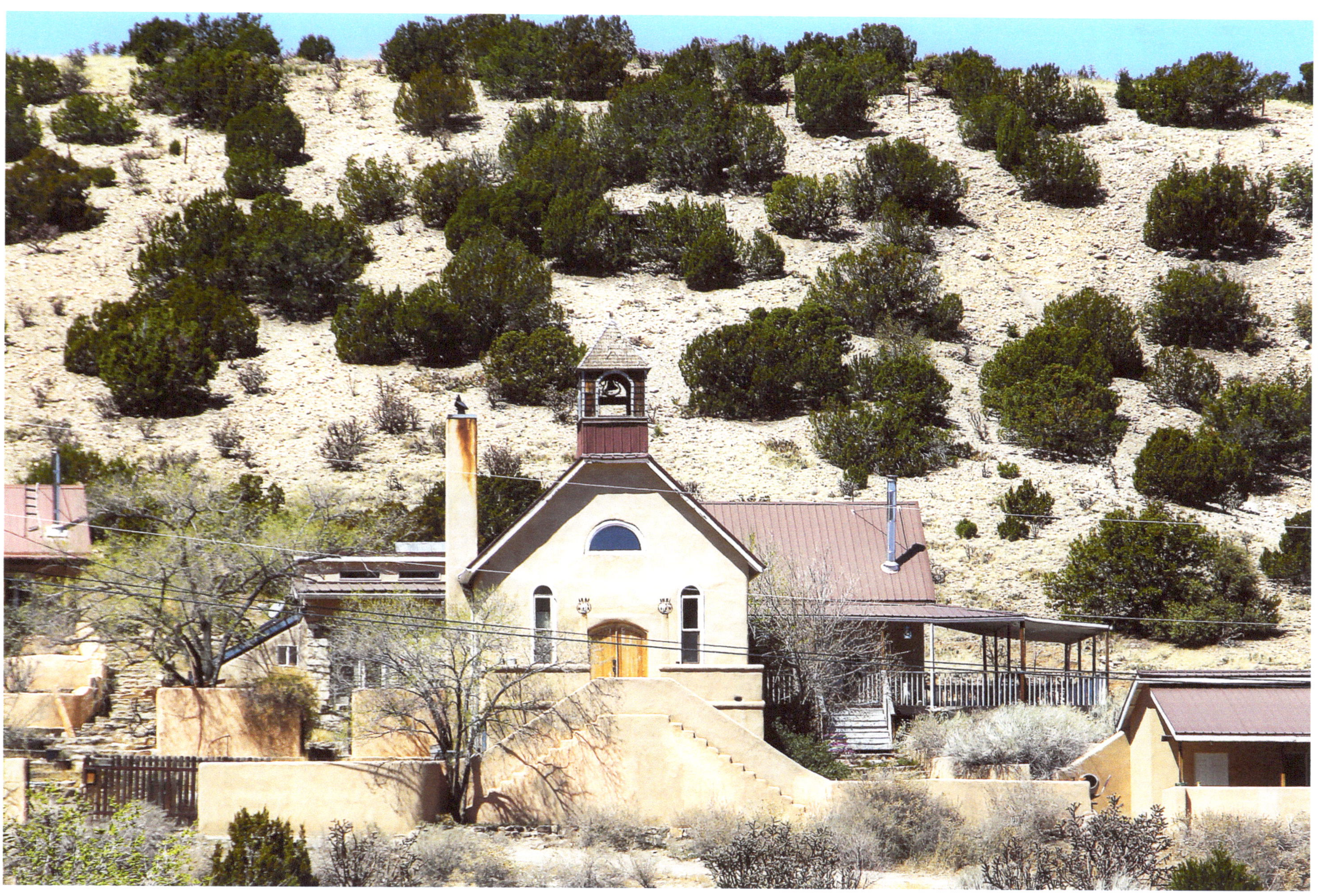

St. Anne Catholic Church, Madrid, Santa Fe County. Early 1900s. Never consecrated, this building is now a private residence. The exterior is little changed since its original construction. On Back Road on the west side of Madrid. Photograph taken in 2022.

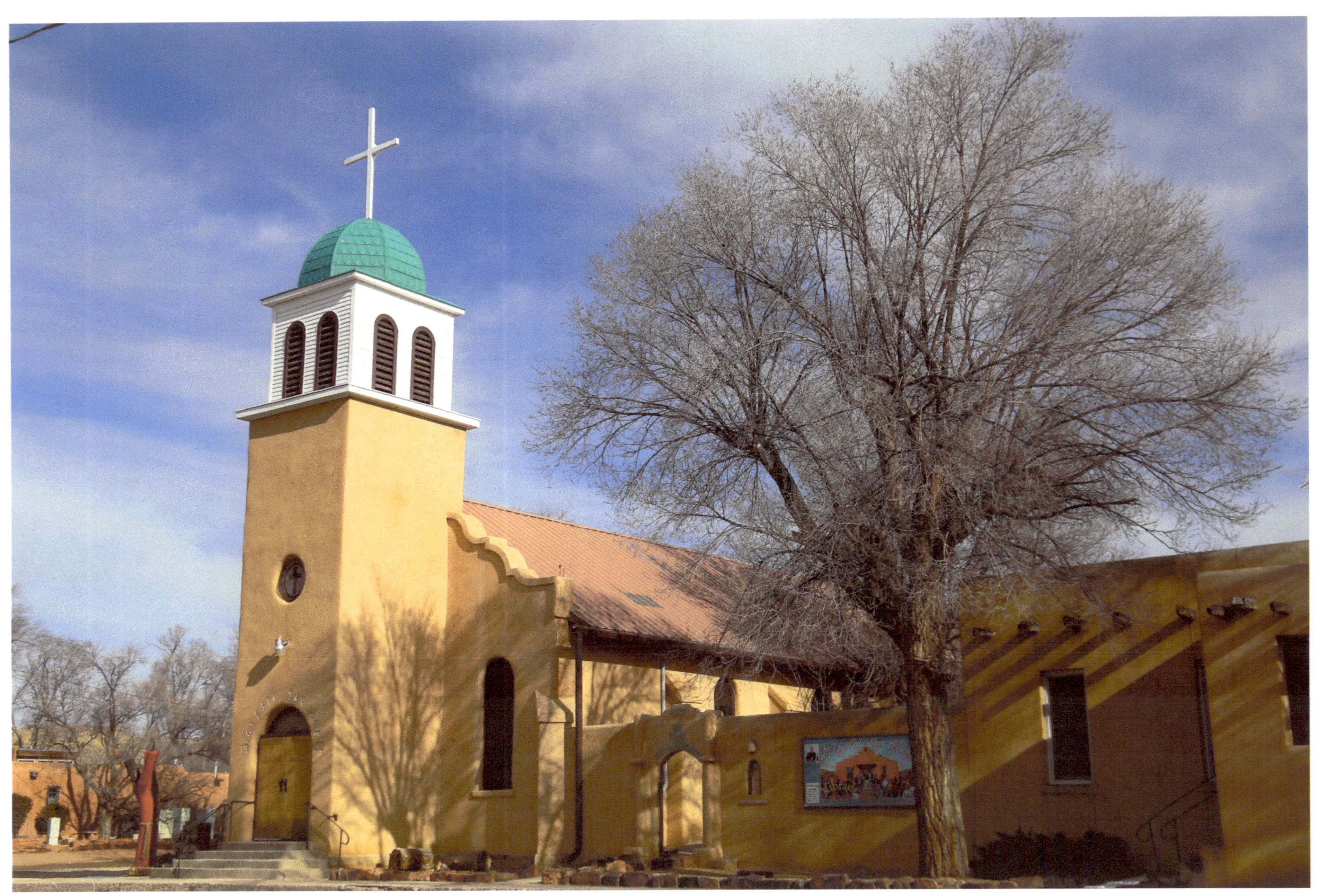

St. Joseph Catholic Church, Cerrillos, Santa Fe County. 1922. The adobe church in the California mission style has a lovely sanctuary and garden. On 1st Street. Photograph taken in 2019.

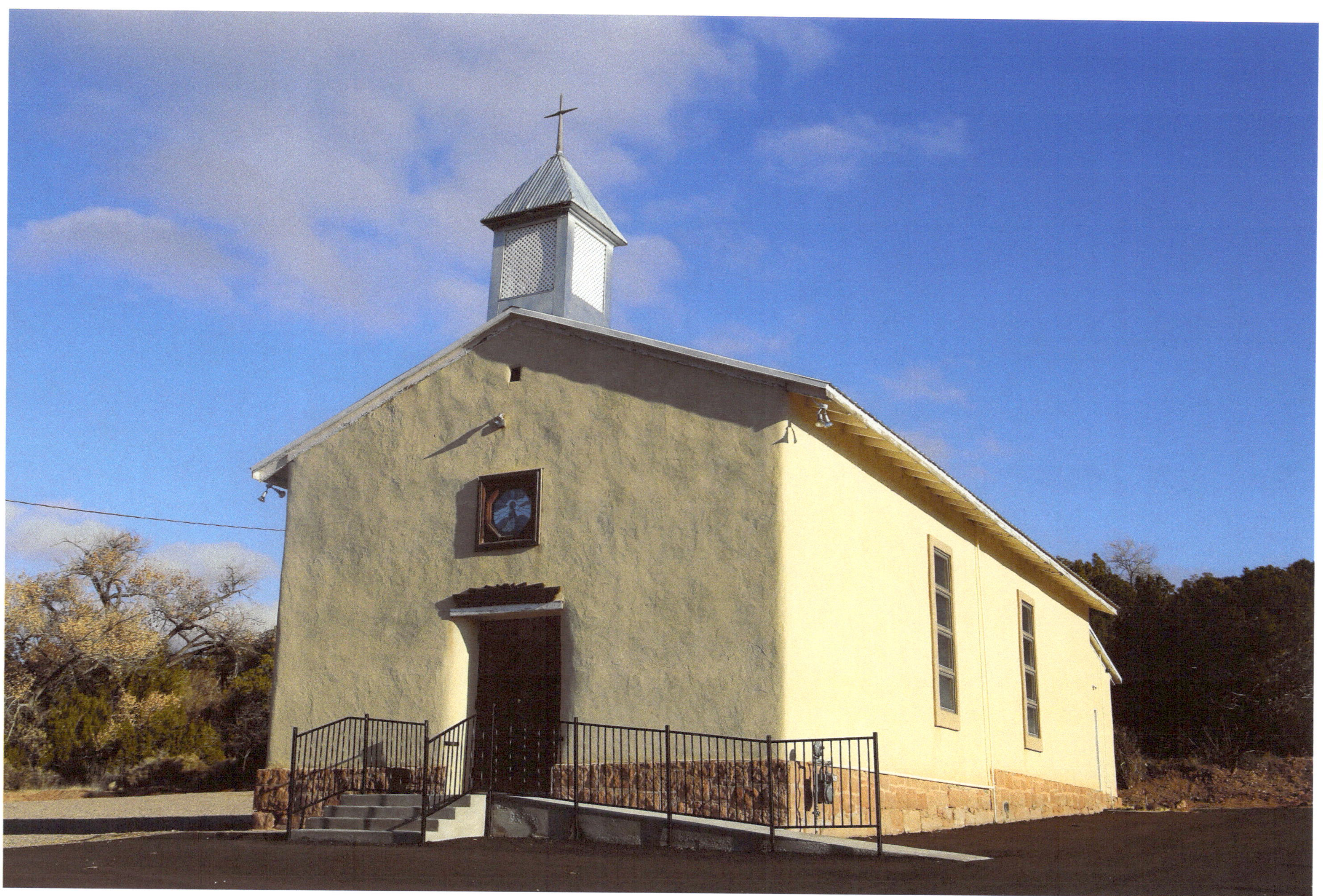

San José Catholic Church, La Cienega, Santa Fe County. 1829 or 1830. This traditional adobe church holds mass weekly. It is co-named for the parish, and thus is labeled above the door as a parish church, but the parish church is San Isidro in Agua Fria. Take Exit 271 off Interstate 25 to Entrada La Cienega, north about a mile to Camino de San José, then about 600 yards to the church. Photograph taken in 2023.

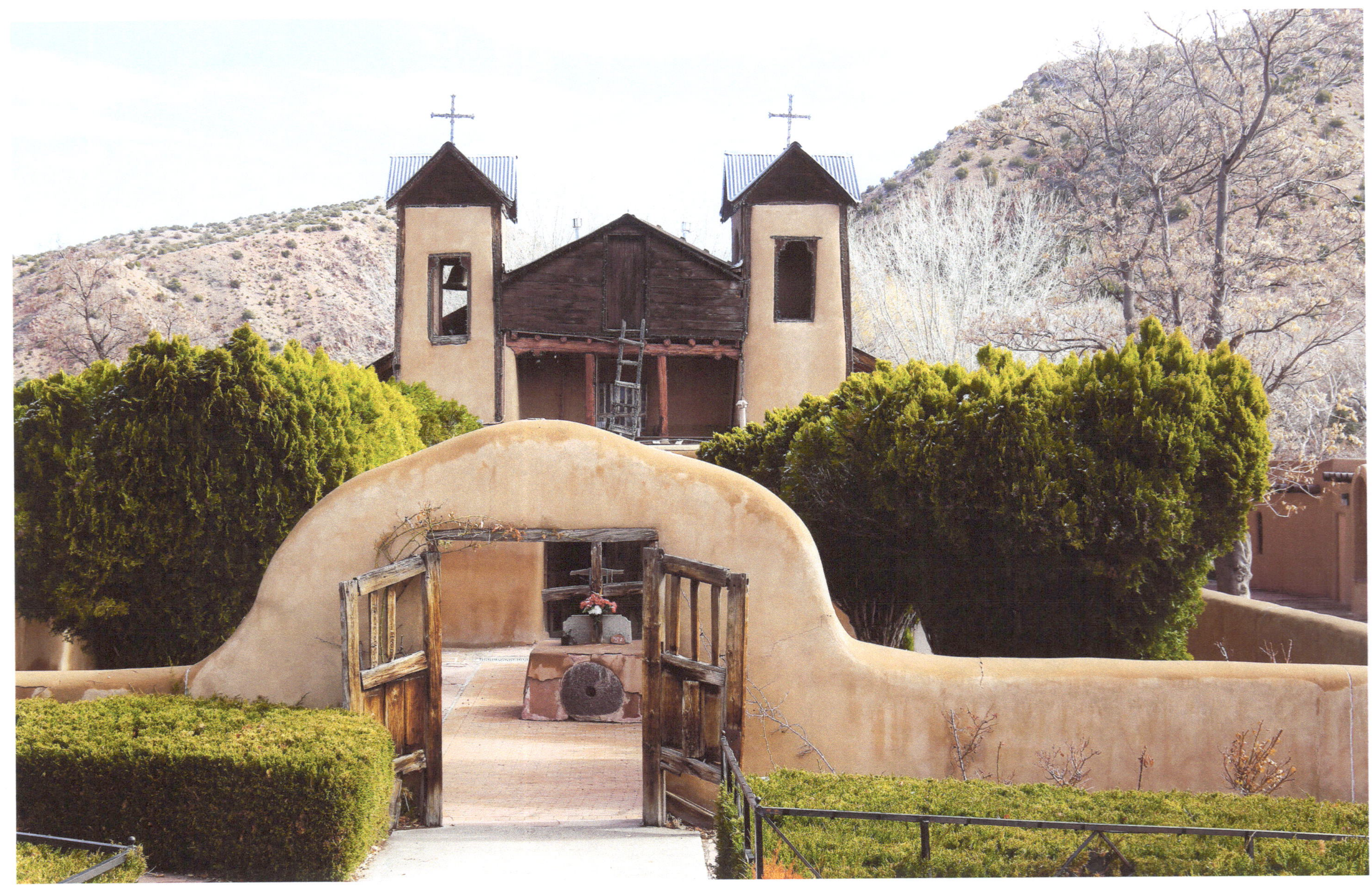

Santuario de Chimayó (Nuestro Señor de Esquípelas Catholic Church), Chimayó, Santa Fe County. 1814. Initially private, the church was bought by several Santa Fe residents in 1929, including architect John Gaw Meem, and donated to the Archdiocese of Santa Fe. It is a famous destination for pilgrims. On Juan Medina Drive. Photograph taken in 2019.

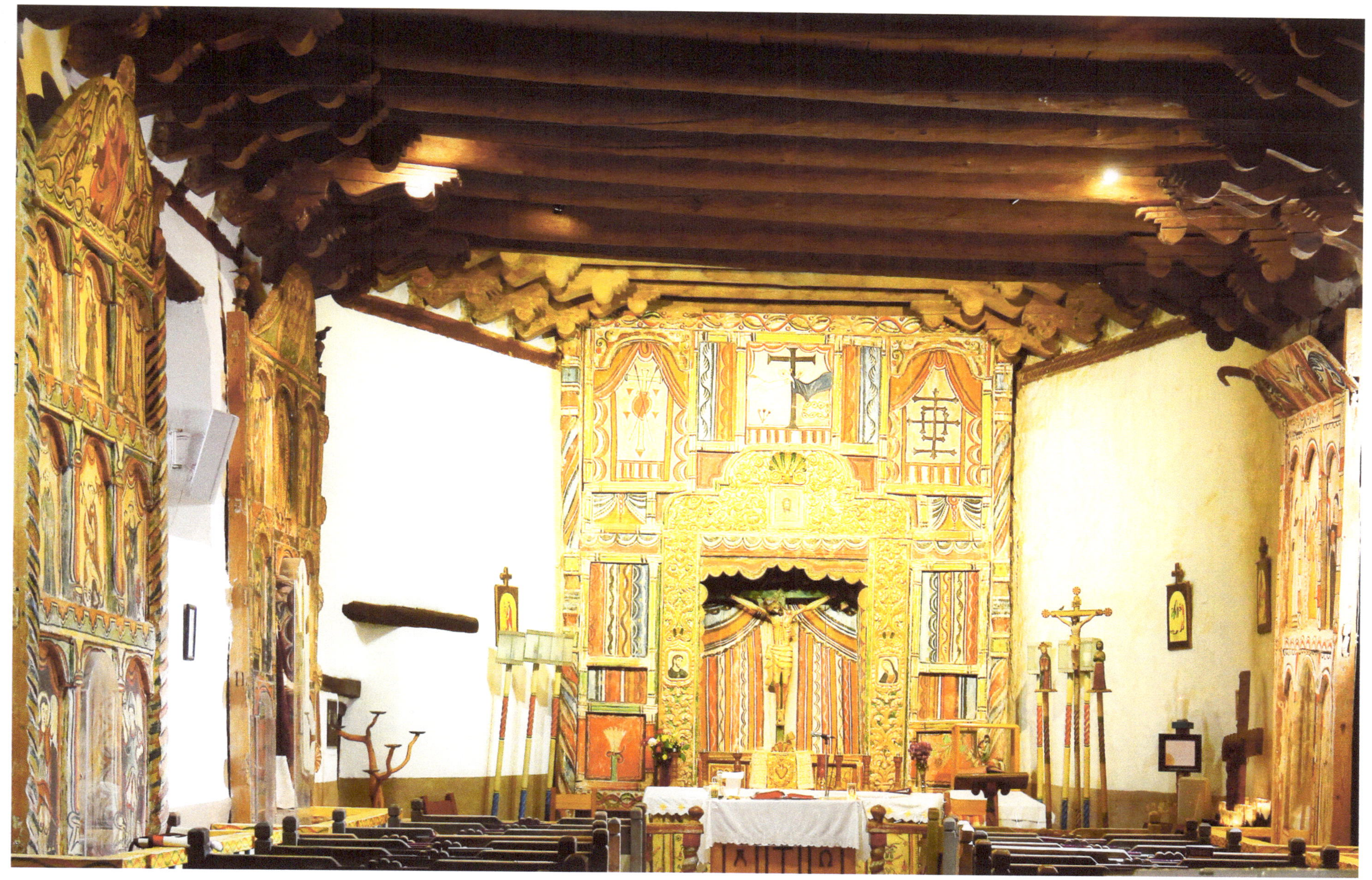

The interior of the Santuario de Chimayó, showing some of the lovely original artwork on display. The main altar screen is by Molleno; other artwork is by José and Rafael Aragon. Photograph taken in 2019.

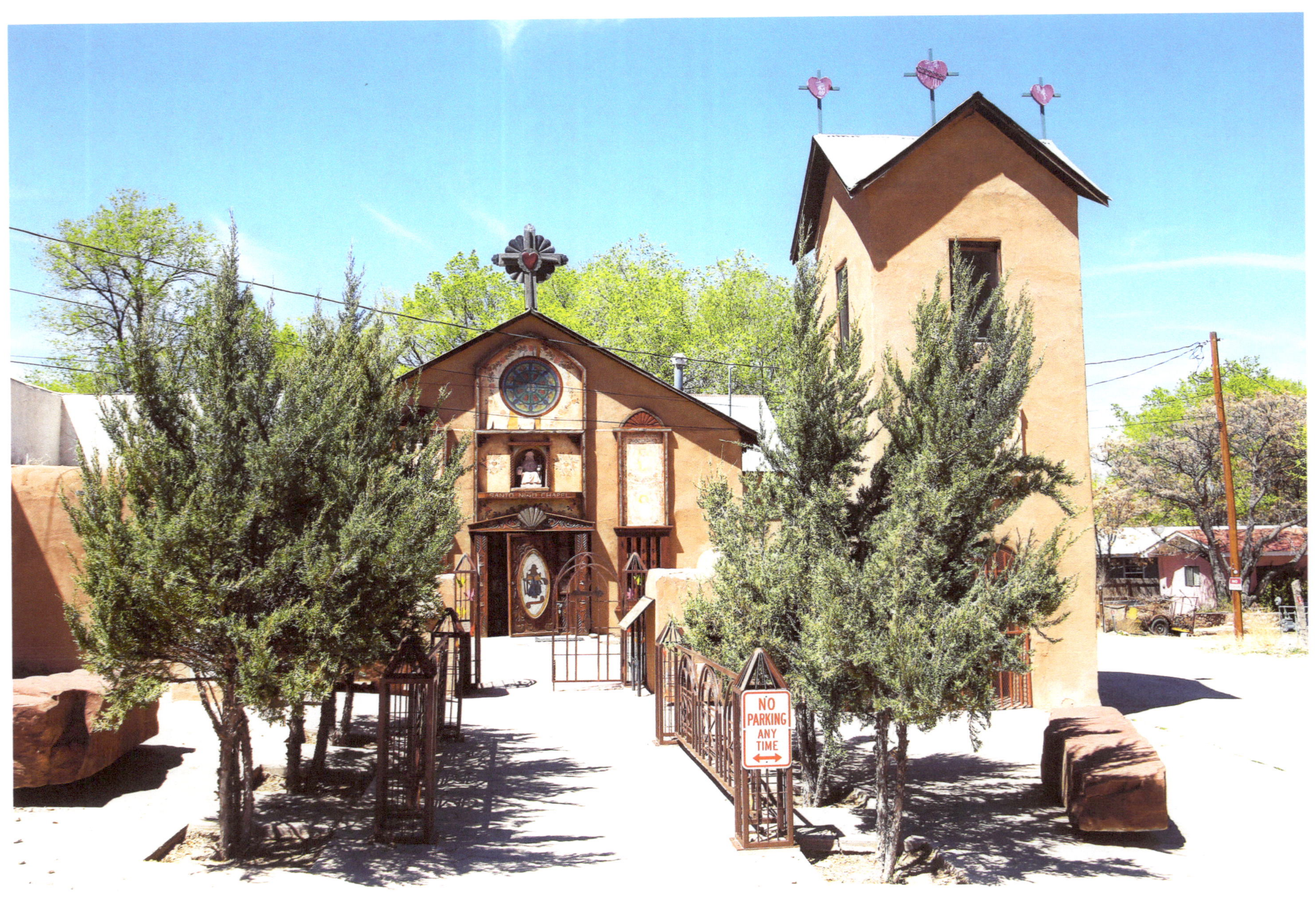

Santo Niño de Atocha Chapel, Chimayó, Santa Fe County. 1856. The chapel is a children's chapel today, and sometimes is festively decorated. On Santo Niño Drive. Photograph taken in 2022.

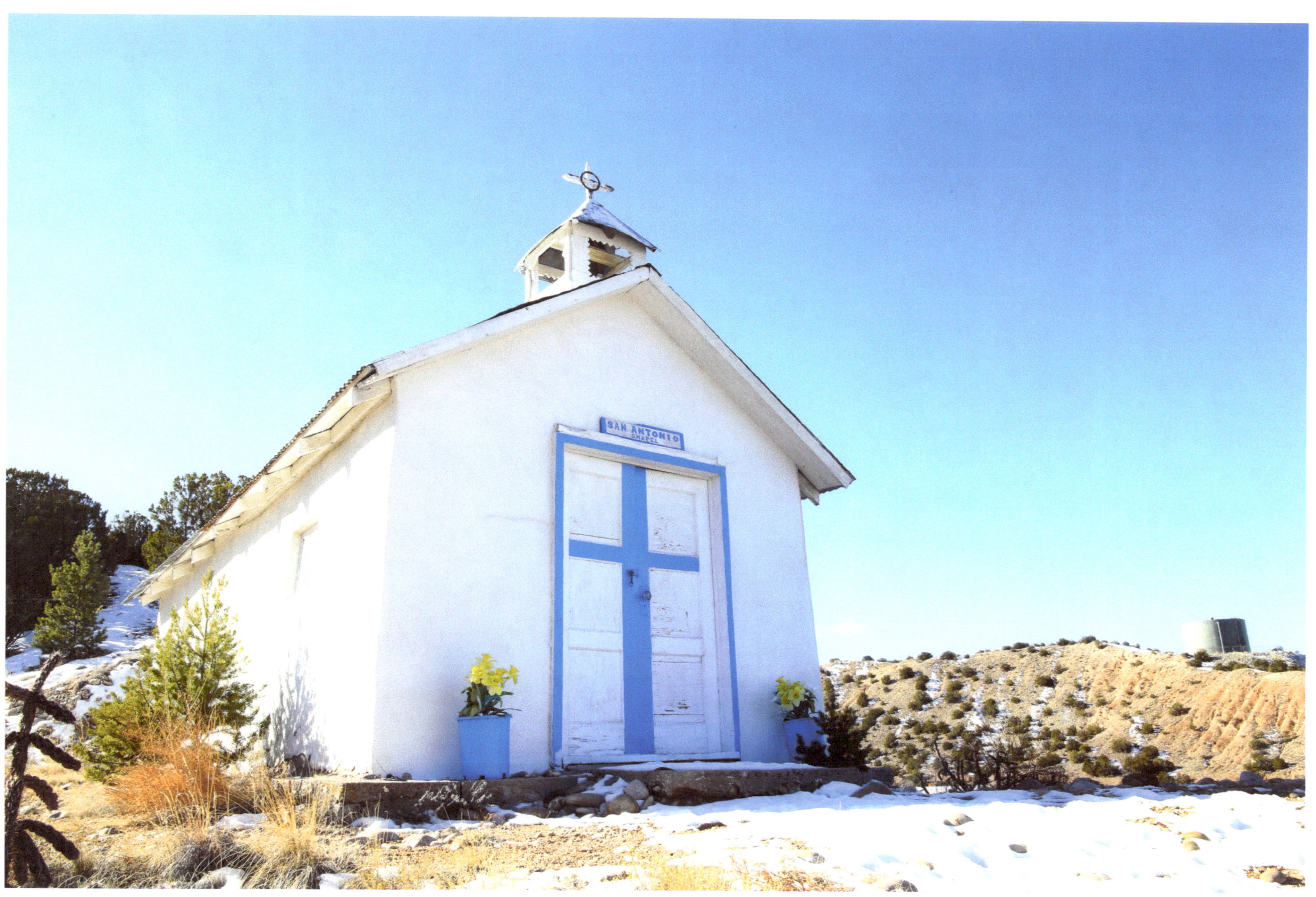

Capilla de San Antonio, Chimayó, Santa Fe County. Early 1940s. This small chapel, which usually is open to visitors, is at the end of a short, steep trail rising from a parking lot at the end of Potrero Road. Photograph taken in 2020.

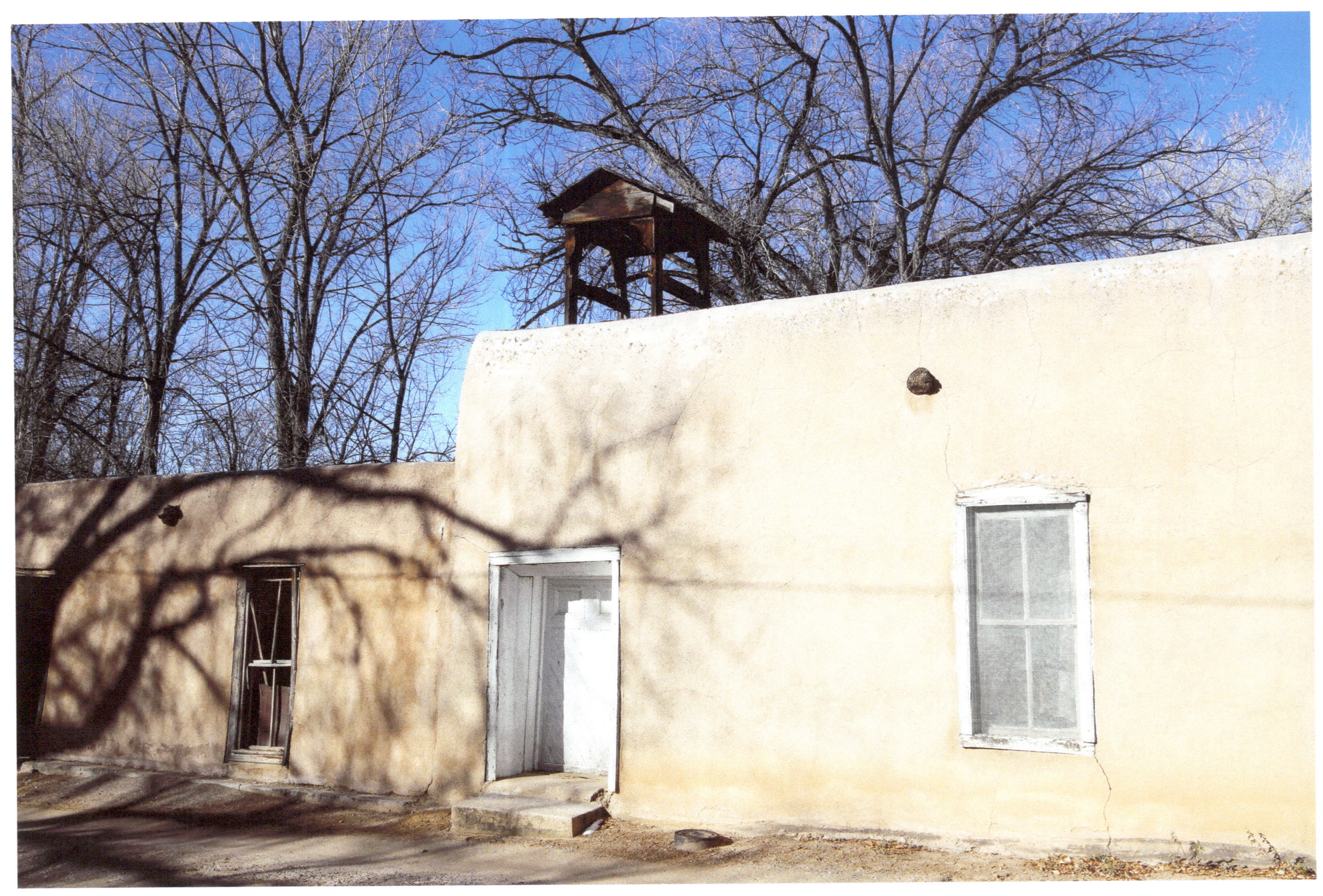

Oratorio (Capilla) de San Buenaventura, Chimayó, Santa Fe County. Likely late 18th or early 19th century. In the Plaza del Cerro. Photograph taken in 2020.

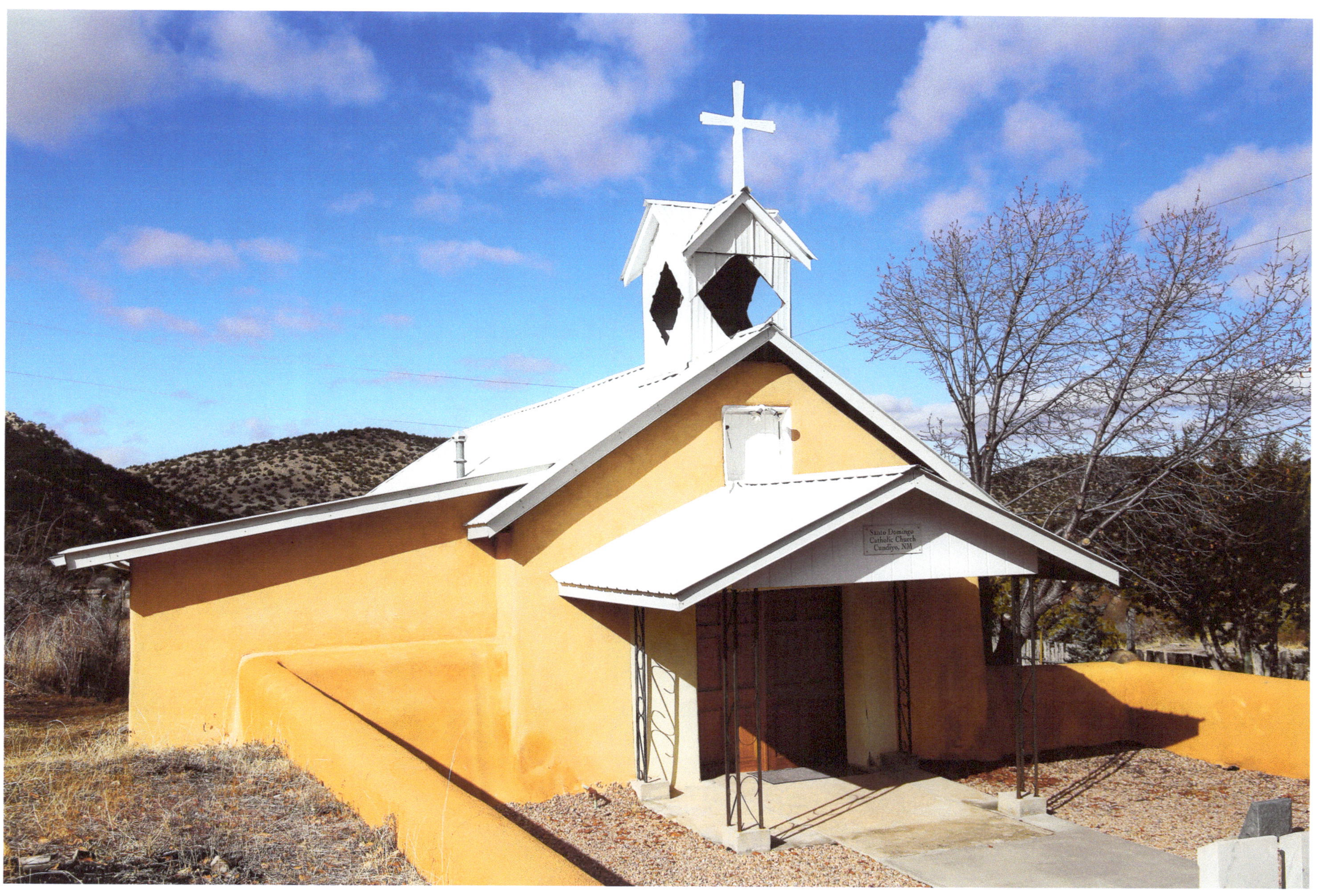

Santo Domingo Catholic Church, Cundiyó Santa Fe County. 1838. This charming adobe church is in a small mountain town on New Mexico Highway 503. Photograph taken in 2019.

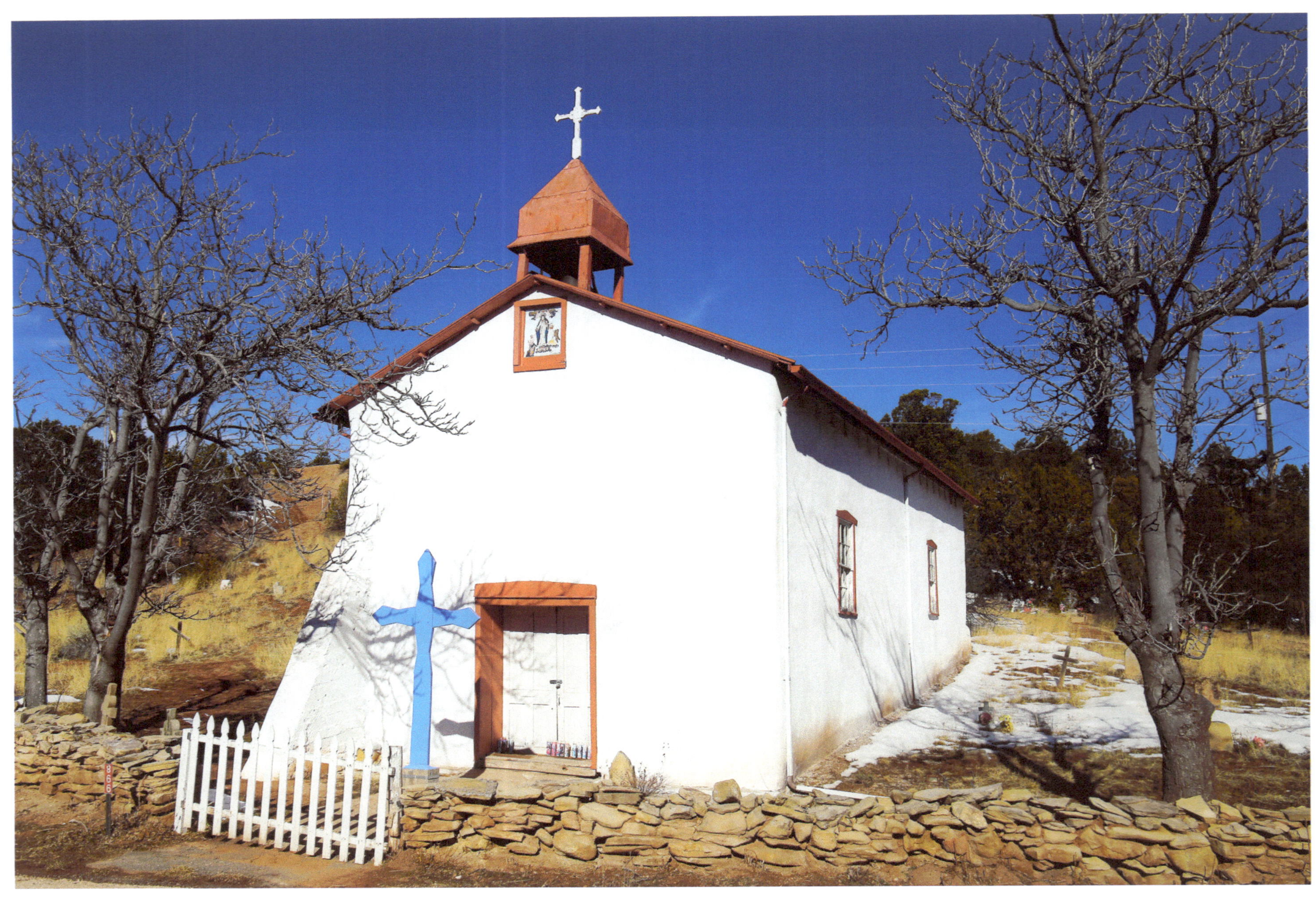

Nuestra Señora de la Luz Catholic Church, Cañoncito, Santa Fe County. 1880. This lovely, small, whitewashed, adobe church is much-photographed. Exit 294 off Interstate 25, then take the north-side frontage road. Photograph taken in 2019.

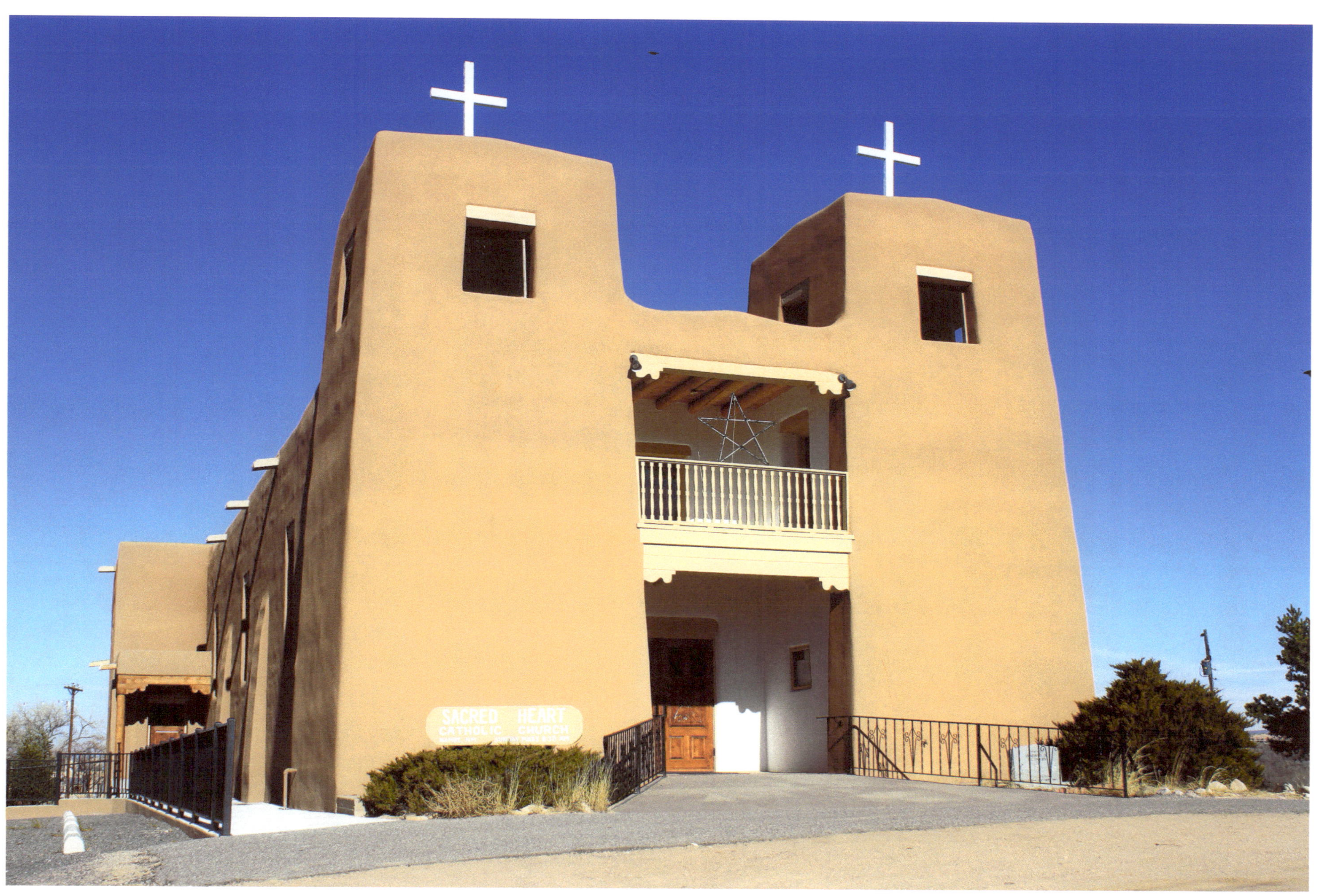

Sacred Heart Catholic Church, Nambé, Santa Fe County. 1947/1974. This large, pueblo-style adobe church was rebuilt after a fire in 1947 and rehabilitated in 1974. Just off New Mexico Highway 503. Photograph taken in 2020.

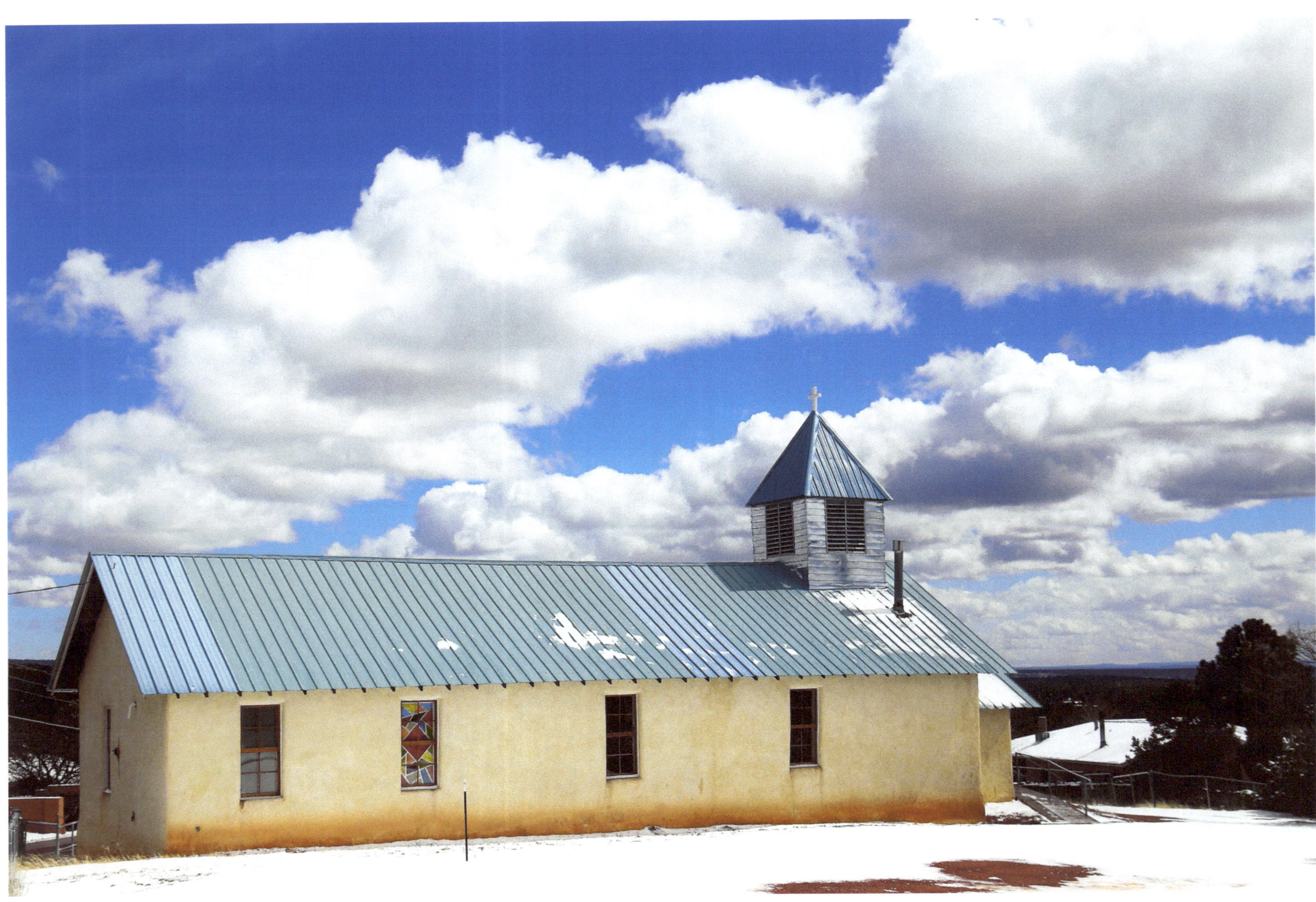

Nuestra Señora de Guadalupe Catholic Church, Cañada de los Alamos (near Santa Fe), Santa Fe County. 1922. A front view of this traditional adobe church was not accessible. Take New Mexico Highway 67 (Old Santa Fe Trail) to Ridge Road. Photograph taken in 2019.

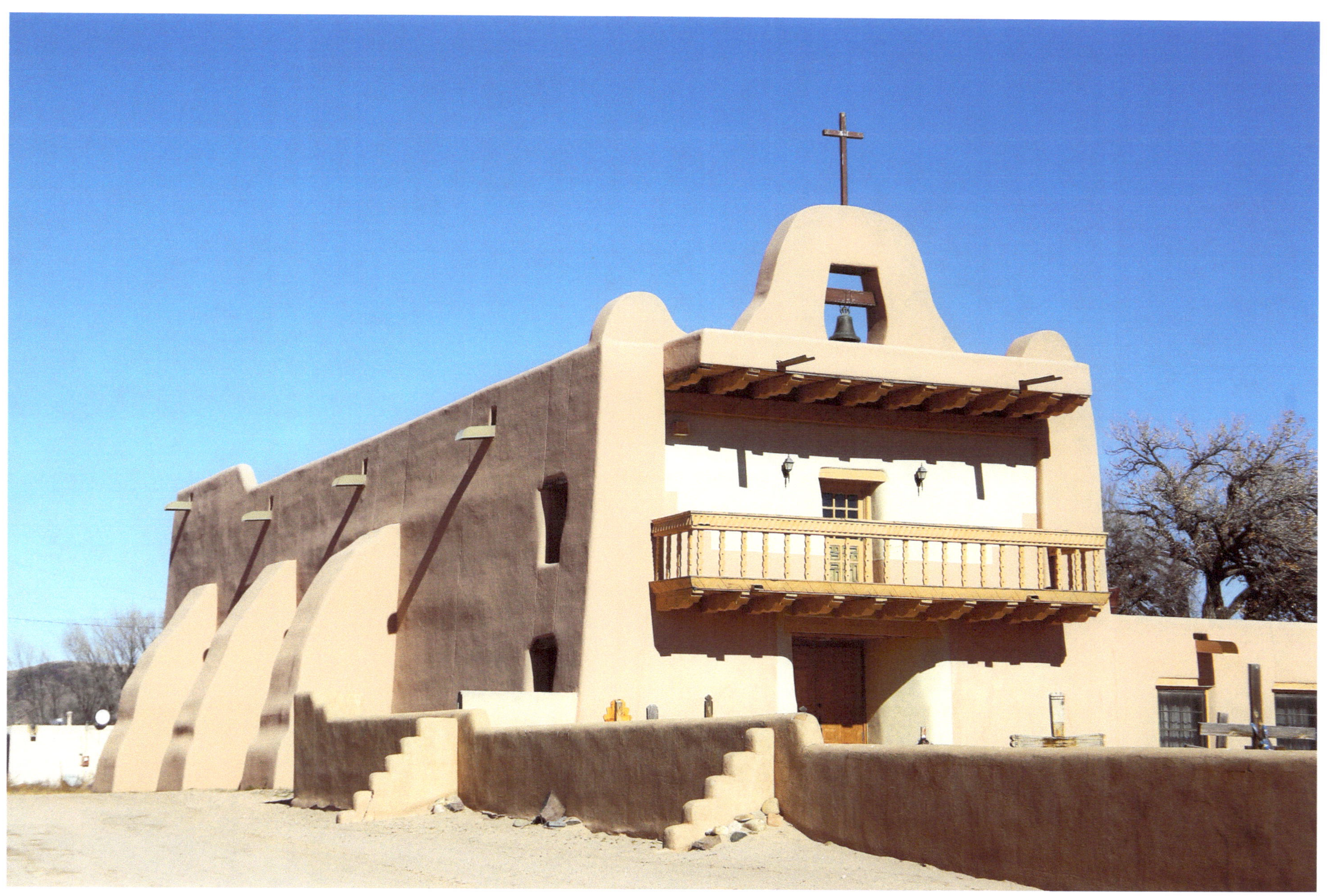

San Ildefonso Catholic Church, San Ildefonso Pueblo, Santa Fe County. 1968. This large adobe church, in the plaza of the pueblo, is a close replica of a church built in 1711 and demolished in 1905. Photograph taken in 2022.

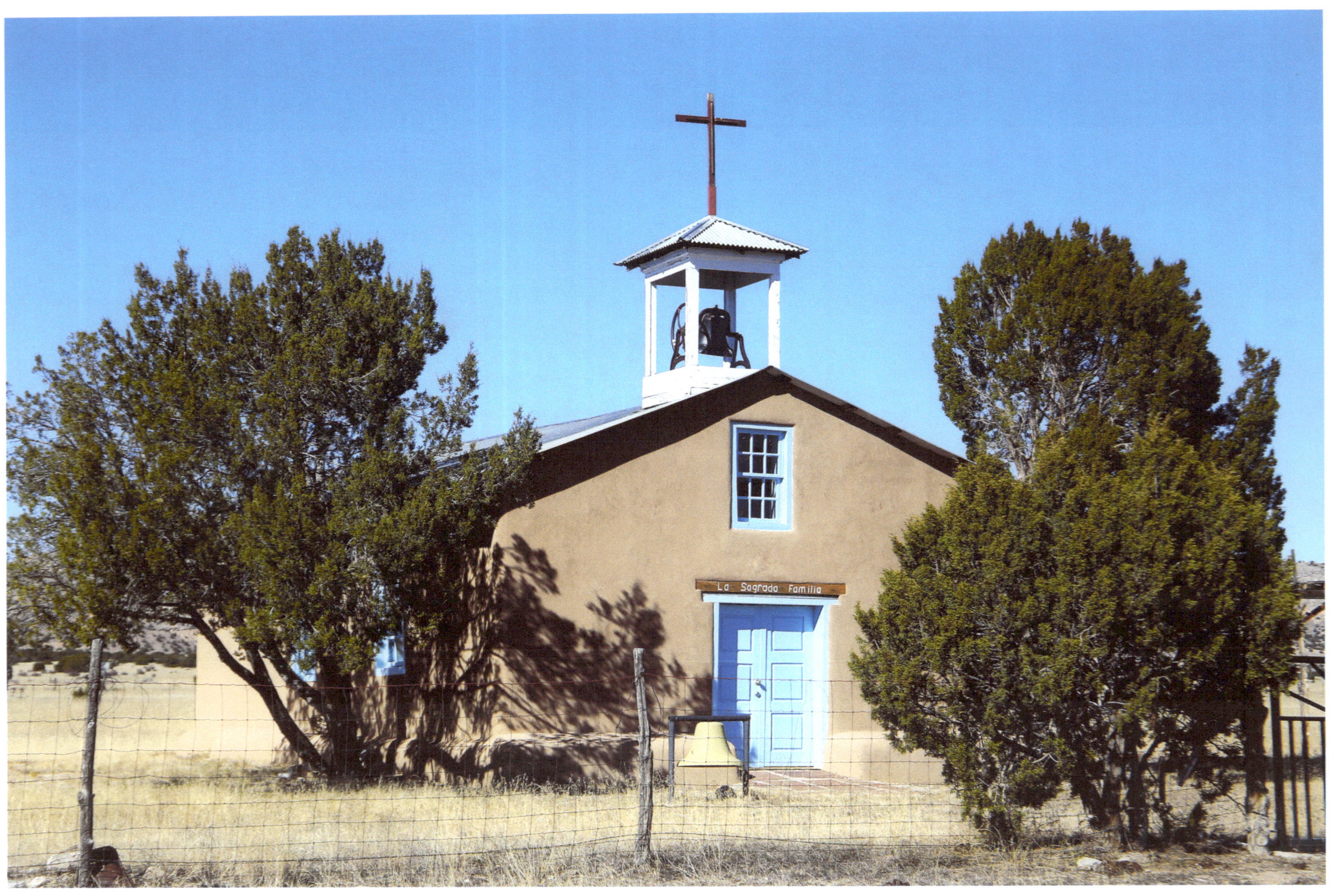

La Sagrada Familia Catholic Church, Pajarito, Santa Fe County. Early 1920s, restored in the 1990s. Surrounded by San Ildefonso Pueblo, but not in it, this church is usually seen and illustrated from the rear, from New Mexico Highway 30, as shown on page 89 of my first book. Reached via 4WD trails through San Ildefonso Pueblo. Photograph taken in 2022.

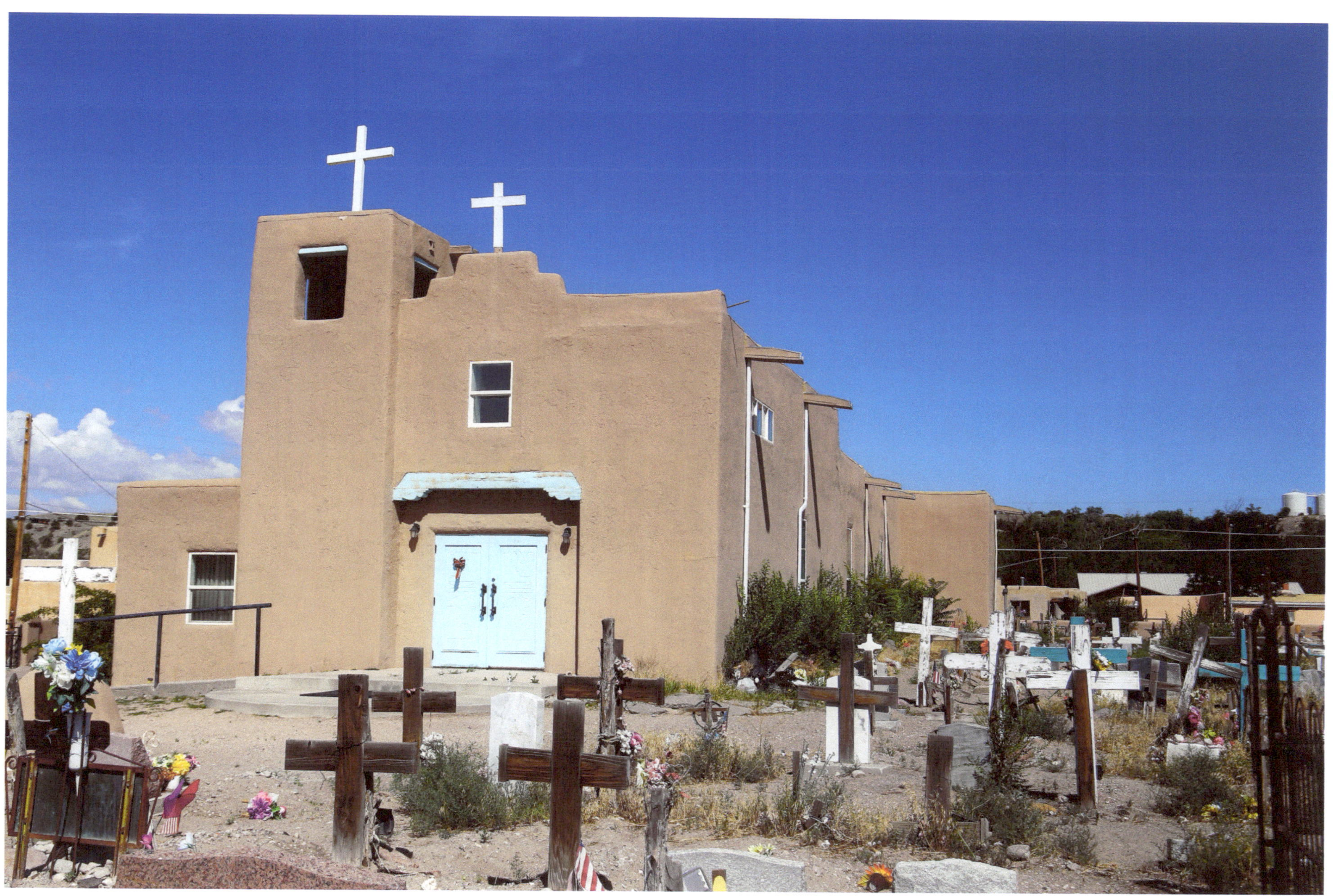

Santa Clara Catholic Church, Santa Clara Pueblo, Santa Fe County. 1918. This church is a much smaller "replica" of a church originally built in 1756. The massive old adobe church collapsed in 1909 after a pitched metal roof was added. Just northwest of the plaza. The pueblo entrances are on New Mexico Highway 30 about two miles south of Española. Photograph taken in 2024.

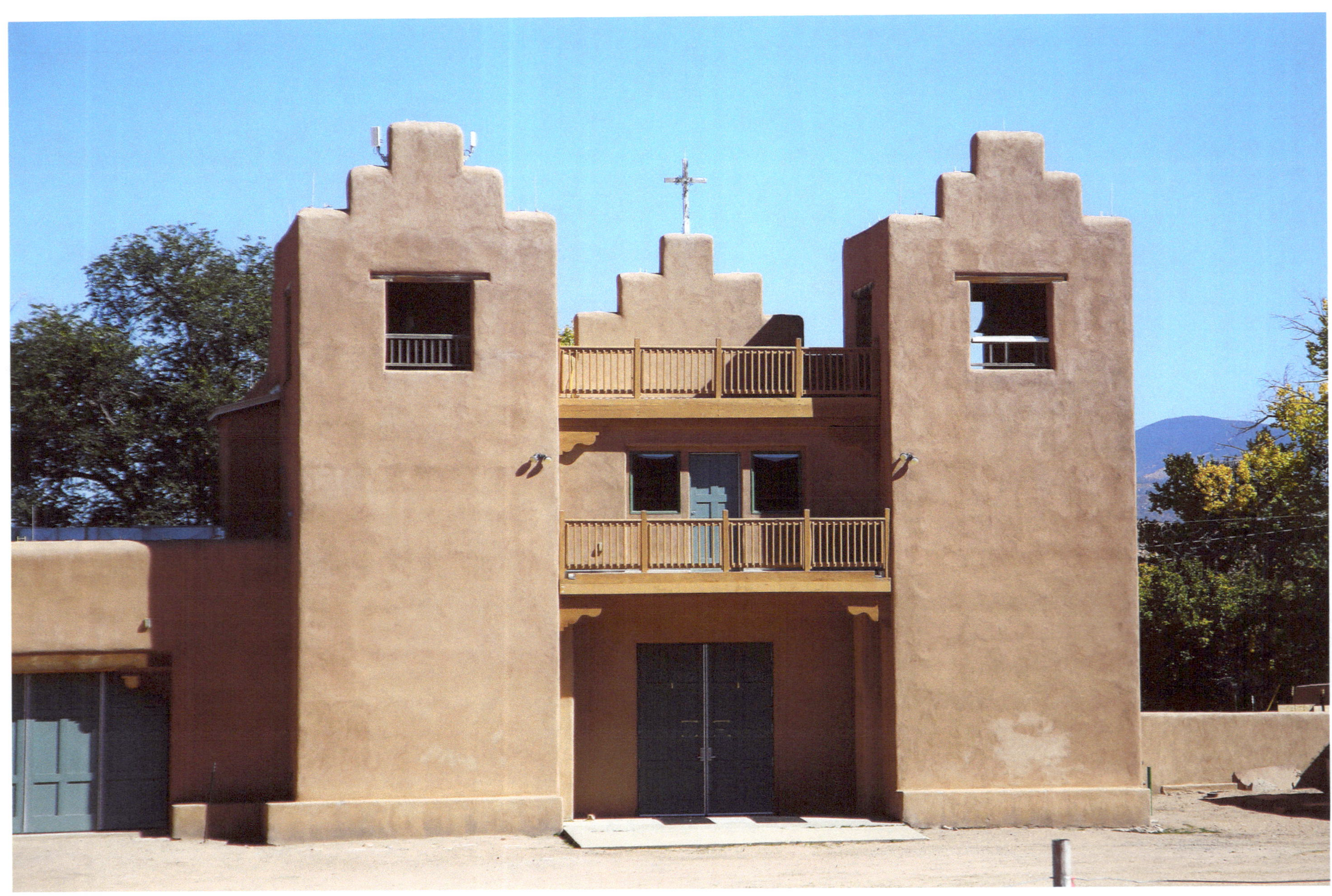

San Diego de Tesuque Catholic Church, Tesuque Pueblo, Santa Fe County. Several churches have stood on this site since 1695. One built in the 1880s and renovated in 1978 was a victim of arson in 2002. The current one was built in the Pueblo style around 2005. Take Camel Rock Road off New Mexico Highway 84/285 to the frontage road to Pueblo Road 806 to the plaza. Photograph taken in 2023.

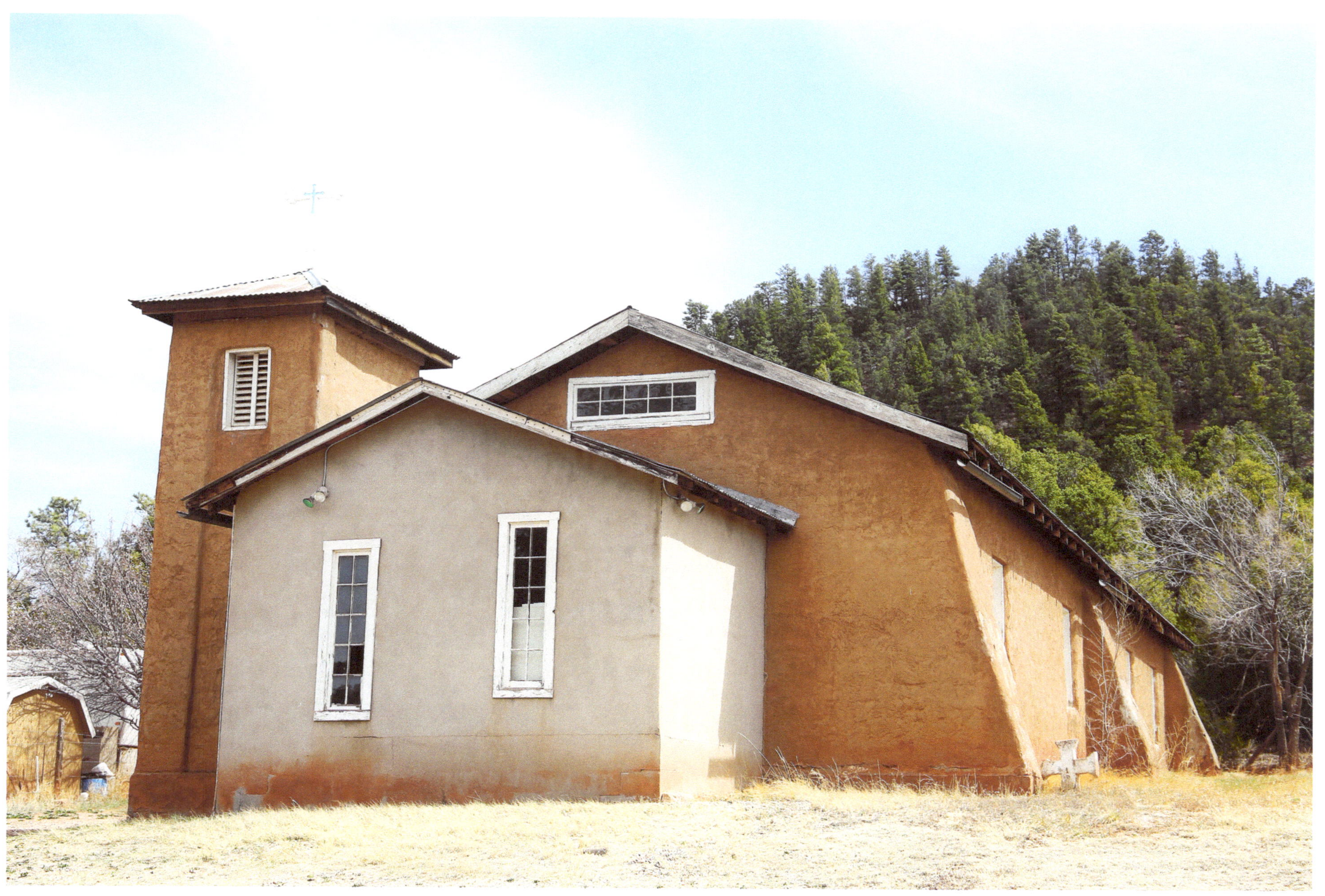

Nuestra Señora de Guadalupe Catholic Church, Glorieta, Santa Fe County. 1950. Glorieta Pass was the site of a major battle of the U.S. Civil War in March, 1862. Exit 299 off Interstate 25 to Fire Station Road, left on Avenida Ponderosa, right on Calle Lomita. Photograph taken in 2021.

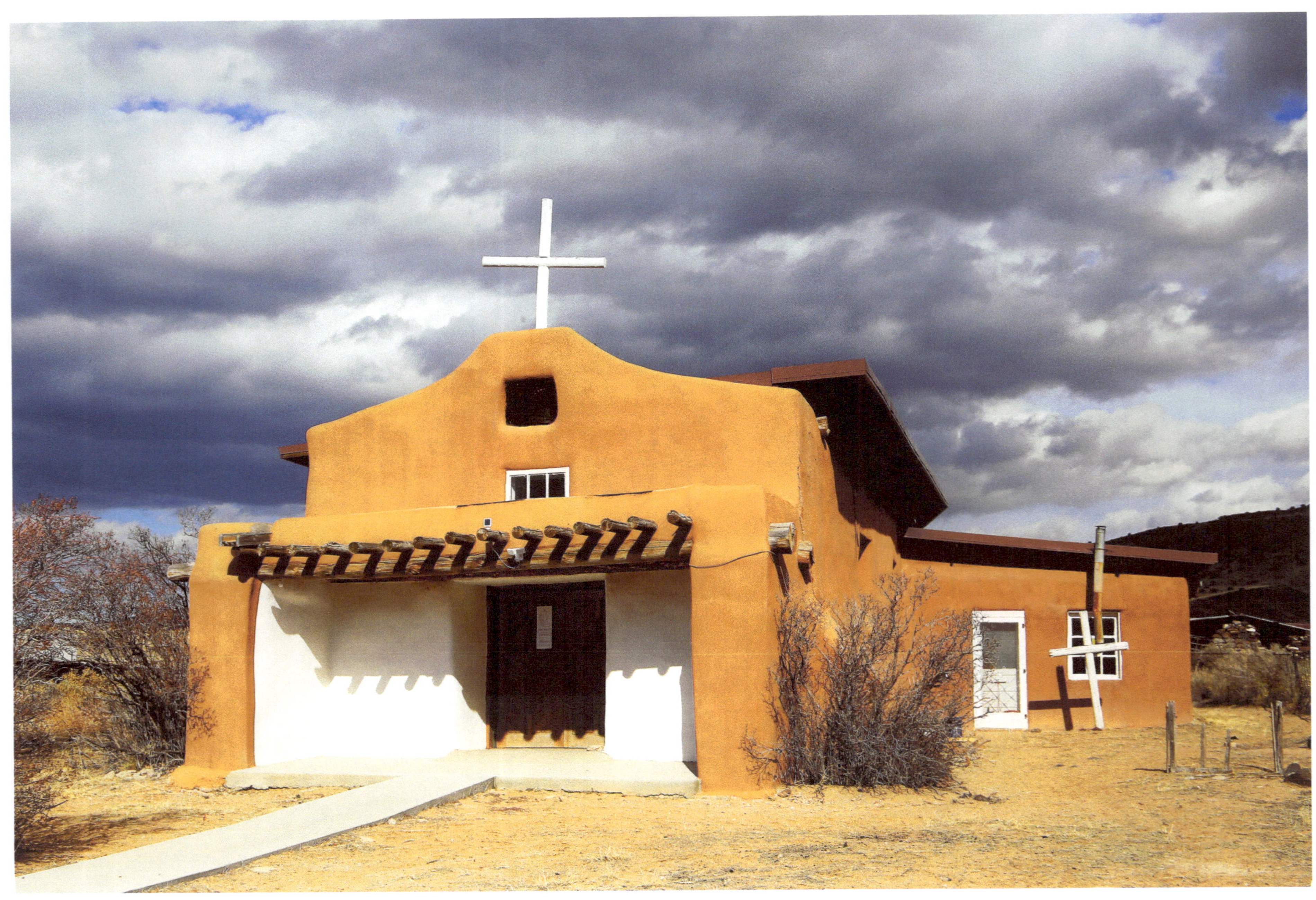

Capilla de San Miguel, La Bajada, Santa Fe County. 1837/1976. This lovely adobe church in the small village of La Bajada was grievously burglarized in 2019. Take New Mexico Highway 16 to Tetilla Peak Road to La Bajada Village Road. Photograph taken in 2020.

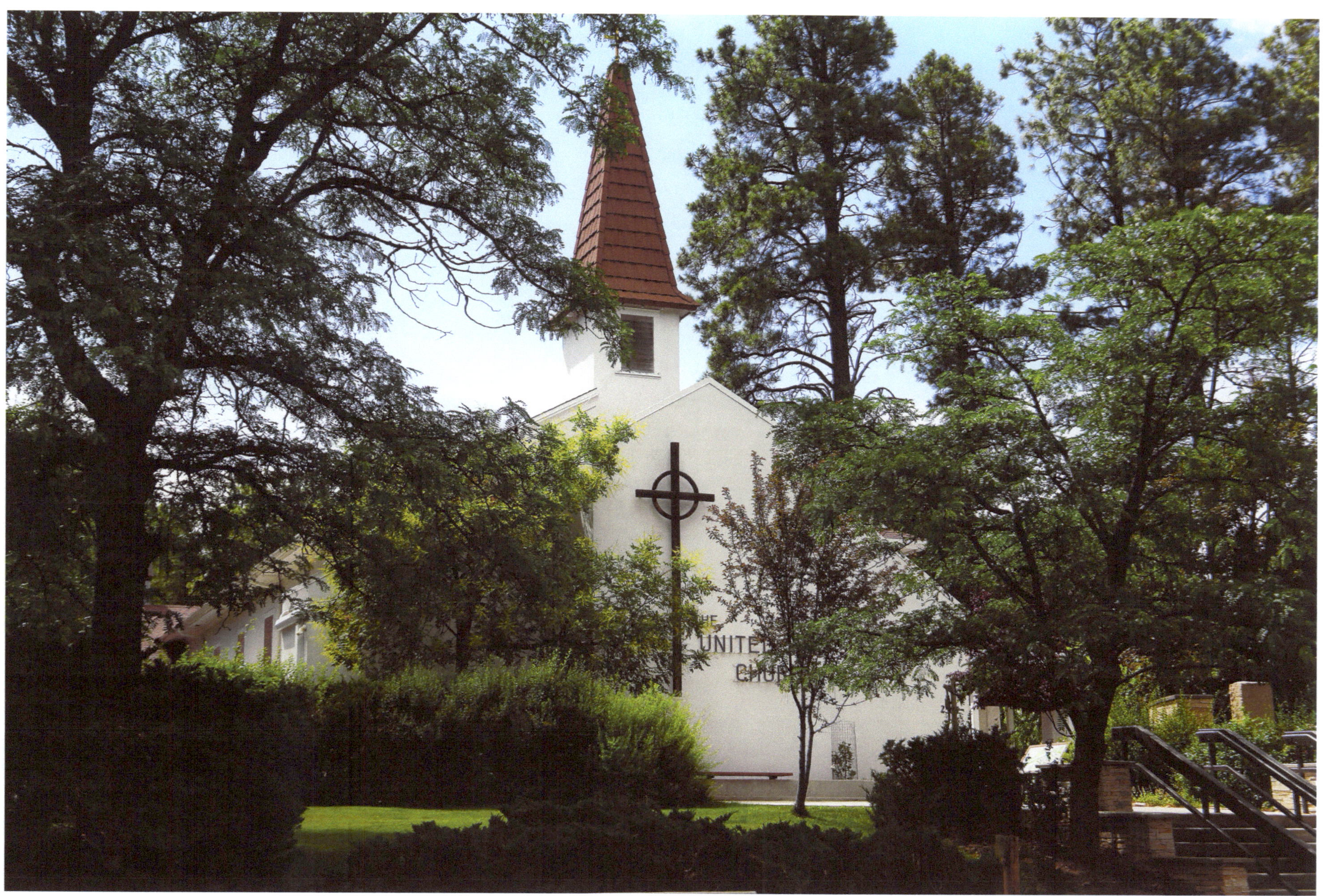

Immaculate Heart of Mary Catholic Church (now United Church of Los Alamos), Los Alamos, Los Alamos County. 1948. This building was moved from Santa Fe to Los Alamos and mass was celebrated here beginning in 1948. The current church in nearby White Rock was dedicated in 1968. At 2525 Canyon Road. Photograph taken in 2024.

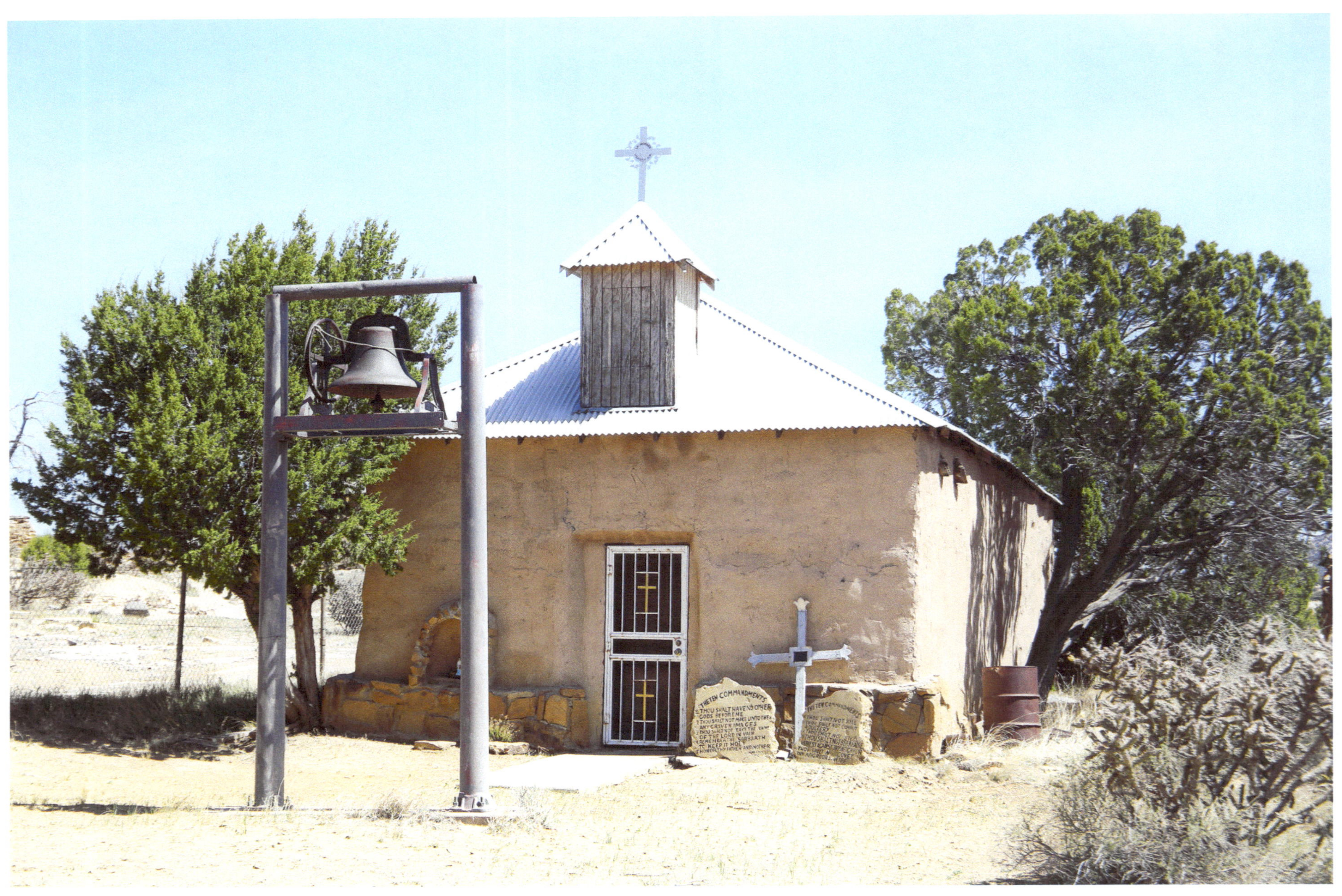

La Morada, Marquez, Sandoval County. Likely late 1800s. San Juan Nepomucemo Catholic Church was nearby, but it has not survived. Its bell is in front of this very remote Penitente Brotherhood morada and its statue of San Juan Nepomucemo is inside. Church services are held there. Take Marquez Road (Cibola County Road 1) 17.6 miles east from New Mexico Highway 279 to the village. Photograph taken in 2023.

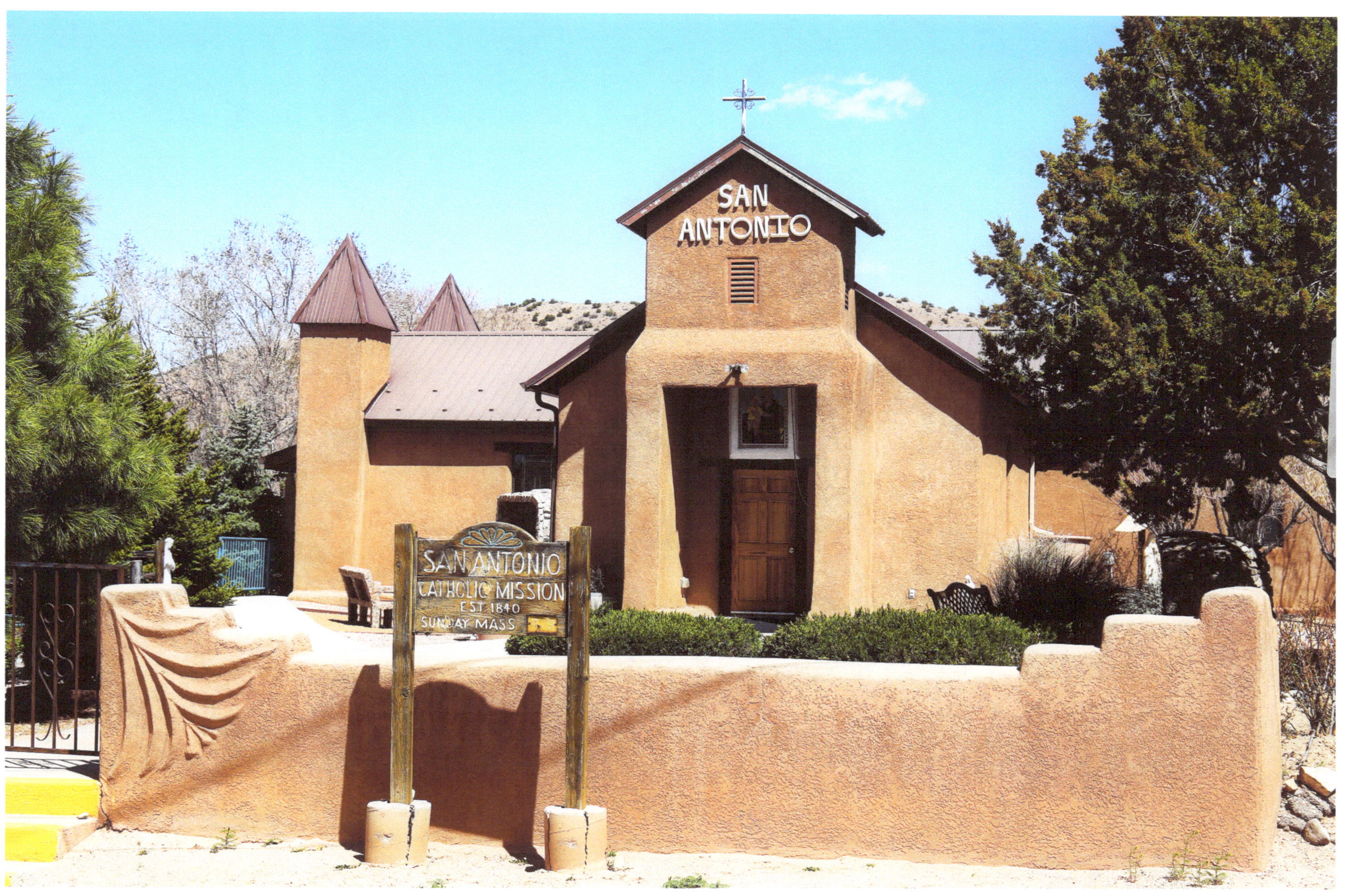

San Antonio Catholic Mission Church, Placitas, Sandoval County. 1919. The mission was established in 1840, as per the sign, but the adobe church was built later. Notice the relief sculpting on the wall. Take Paseo de San Antonio Road off New Mexico Highway 165 to the church. Photograph taken in 2019.

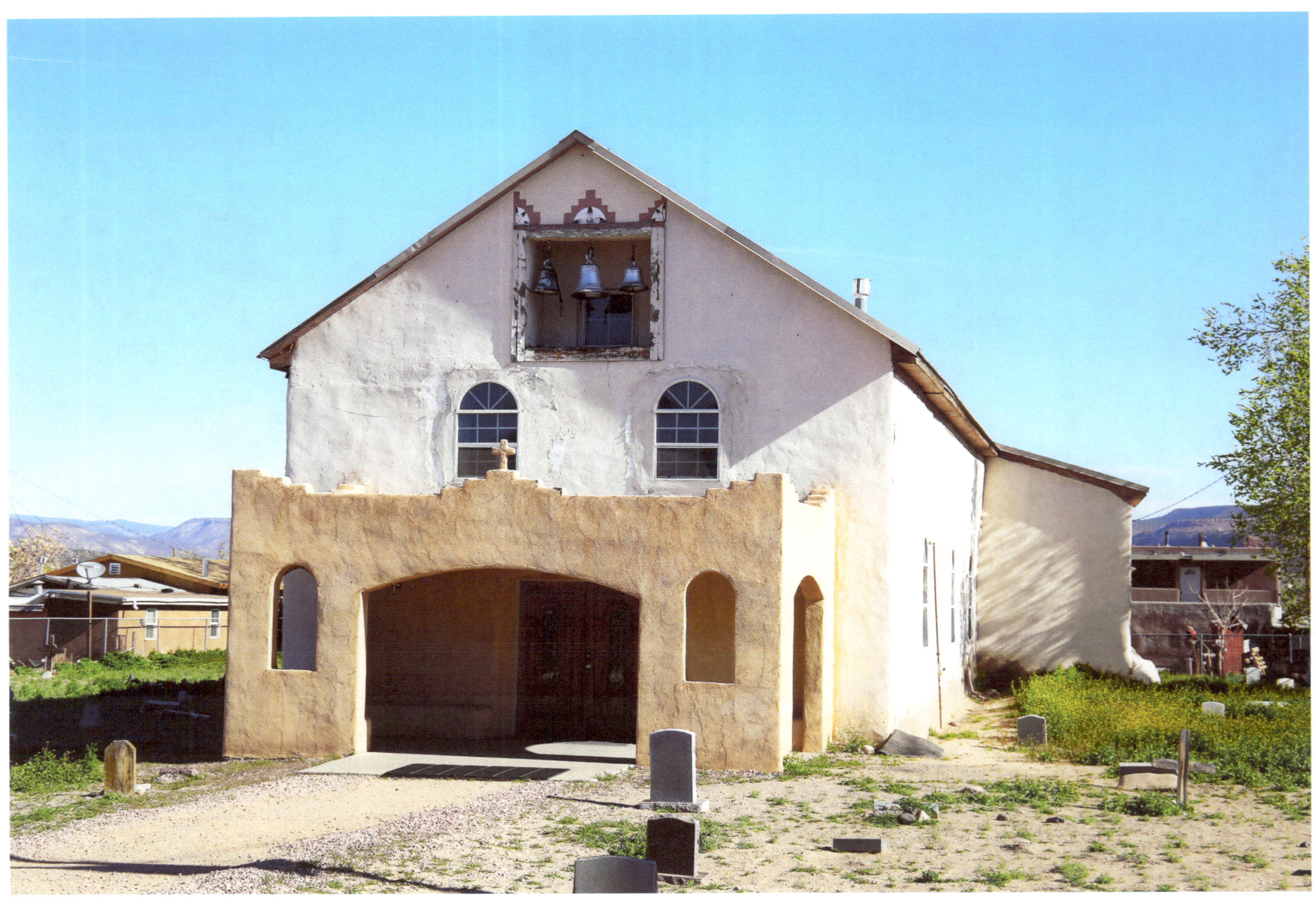

San Diego Mission Church, Jémez Pueblo, Sandoval County. Mid-1700s/1887. The cross is on the adobe portico in front of the church, which is called "the pueblo church" by residents. On Mission Road. Photograph taken in 2019.

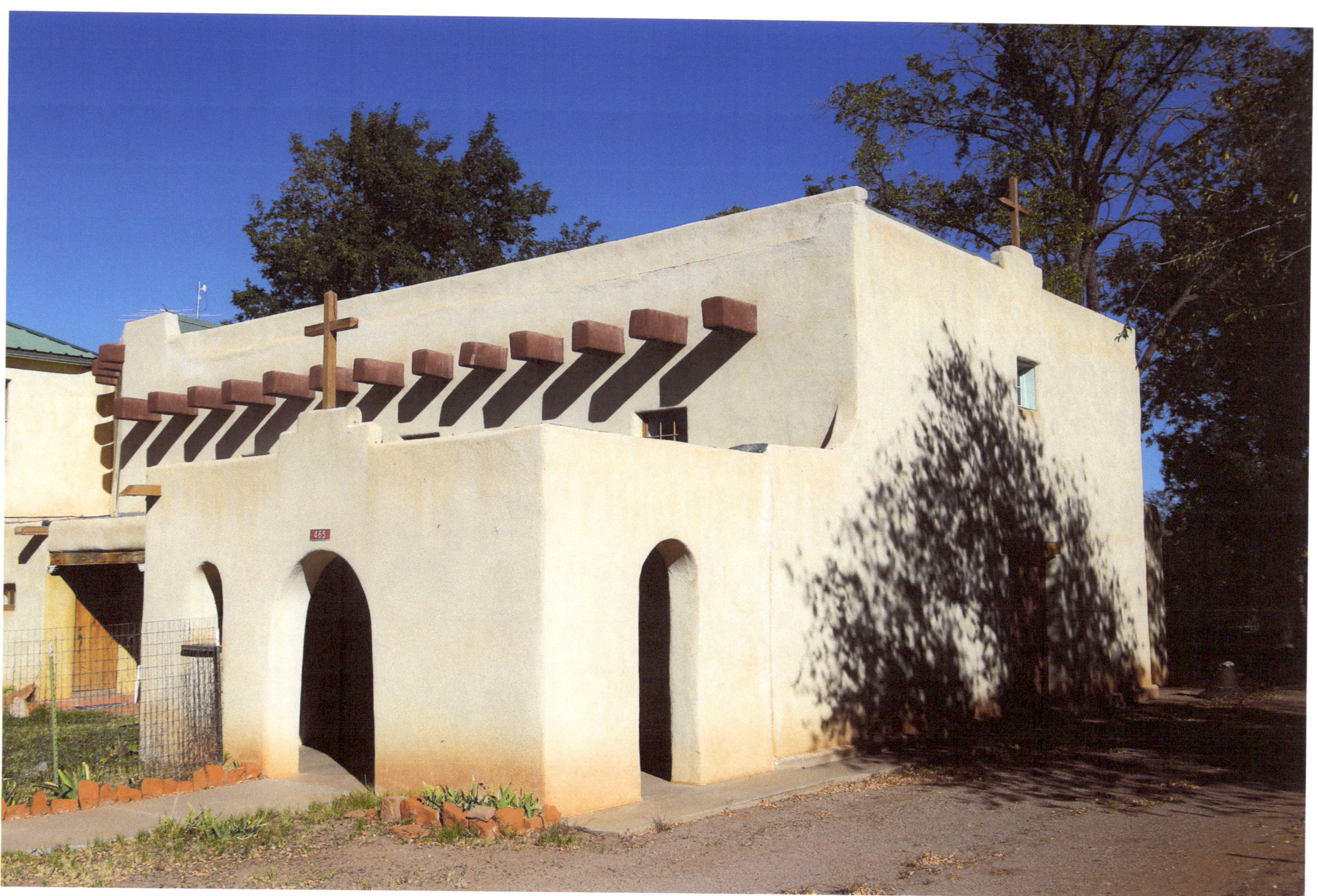

San Diego Parish Church, Jémez Pueblo, Sandoval County. Early 1900s. This adobe church is across from the school, about half a mile down from the pueblo church. The interior (not pictured) has remarkable wooden carvings in front of and behind the altar. It is currently used for services. Photograph taken in 2023.

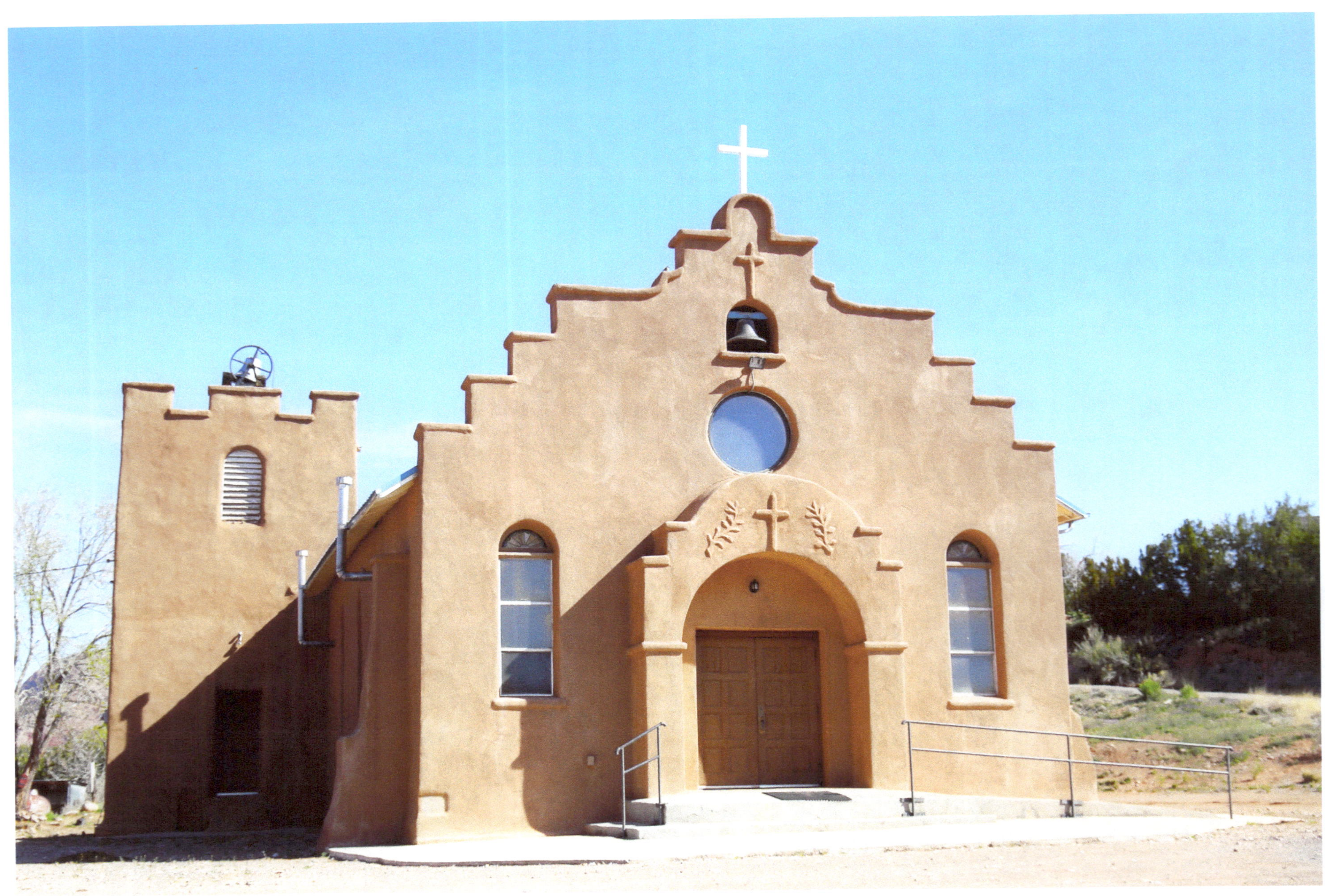

Nuestra Señora de Guadalupe Catholic Church, Jémez Pueblo, Sandoval County. 1921. This adobe church is in the California mission style and has another bell on the far side. About 200 yards down Los Luceros Road off New Mexico Highway 4. Photograph taken in 2019.

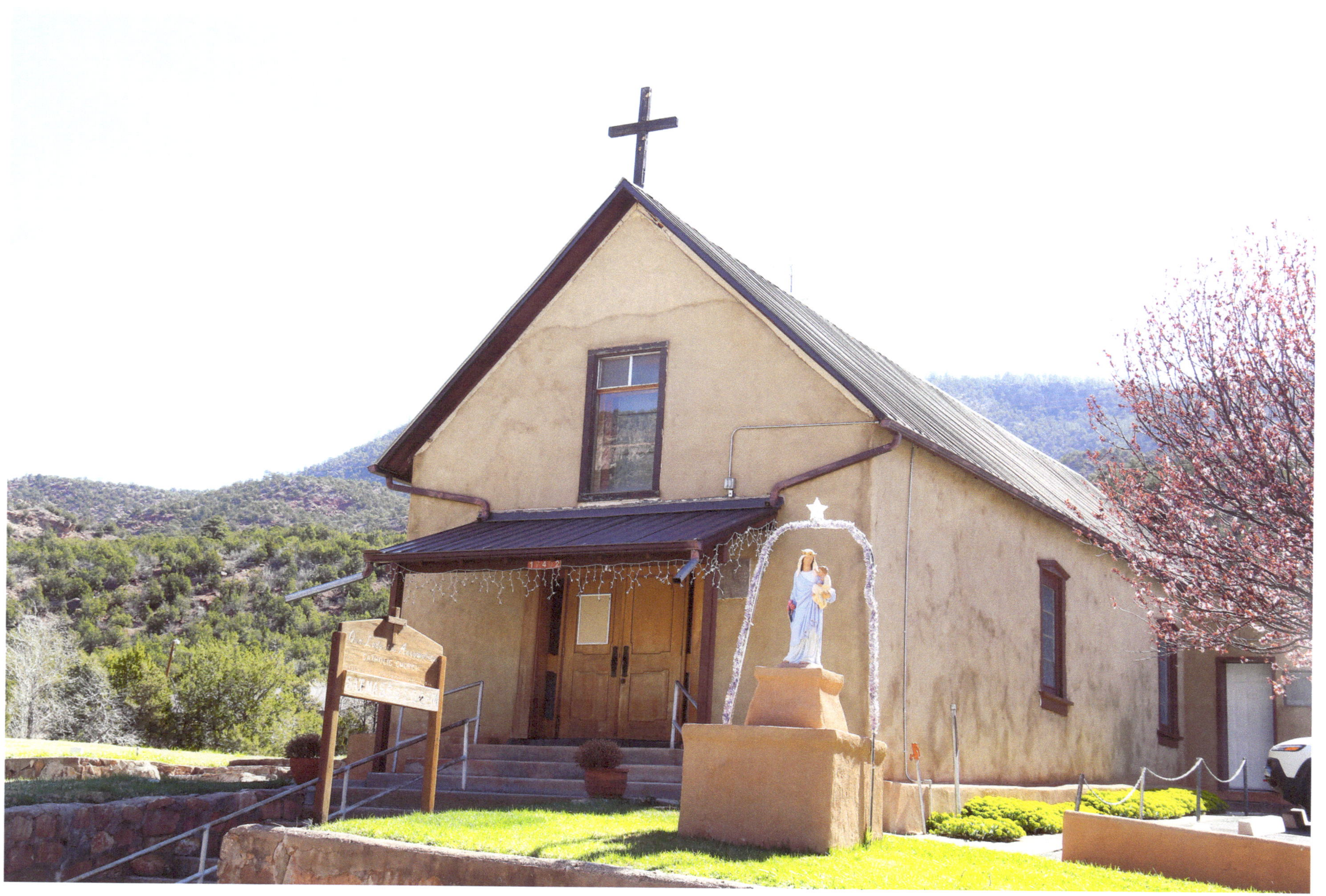

Our Lady of the Assumption Catholic Church, Jémez Springs, Sandoval County. 1916. The wooden bell tower is at the rear of this adobe church and not visible from this viewpoint. On New Mexico Highway 4. Photograph taken in 2019.

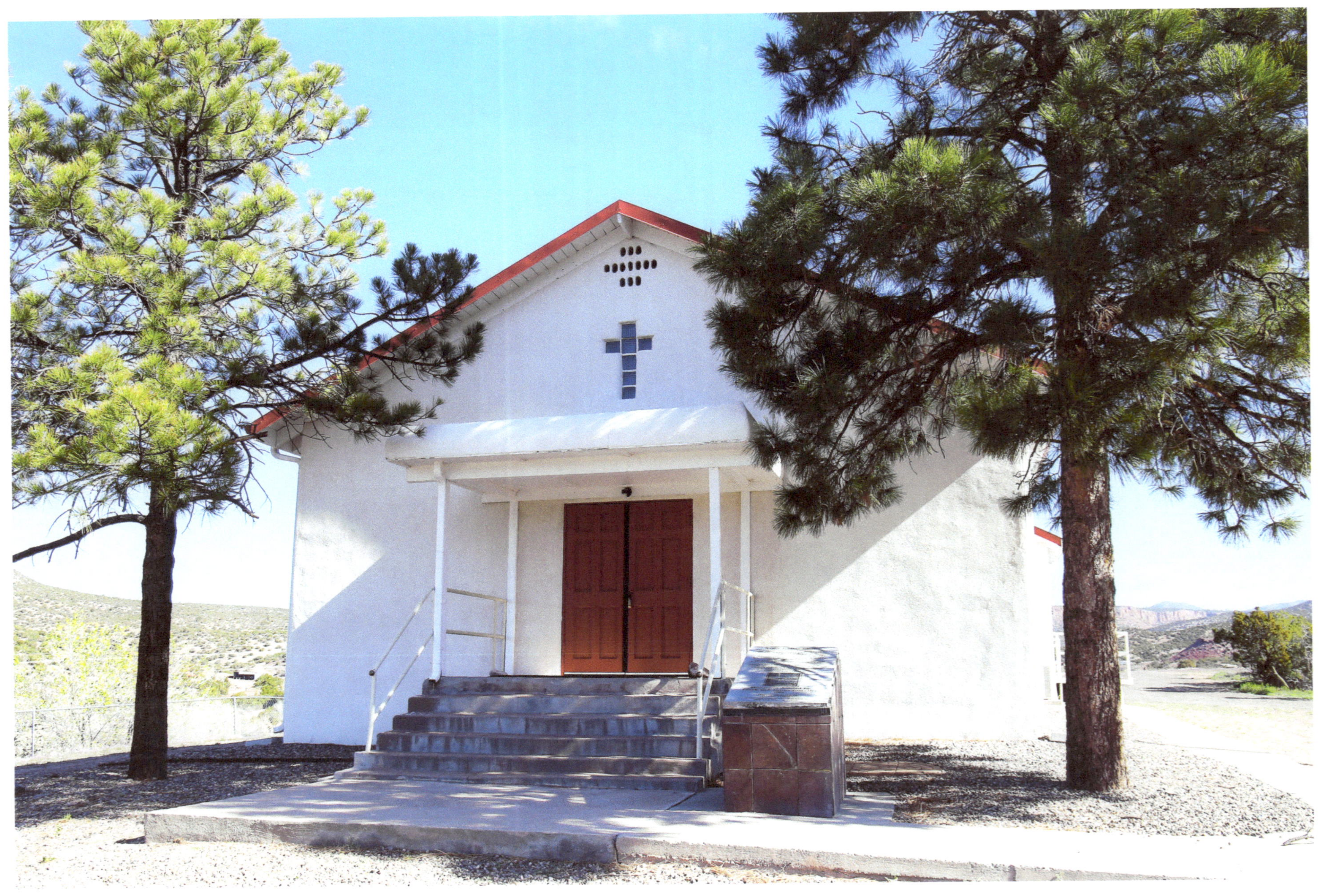

Santo Toribio Catholic Church, Ponderosa (Vallecito), Sandoval County. Around 1950. On the east side of New Mexico Highway 290. Photograph taken in 2019.

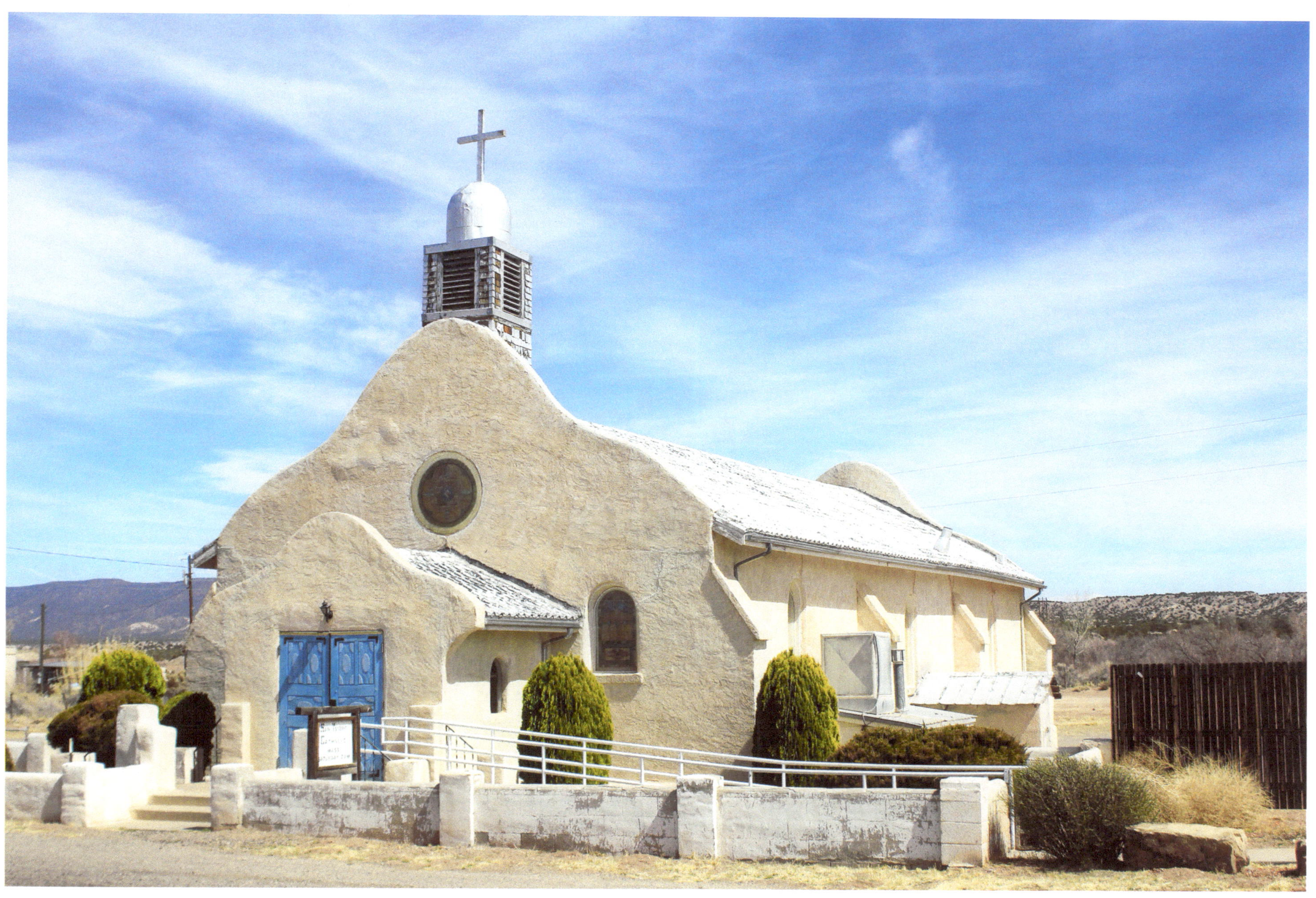

San Ysidro Catholic Church, San Ysidro, Sandoval County. 1858. This adobe church is a favorite of mine because its gables remind me of the Cape Dutch architecture of many wineries in my native South Africa. On New Mexico Highway 4 one mile from U.S. Highway 550. Photograph taken in 2022.

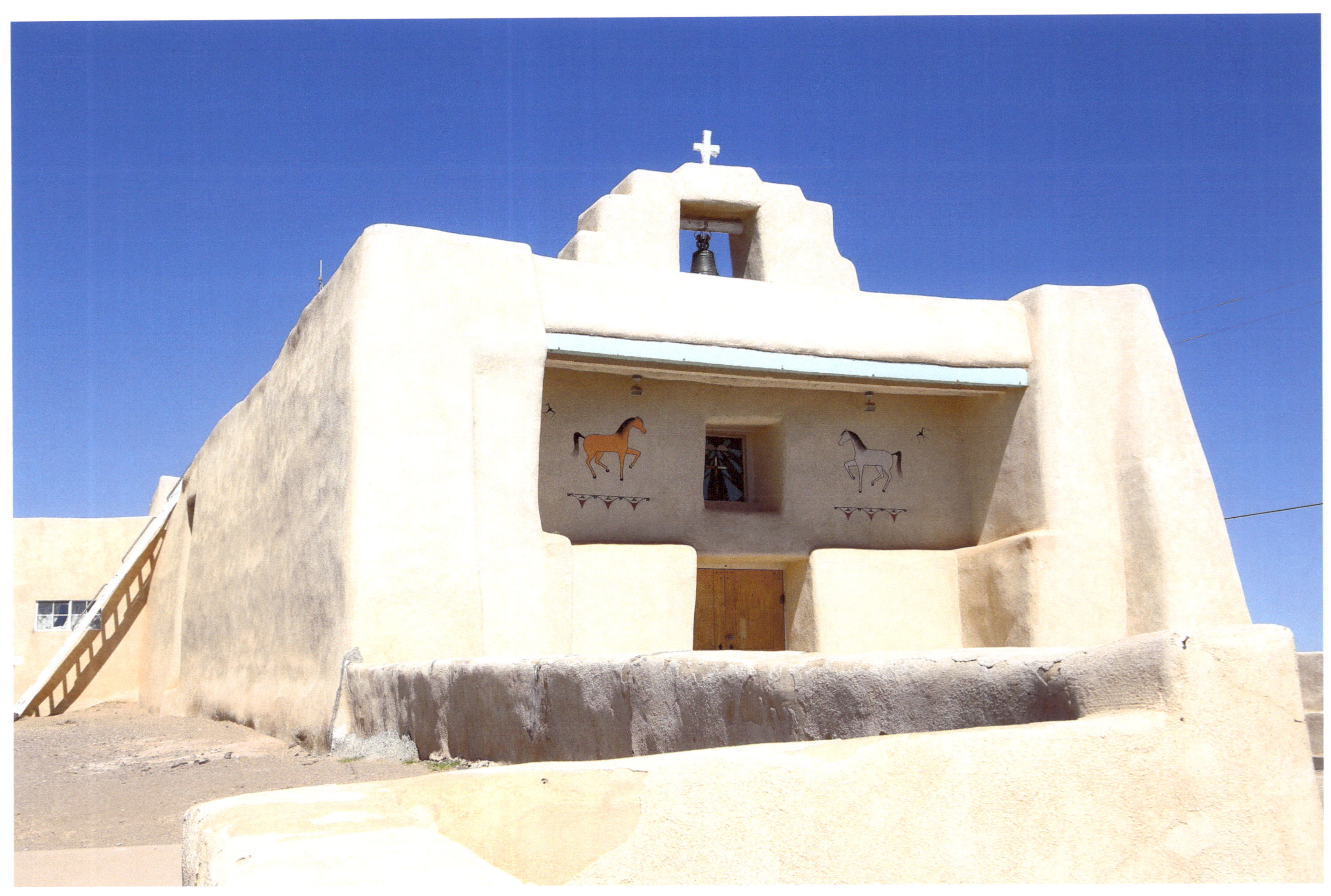

Nuestra Señora de Asunción Catholic Church, Zia Pueblo, Sandoval County. After the original church was mostly destroyed in Pueblo Revolt of 1680, a new church was built, starting around 1704 and completed around 1752. It probably includes some walls of the pre-1680 church. A classic, beautifully maintained pueblo church. The horses were painted by pueblo artist Ralph Aragon. Photograph taken with permission of Zia Pueblo in 2024.

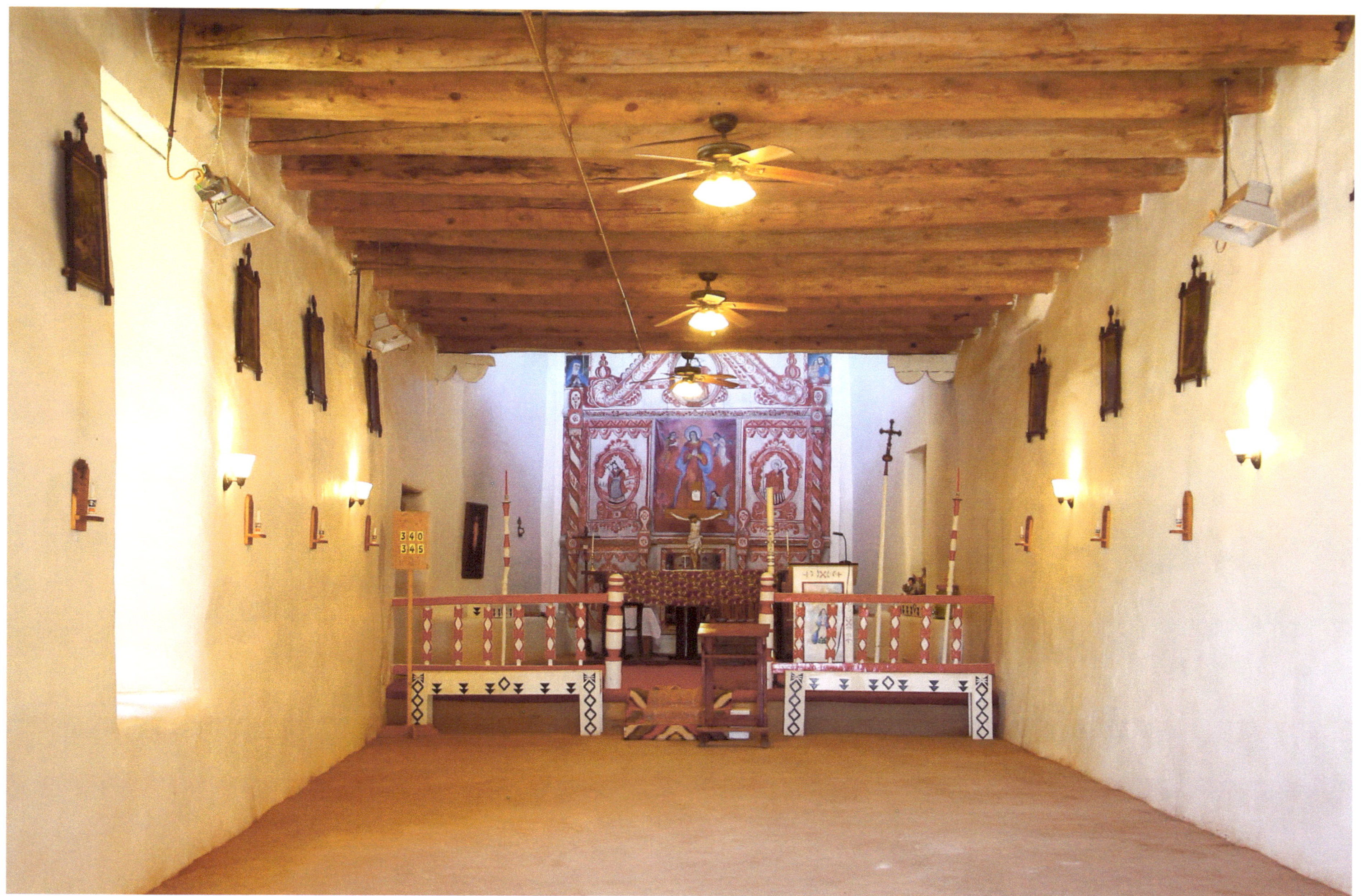

The lovely interior of Nuestra Señora de Asunción. The restored altar screen was created by the Laguna Santero in the late 1700s. The south (left) wall is double-thick because the vigas were cut too short to reach both walls, and rather than haul more logs from the mountains, the residents thickened the wall from inside. Notice the packed-earth floor. Photograph taken with permission of Zia Pueblo in 2024.

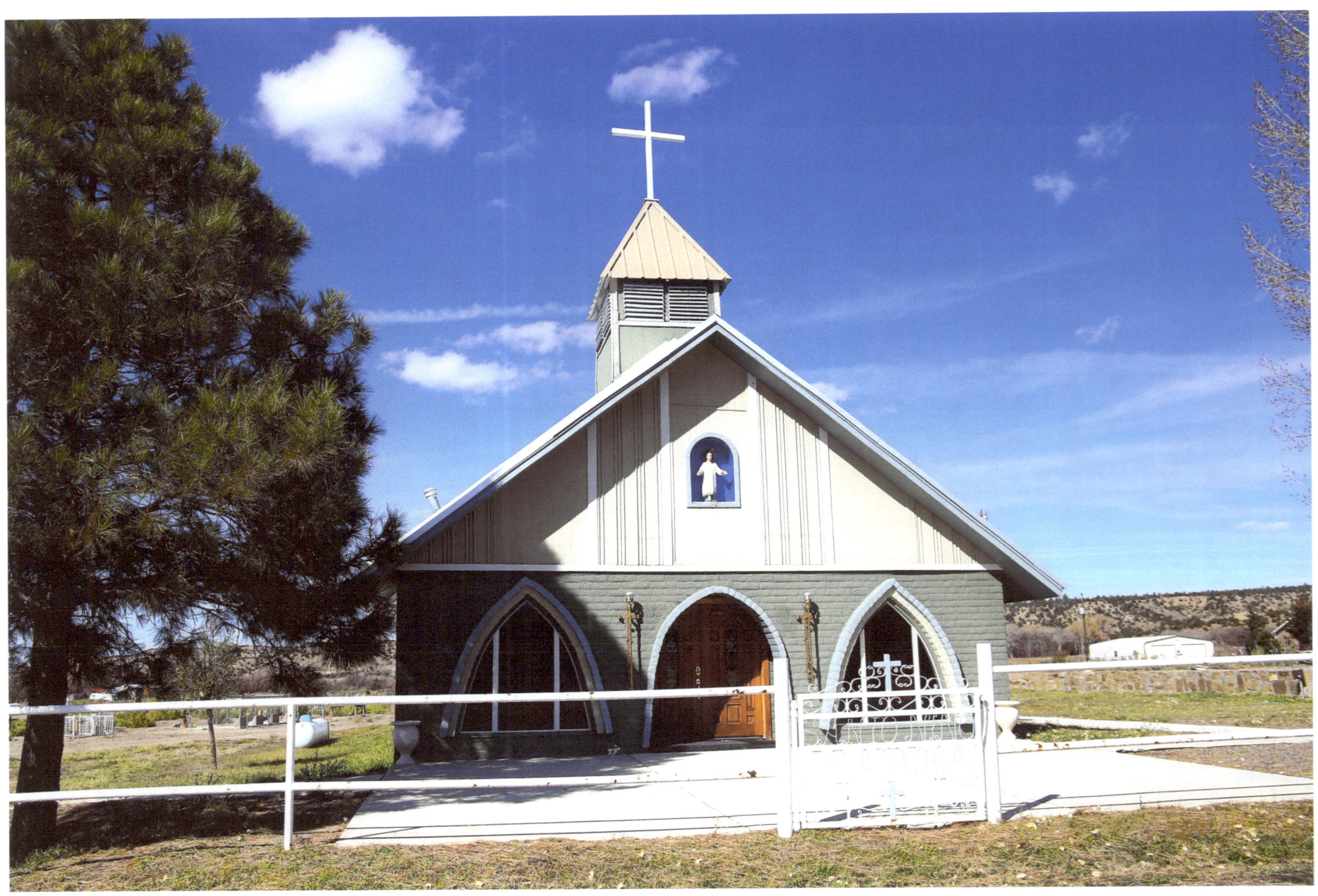

Santo Niño Catholic Church, La Jara, Sandoval County. Likely a building from the 1940s recently refurbished. A church has been here since around 1890. From New Mexico Highway 96 take County Road 496 1.3 miles east to the church. Photograph taken in 2021.

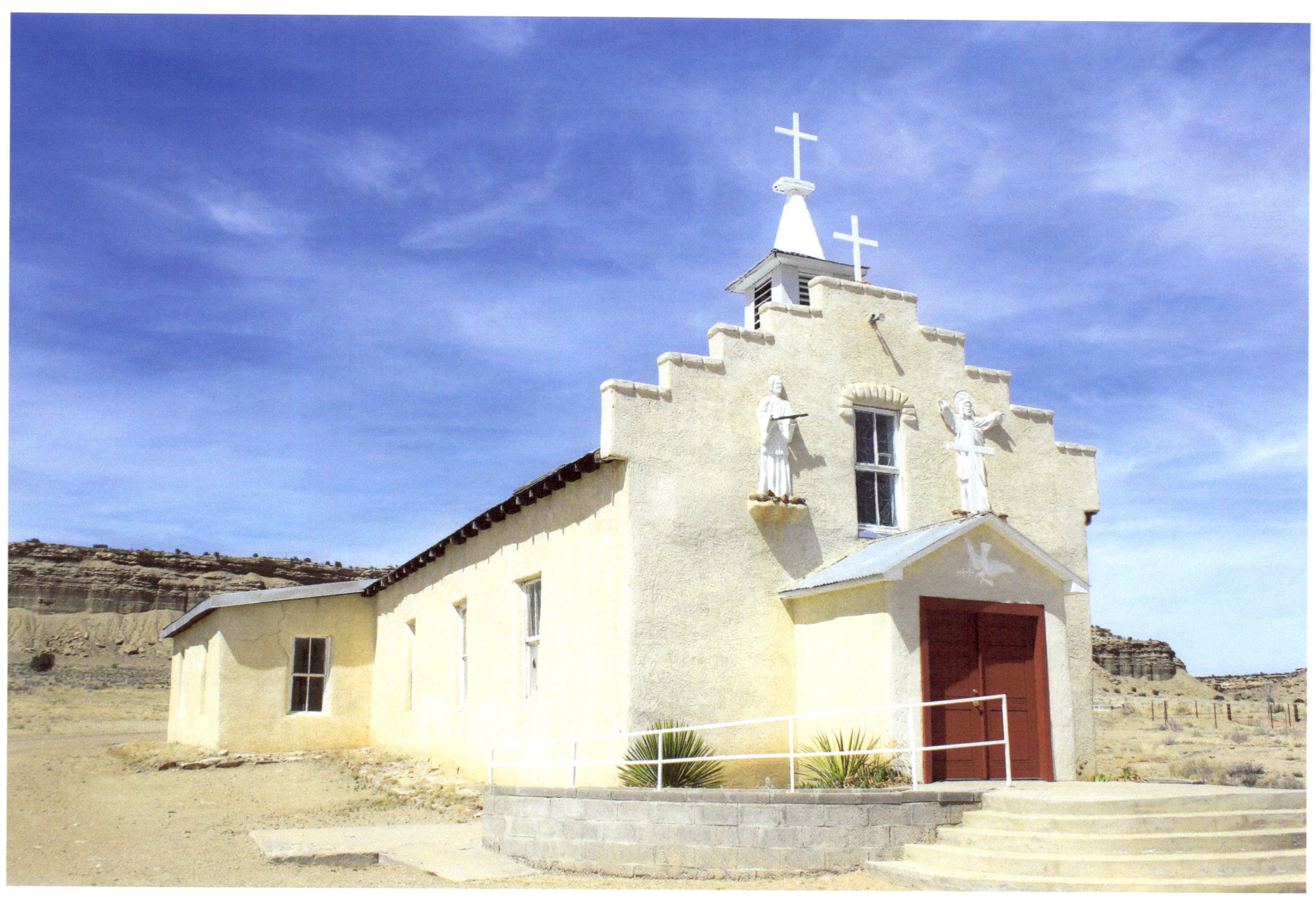

San Luis Gonzaga Catholic Church, San Luis, Sandoval County. 1917. The adobe church's design, including the two large statues above the vestibule, is striking. Take New Mexico Highway 279 (Cerro de los Piños Road) south 7.3 miles from U.S. Highway 550. Photograph taken in 2022.

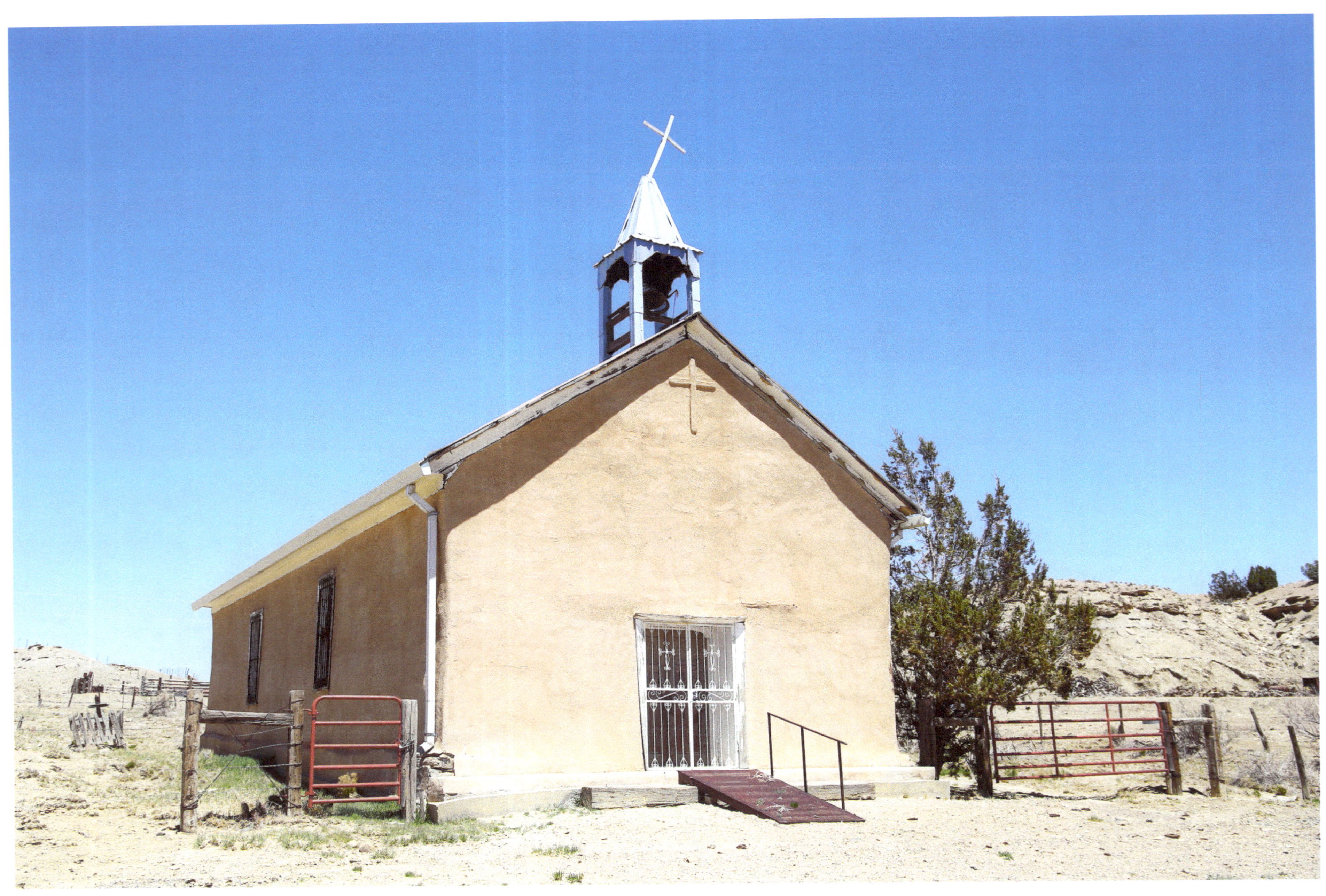

San José Catholic Church, Cabezon, Sandoval County. Likely around 1900. The adobe church is still used occasionally for masses and other events. The church is not easy to access; it is about 11.5 miles down New Mexico Highway 279 (Cerro de los Piños Road) from U.S. Highway 550, then left one mile through two unlocked gates. Photograph taken in 2021.

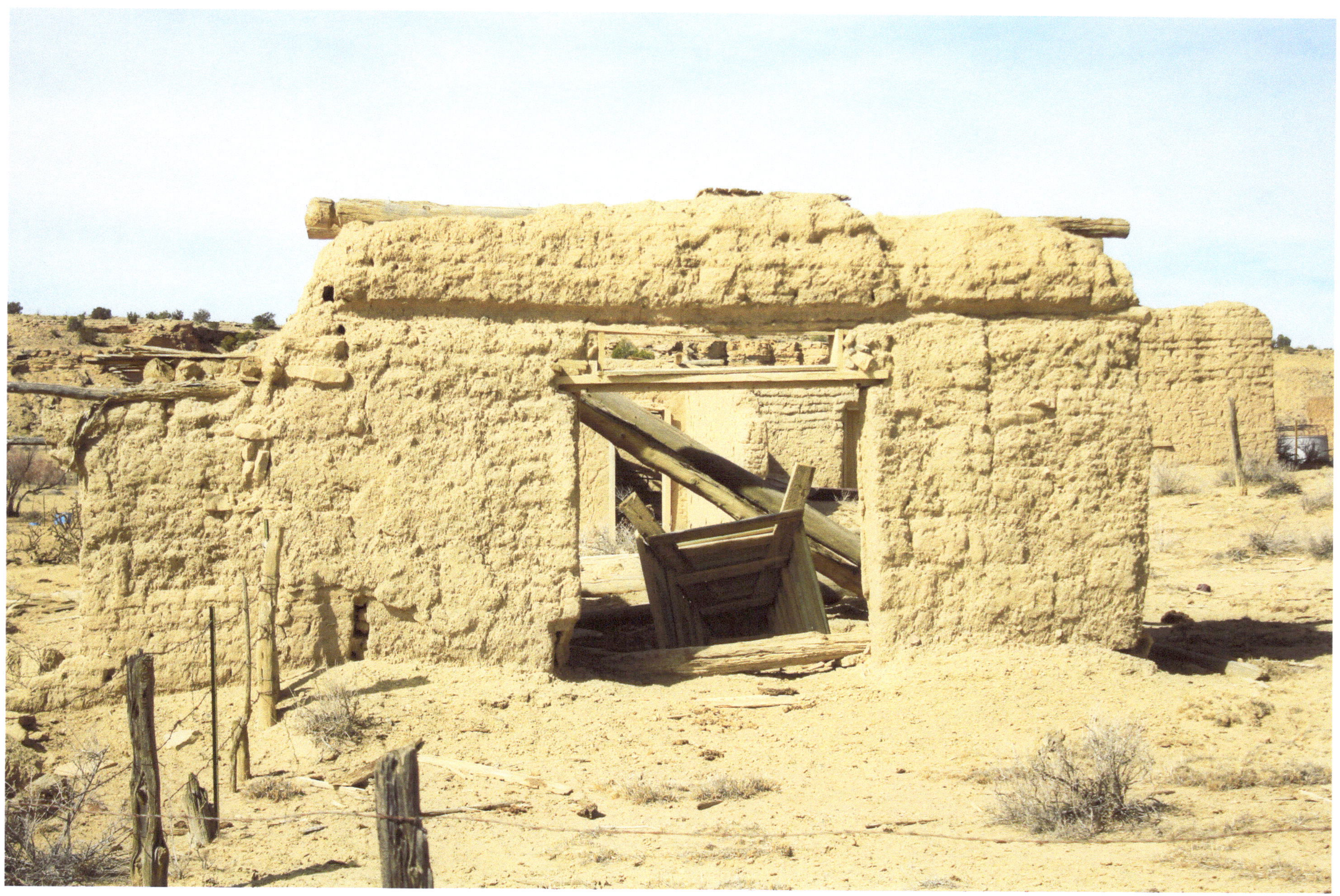

Our Lady of Guadalupe Catholic Church ruin, Guadalupe, Sandoval County. Late 1800s. Notice the wooden bell tower in the doorway of this ruined adobe church. Guadalupe is a ghost town. Continue on New Mexico Highway 279 past San Luis and Cabezon; take the left fork at 21.5 miles from U.S. Highway 550 to Guadalupe. The road can be rough. Photograph taken in 2022.

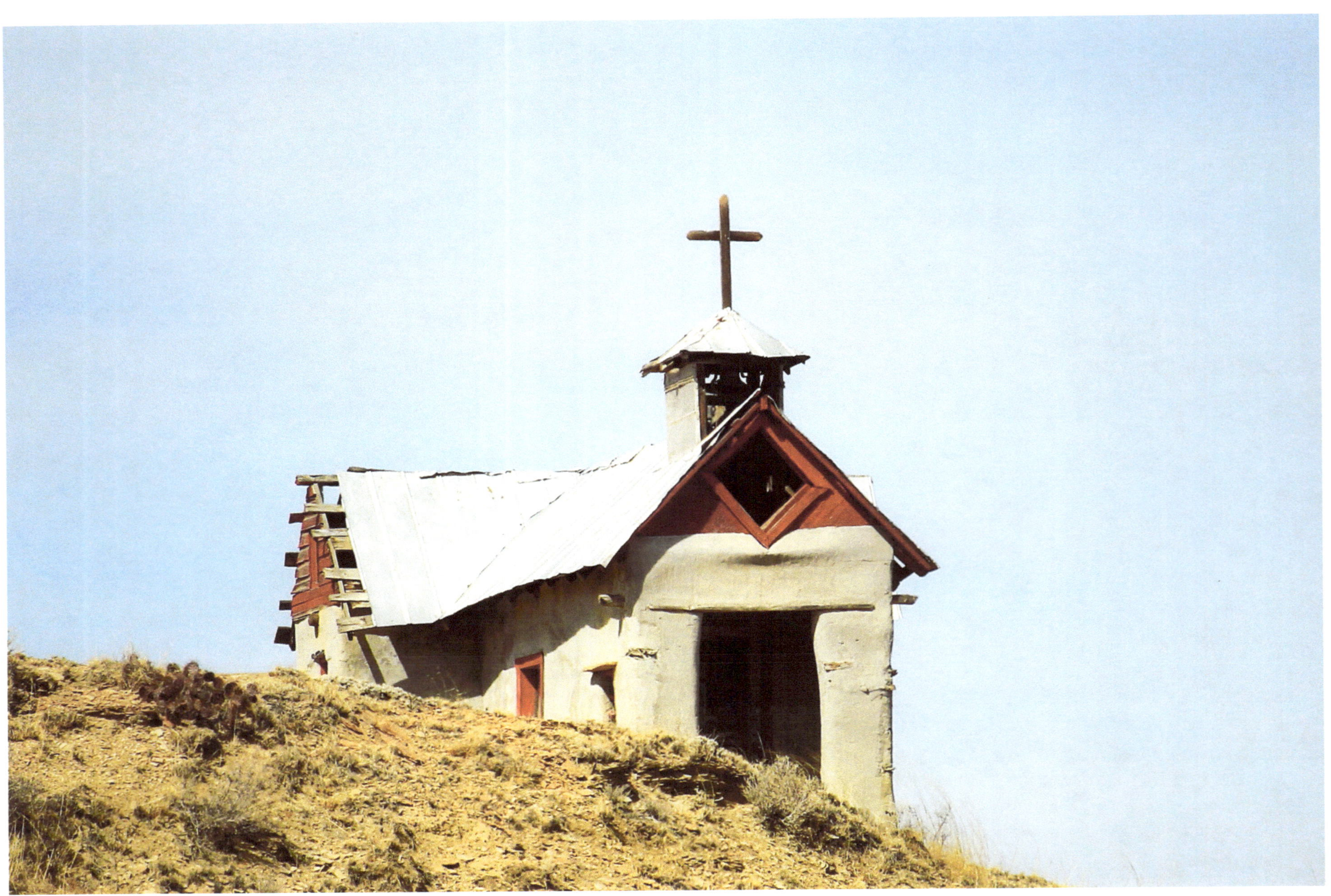

Santo Niño Catholic Chapel, Casa Salazar, Sandoval County. Around 1900. This remote, small chapel overlooks the remnants of the settlement, which is now privately owned and is behind a gate. Continue about 6.3 miles past Guadalupe. The road, which is gravel past San Luis, can be impassable in or after wet weather. Photograph taken in 2022.

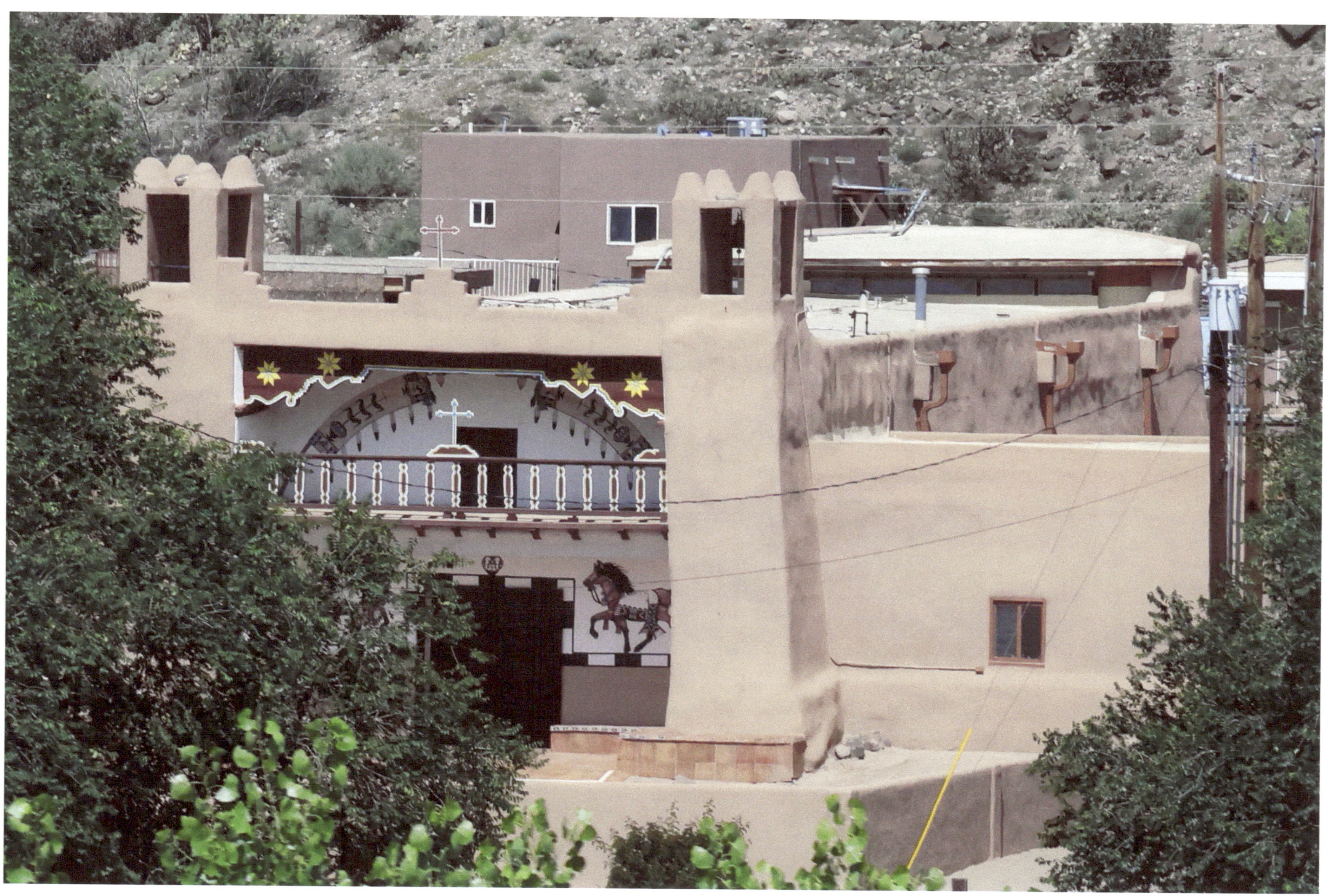

San Felipe Catholic Church, San Felipe Pueblo, Sandoval County. 1736, rebuilt in the early 1800s. This well-maintained and strikingly decorated church is in the middle of the pueblo. Photograph taken in 2024.

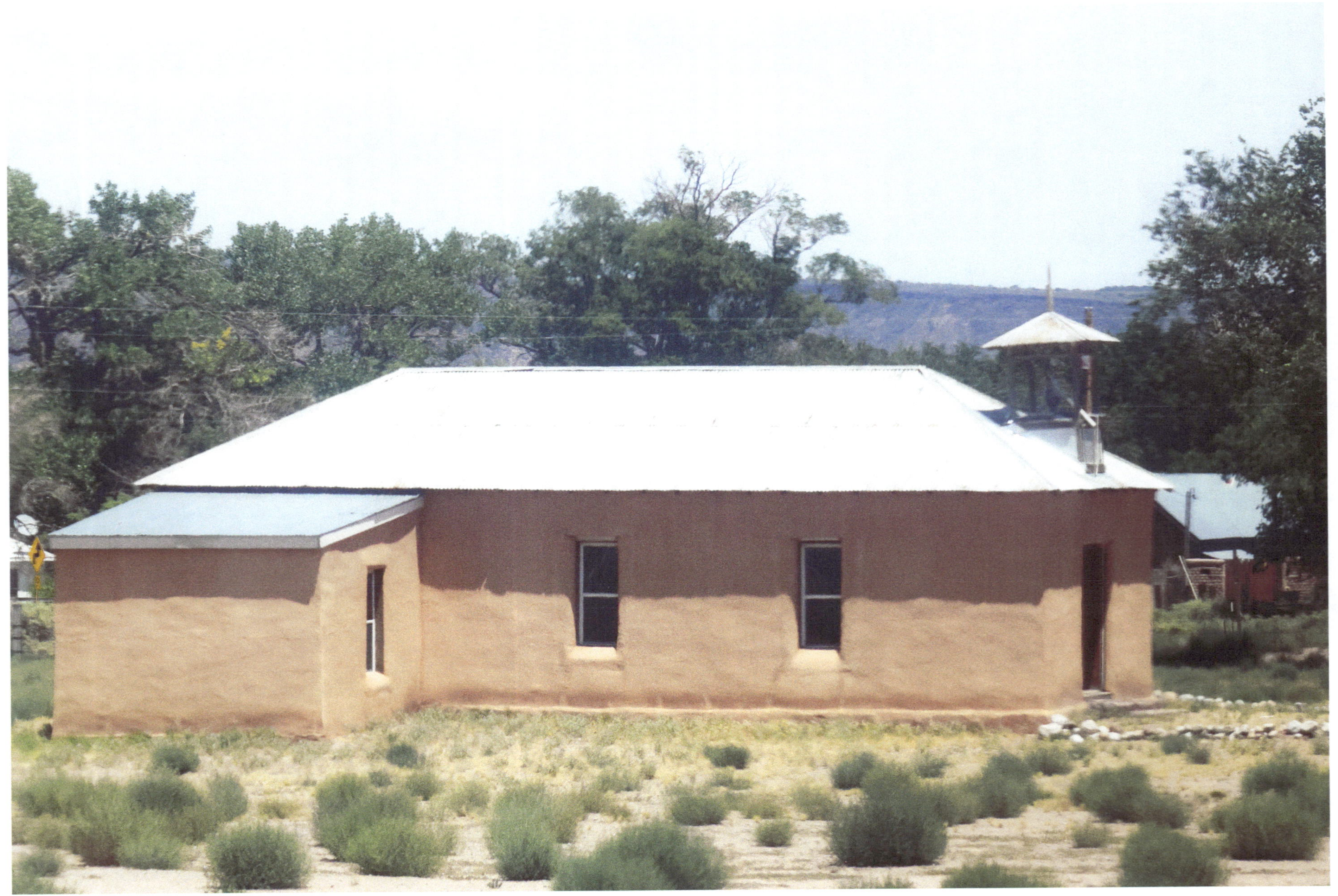

San Miguel Catholic Mission Church, Algodones (Angostura area), Sandoval County. Around 1900. The adobe church, formerly a mission of Our Lady of Sorrows Parish in Bernalillo, was turned over to San Felipe Pueblo in 1967. San Miguel's feast day, September 29, is celebrated here. It is on the east side of North Camino del Pueblo. Photograph taken in 2024.

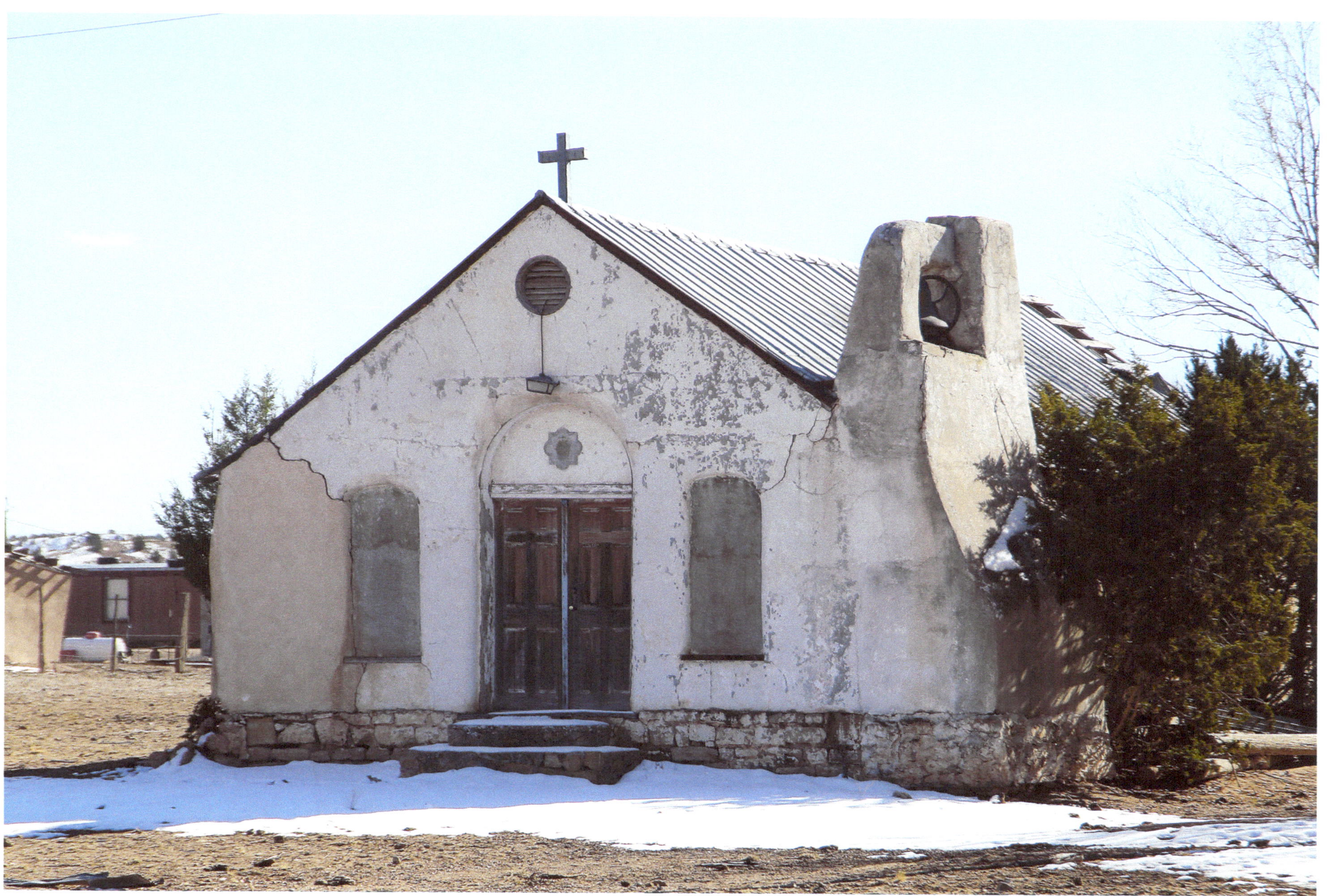

Santa Dorotea Mission Catholic Church, near the Kewa Pueblo Rail Runner station, outside the village; Sandoval County. 1910. According to the New Mexico Historic Preservation Division, this adobe church was already abandoned and deteriorating in 1986. Photograph taken in 2023.

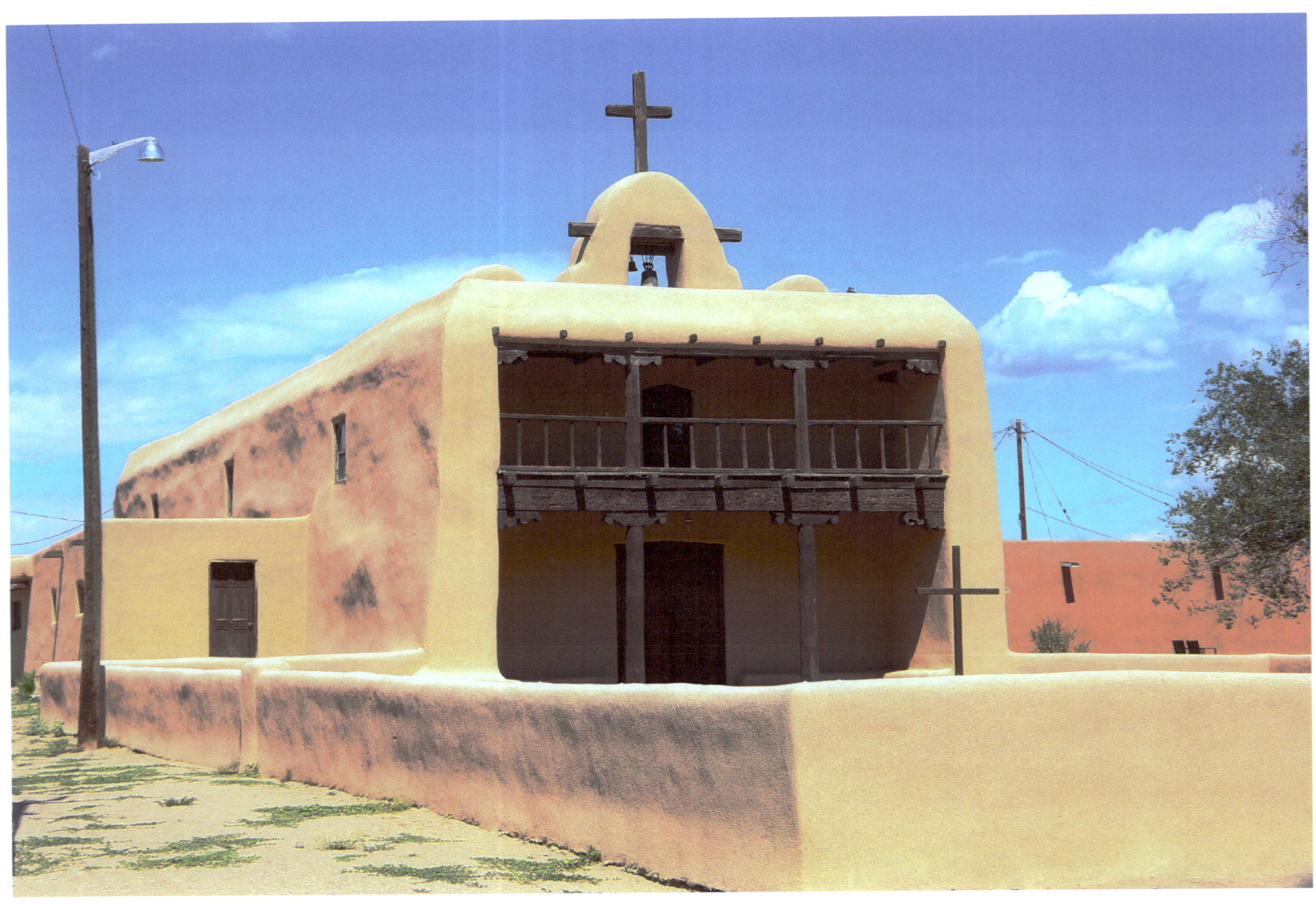

Mission San Buenaventura de Cochiti, Cochiti Pueblo. Sandoval County. The attractive church was built before 1776 and restored in the 1960s, and is well maintained today. South of the pueblo plaza off New Mexico Highway 22. Photograph taken in 2024.

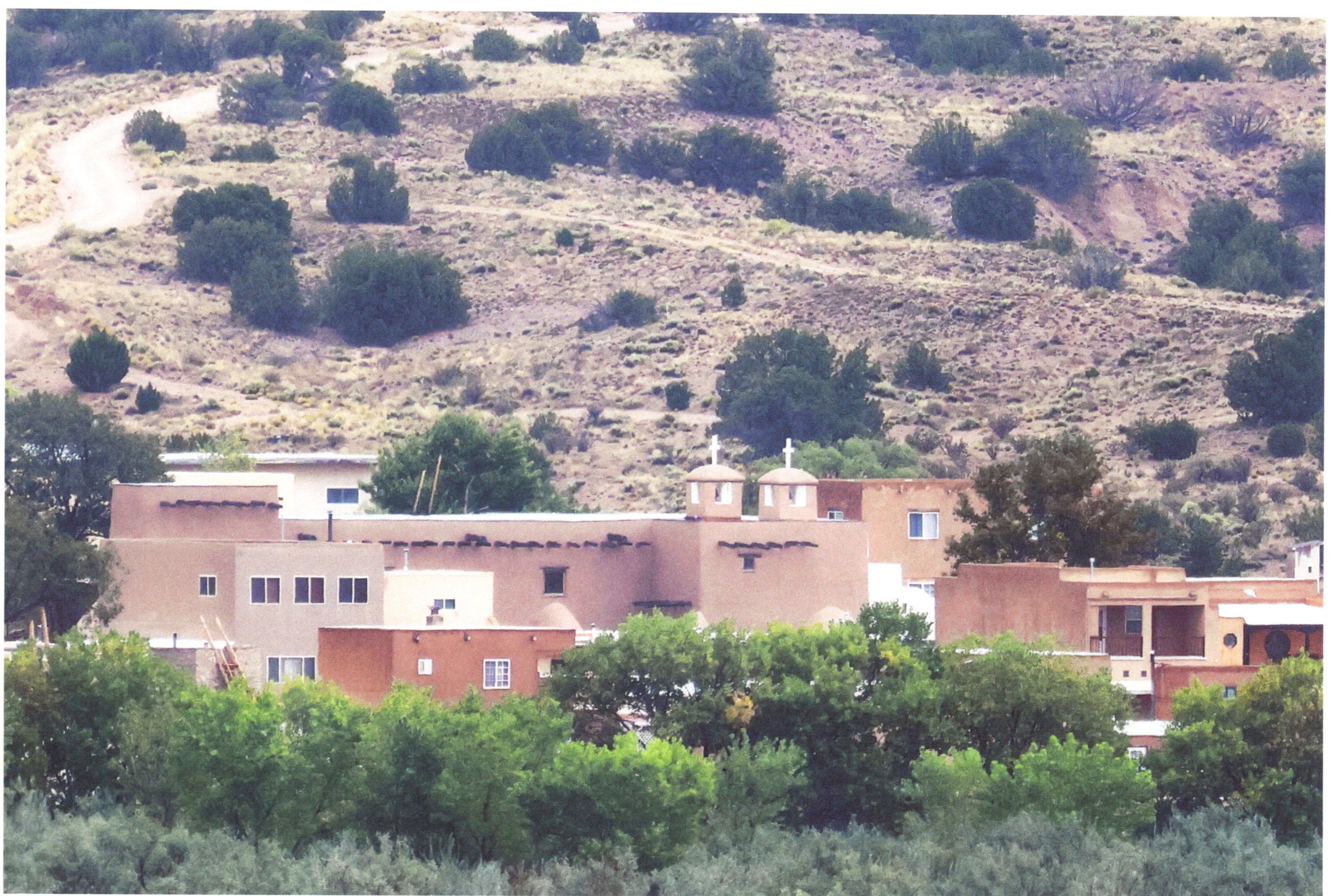

Santa Ana de Tamaya Mission Catholic Church, Tamaya Village, Sandoval County. 1750/2012. The historic adobe church, completed in 1750, is the third at the site. It has been remodeled several times, at times having no bell, then two, then one. In 2012, the church was restored, stabilized and remodeled, retaining its façade with six bays and two bell towers. Photograph taken from New Mexico Highway 550 near mile marker 10 in 2024.

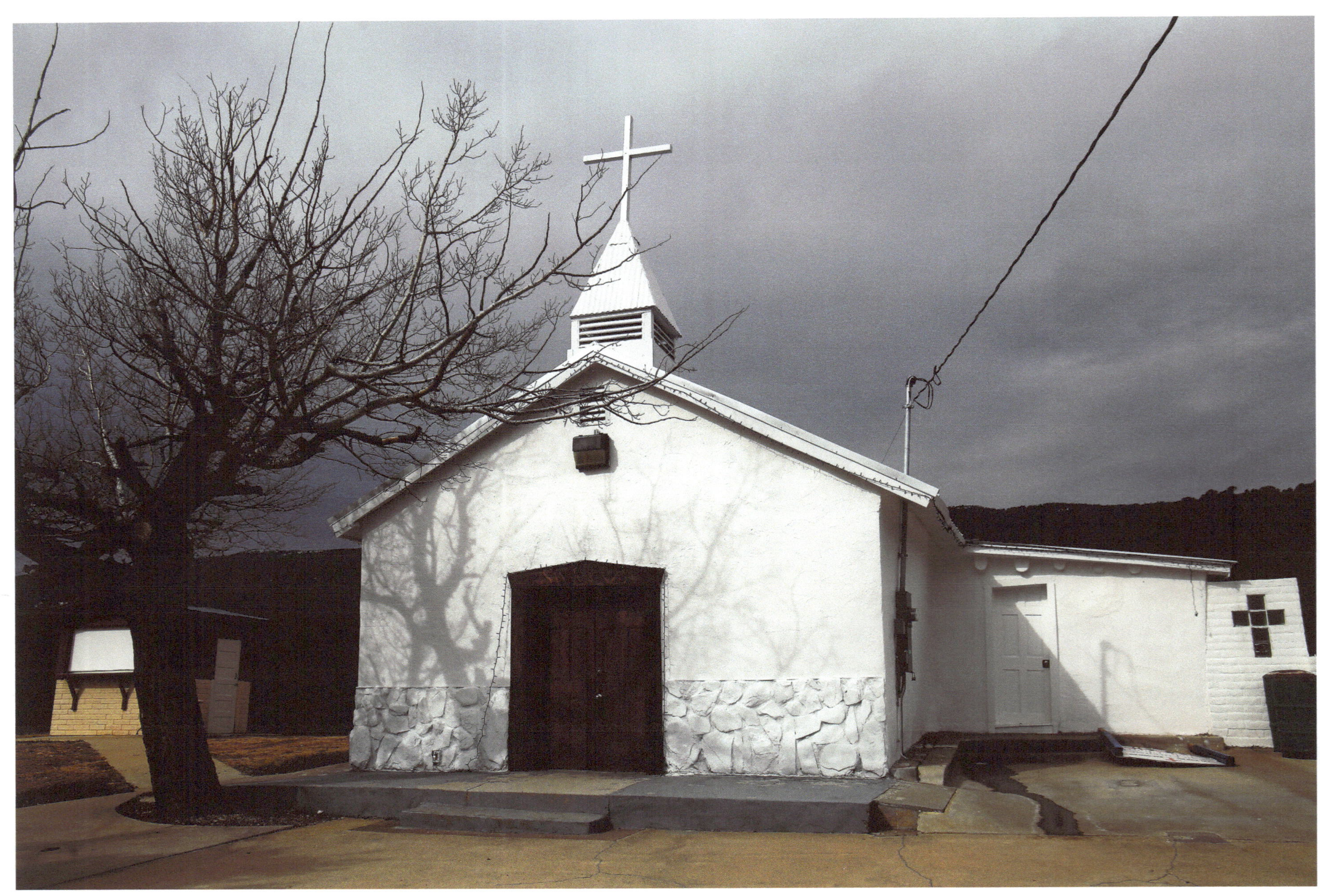

San Lorenzo Catholic Church, Cañoncito, Bernalillo County. 1870. This traditional, whitewashed, adobe church has too many trees for good photography. Take Cañoncito Road west off New Mexico Highway 14 about half a mile. Photograph taken in 2019.

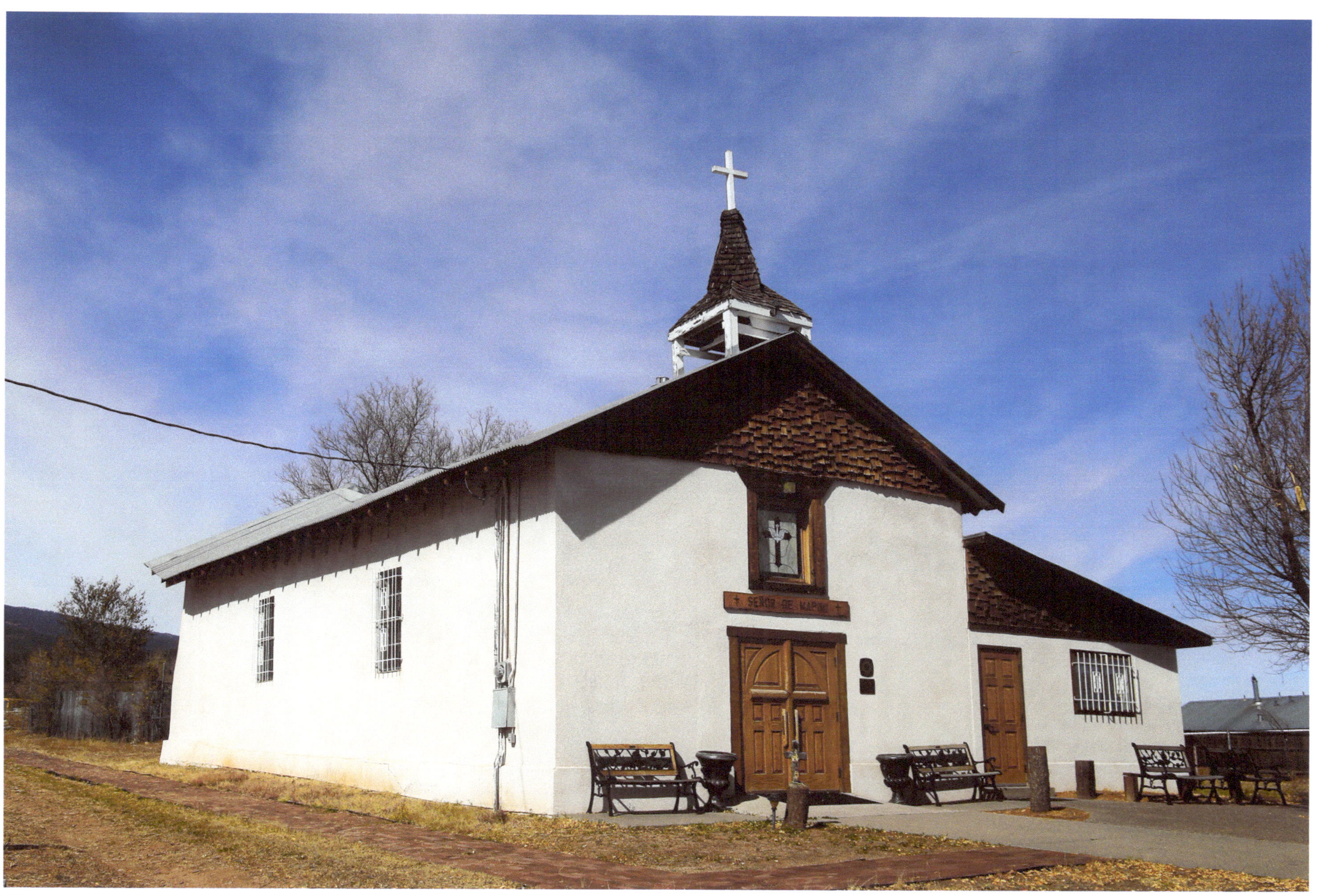

Nuestro Señor de Mapimi Catholic Church, San Antonito, Bernalillo County. 1886. Also known as Iglesia de la Santa Cruz, the adobe church has an unusual rounded hump in the rear, over the altar, barely visible in this 2021 photograph. Near the junction of New Mexico highways 14 and 306.

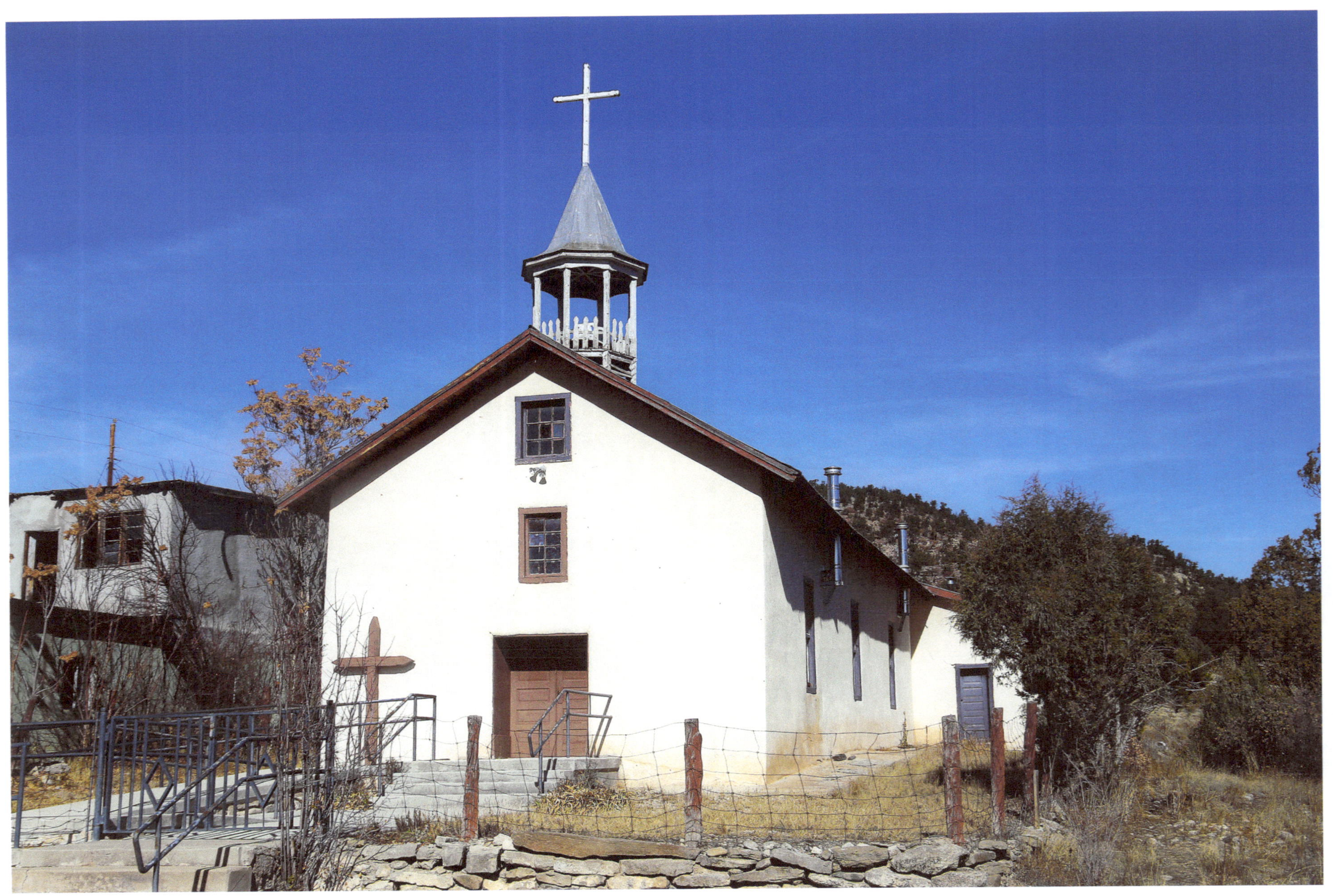

Holy Family (Santo Niño) Mission, Lower Colonias, San Miguel County. 1867. Regular masses are provided in this traditional adobe church, a mission of St. Anthony Parish in Pecos. From its junction with New Mexico Highway 63, head east 2.1 miles on New Mexico Highway 223 to County Road B44a (signed "To Upper and Lower Colonias"). After 5.3 miles take County Road B44C just under a mile to the church. Photograph taken in 2023.

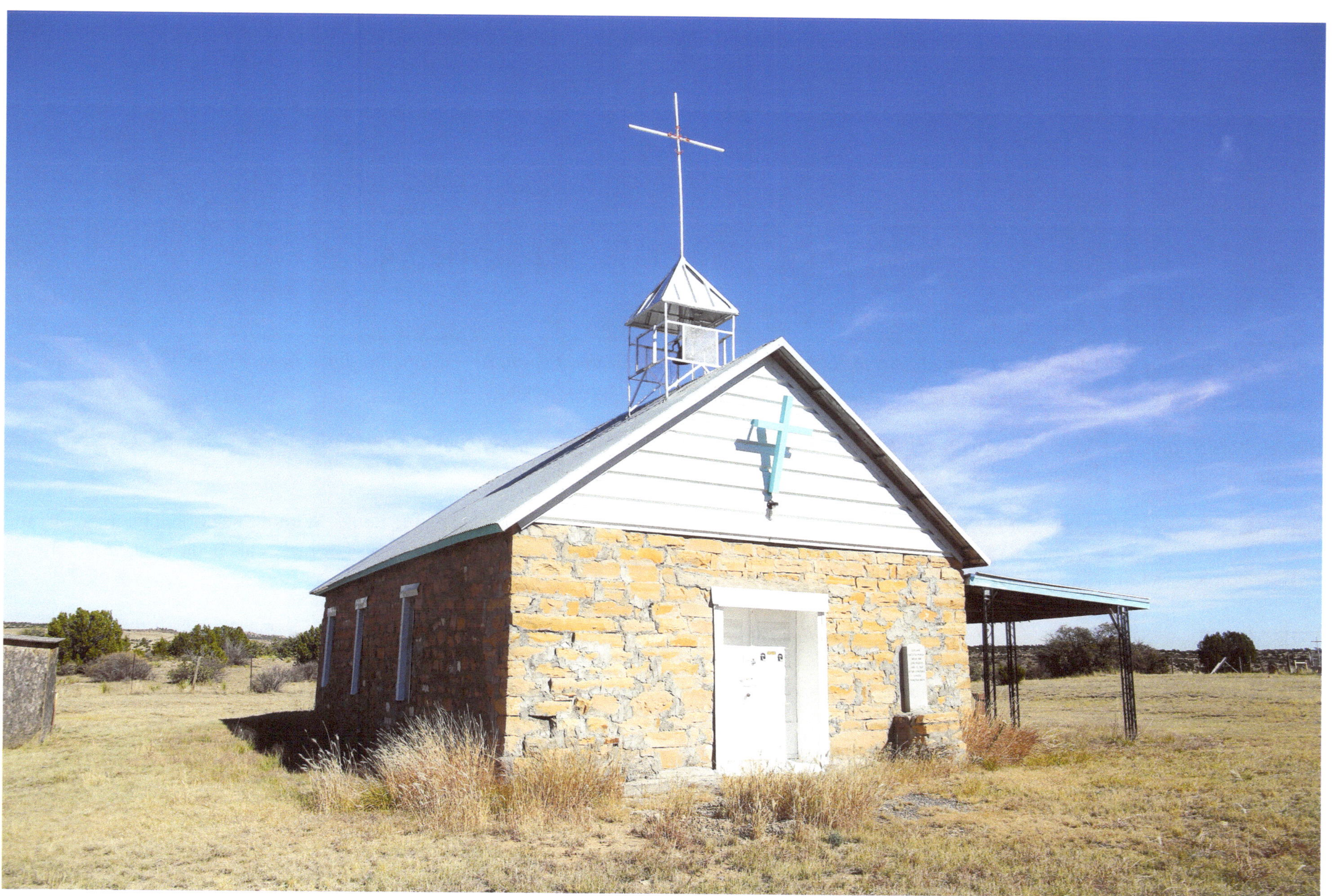

San Juan Bautista Catholic Church, Miera, Union County. 1906. This remote, traditional, stone church is on the Brockman Ranch. Just east of Bueyeros on New Mexico Highway 102, take Gap Road (County Road M on some maps) 10.2 miles to County Road C022 (Bluefoot Road on the sign but not on the GPS), then 2.2 miles to the church. Photograph taken in 2023.

Selected Further Readings

Archdiocese of Santa Fe. 1998. *Four Hundred Years of Faith: Seeds of Struggle, Harvest of Faith.* An information-filled history of the Catholic Church in New Mexico with information about every parish in the archdiocese and photographs of each parish church.

Brewer, Robert, and Steve McDowell. 1990. *The Persistence of Memory: New Mexico's Churches.* Museum of New Mexico Press. An historical approach with idiosyncratically chosen photographic illustrations. The emphasis is on northern New Mexico.

Cash, Marie Romero. 1993. *Built of Earth and Song: Churches of Northern New Mexico. A Guide.* Red Crane Books. With monochrome photographs and maps. About 80 churches are pictured and more are mentioned. Many are in this book. Her expertise and insight make this book valuable for anyone interested in New Mexico's historic Catholic churches.

Cash, Marie Romero. 1999. *Santos: Enduring Images of Northern New Mexican Village Churches.* University Press of Colorado. Cash, herself a noted *santera* (church artist) and steeped in the history and artwork of Northern New Mexico's Catholic churches, also brings a rigorous scholarly approach to her work. This informative book has ample documentation and is graced with many monochrome and color photographs.

Cunningham, Elizabeth. 2011. *Historic Churches of Taos and Northern New Mexico: A Self-Guided Driving Tour of 24 Historic Iglesias.* Taos County Lodgers Association and the Town of Taos. A helpful booklet, with illustrations; a map; directions; and brief histories, including construction dates, for each of 24 churches. Available at the Taos Visitor Center, also on line at https://taos.org/explore/landmarks/churches/

Dakin, William. 2013. *Rural Churches of Northern New Mexico: A Personal Selection.* Beech River Books. A charming book of Dakin's paintings of churches, with descriptions and rough directions to them. The book has some errors in church identifications and construction materials, but it helped me considerably.

DeLorne Publishing. 2019. *DeLorne Atlas & Gazetter: New Mexico, 8th Edition.*

Drain, Thomas, and David Wakely. 1994. *A Sense of Mission: Historic Churches of the Southwest*. Chronicle Books. Covers several mission churches in Texas, New Mexico, and California, and one small adobe church in Colorado. Drain wrote the text and Wakely took the color photographs.

Espinosa, J. Manuel. 1991. *The Pueblo Indian Revolt of 1696 and the Franciscan Missions in New Mexico*. University of Oklahoma Press. Less well known than the 1680 revolt, the 1696 revolt had similar causes. The book contains letters from friars (translated into English) as well as a long introduction by Espinosa, and includes information about Catholic mission churches that were damaged or destroyed in the 1680 revolt. Of special interest for those who wish to take a deep dive into primary sources rather than relying on secondary sources such as Kessell's book and others.

Gibson, Daniel. 2011. *Pueblos of the Rio Grande: A Visitor's Guide*. Rio Nuevo Publishers. Covers all 19 of New Mexico's active pueblos, most of which have historic churches, and includes useful information for visitors to the pueblos.

Graziano, Frank. 2019. *Historic Churches of New Mexico Today*. Oxford University Press. An in-depth look at the history of Catholicism and Catholic churches in New Mexico with an emphasis on current conditions. This excellent book has few illustrations of churches but provides detailed directions to quite a few of them.

Iowa, Jeremy. 1985. *Ageless Adobe: History and Preservation in Southwestern Architecture*. Sunstone Press. A history of southwestern architectural styles, with a strong focus on New Mexico and covering far more than only adobe. No church in this book is discussed in much detail, but the book covers locations and the architectural styles of many of them. The part on historic preservation likely will be useful to those undertaking such projects, although more-recent works should be consulted as well.

Jaramillo, Victor Dan. 2019. *Los Chimayosos: A Community History*. Outskirts Press. Jaramillo, a lifelong resident of Chimayó, writes with personal and scholarly knowledge about a northern New Mexico community, including many of its churches. With monochrome photographs.

Julyan, Robert. 1998. *The Place Names of New Mexico,* 2nd Edition. University of New Mexico Press. An indispensable guide, written with insight, humor, and great erudition. A third edition is being prepared as of 2024.

Kessell, John. 2012. *The Missions of New Mexico Since 1776*. Sunstone Press. First published in 1980 by the University of New Mexico Press. Kessell writes engagingly and authoritatively about New Mexico's surviving mission churches, including several in this book. Illustrated with drawings, photographs, and maps.

Lehmberg, Stanford. 2005. *Churches for the Southwest: The Ecclesiastical Architecture of John Gaw Meem*. Norton. An illustrated and analytical catalogue of the famous New Mexico architect's work on churches.

Lux, Annie, and Daniel Nadelbach. 2007. *Historic New Mexico Churches*. Gibbs Smith Press. Informative histories of a selection of churches graced with Nadelbach's glorious color photographs.

Museum of New Mexico Press. 1994. *The Churches of New Mexico: The Postcard Archive Series.* Historic monochrome photographs in postcard form of New Mexico Catholic churches from the museum's extensive collection. The photographs are dated from 1882 to 1975, with a few undated ones.

Nava, Margaret. 2004. *Along the High Road: A Guide to the Scenic Route Between Española and Taos.* Sunstone Press. Despite its age, it still is a useful guide to the history, art, and culture of the region, including information about lodging and restaurants. It describes several historic Catholic churches. With monochrome photographs.

New Mexico Historical Records Survey. 1940. Reprinted by Prenava Books, India, no date. *Directory of Churches and Religious Organizations in New Mexico.* This useful compilation covers all denominations that were in New Mexico at the time.

Pallen, C.B., and J.J. Wynne, editors. 1929. *The New Catholic Dictionary.* The Universal Knowledge Foundation. More an encyclopedia than a dictionary, the book is an informative and authoritative compilation of all matters Catholic in the first third of the twentieth century, including information about New Mexico.

Policansky, David. 2022. *Historic Catholic Churches Along the Rio Grande in New Mexico.* Sunstone Press. Similar in format to this book, with color photographs and detailed directions to the churches. Covers the historic churches along and near the great river from the southern border of New Mexico to Taos County.

Policansky, David. 2022. *Historic Catholic Churches of Central and Southern New Mexico.* Sunstone Press. Similar in format to this book, with color photographs and detailed directions to the churches. Covers the historic Catholic churches in New Mexico south of Interstate 40 except for those along and near the Rio Grande, which are in the first book.

Policansky, David. 2023. *Historic Catholic Churches of Northeastern New Mexico.* Sunstone Press. Similar in format to this book, with color photographs and detailed directions to the churches. Covers the historic Catholic churches in New Mexico north of Interstate 40 and east of those in this book. The three books cover churches in areas adjacent to those in this book.

Taylor, John. 2011. *Catholics Along the Rio Grande.* Arcadia Publishing. An account of the spread of Catholics and their churches along New Mexico's great river, with monochrome photographs. The book is organized by parish and hence includes many churches far from the river; with much information about their construction dates. Although Taylor's area is mainly south of that covered here, the information is relevant to the area in this book.

United States Conference of Catholic Bishops. 2024. *Keeping Christ's Sacred Promise: A Pastoral Framework for Indigenous Ministry.* An important document that reflects a welcome departure from some previous church practice in New Mexico. Available on line at https://www.usccb.org/resources/Indigenous%20Pastoral%20Framework%20-June%202024-Final%20Text.pdf

Glossary of Spanish Terms and Names

Adobe: Building material made from earth and organic material.

Acacio: Acacius, Greek priest of the 3rd century, also a soldier of that name who was martyred. Also 5th century Turkish priest who commanded swallows (see Golondrinas) not to impede his sermon. The name means thorny tree in Greek, and its feminine form (Acacia) also is the name of a widespread genus of trees, usually thorny, found in the southwestern U.S. and elsewhere.

Acequia: A community irrigation canal or ditch.

Agustín: Augustine. Saint Augustine of Hippo, North Africa, 354–430 AD.

Alamo: Cottonwood.

Ana: Ann, Anne. Saint Anne was Mary's mother, Jesus's grandmother.

Antonio: Anthony. Saint Anthony of Padua, born in Lisbon 1195, died 1231 in Padua.

Arroyo: A usually dry river bed or its gully, subject to occasional flooding.

Asís: Assisi, town in Italy, home of Saint Francis.

Asunción: Assumption. The belief that the Virgin Mary, having completed her earthly life, was assumed body and soul into heaven.

Bárbara: Barbara. Saint Barbara, Greek virgin martyr, patron saint of armorers, mathematicians, architects, and others, 273–306 AD.

Bautista: Baptist. St. John the Baptist, Jewish preacher in the early 1st century AD.

Buenaventura: Bonaventure. Saint Bonaventure, Italian Franciscan bishop, cardinal, philosopher, 1221–1274.

Bulto: A three-dimensional carved figure of a saint, usually painted.

Campo: Field.

Camposanto: Cemetery.

Candelaria: Candelmas, the Feast of the Purification of the Blessed Virgin Mary.

Capía: Alternate spelling of capilla.

Capilla: Chapel.

Carmen: Carmel. Mount Carmel in the Holy Land, now Israel.

Clara: Clare. Saint Clare of Assisi, 1194–1253.

Concepción Immaculada or Purísima: Immaculate Conception, the Catholic doctrine that Mary was conceived free of original sin.

Corazón: Heart.

Corbel: A structure, usually of wood, supporting the end of a viga (beam).

Cristo: Christ.

Cristóbal: Christopher. Saint Christopher, 3rd century AD, martyr in the Holy Land.

Cruz (plural, cruces): Cross.

Dios: God.

Divina: Divine. See Pastura.

Dolores: Sorrows.

Domingo: Sunday or sabbath. Also Dominic, Saint Dominic, Castilian-French Catholic priest and the founder of the Dominican Order, patron saint of astronomers and natural scientists, 1170–1221.

Dorotea: Dorothea or Dorothy. Saint Dorothea of Caesaria (modern Türkiye), virgin martyr, 279–311 AD; patron saint of gardeners. The historical record of her existence is very sparse.

Esquípulas: A town in Guatemala, site of the Black Christ of Esquípulas (Nuestro Señor de Esquípulas), a darkened wooden image of Christ in the cathedral in Esquípulas.

Estéban (sometimes Estévan): Stephen. Saint Stephen, King Stephen 1 of Hungary, 975–1038.

Familia: Family.

Felipe: Philip. Filippo Neri: Italian priest, 1515–1595.

Francisco: Francis. Saint Francis of Assisi, died 1226, or Saint Francis Xavier, Spanish Missionary, 1506–1552.

Gerónimo: Jerome. Saint Jerome, around 345–420 AD; theologian in the Roman province of Dalmatia.

Golondrinas: Swallows (birds).

Gracia: Grace. San José de Gracia, a name for Saint Joseph. See also José.

Grande: Great, large.

Gregorio: Gregory. Saint Gregory the Great, Bishop of Rome, 540–604 AD.

Iglesia: Church.

Ignacio: Ignatius. Saint Ignatius, Spanish priest, 1491–1556.

Inez: Agnes. Saint Agnes of Rome, virgin martyr, 291–304 AD.

Isidro: Isidore. Usually Saint Isidore the Farmer (Labrador), Spanish farmworker, 1082–1172.

Joaquin: Joachim. Saint Joachim was the husband of Anne and father of the Virgin Mary, 75–15 BCE.

José: Joseph. Saint Joseph, Mary's husband, legal father of Jesus.

Juan: John. Saint John the Apostle, one of Jesus's Twelve Apostles; or Saint John the Baptist (see Bautista) or Saint John of Nepomuk (see Nepomucemo).

Juramento: An oath or vow. See Promesa.

Lagos: Lakes. Our Lady of Saint John of the Lakes is a name for the Virgin Mary in the Americas.

Lorenzo: Lawrence. Saint Lawrence of Rome, deacon and martyr, 225–258 AD.

Luis: Aloysius. Aloysius de Gonzaga, Italian aristocrat and Jesuit, 1568–1591. Also San Luis Gonzalo, a local name for Gonzalo de Amarante, Portuguese Dominican priest, hermit, and Marian devotee, born as Gonçalo de Amarante, 1187–1259.

Luis Rey: Louis the King. Louis IX, king of France and saint, 1214–1270; canonized 1294.

Luz: Light. Nuestra Señora de la Luz, Our Lady of the Light, a name for the Virgin Mary.

Mapimi: A place in Mexico, thought to be the origin of a statue of Christ on the cross that was in the church in San Antonito. It was stolen in the 1970s.

Maria: Mary. Mother of Jesus.

Mayordoma or mayordomo: A caretaker or manager, in New Mexico usually of an acequia or a church.

Miguel: Michael. Archangel Michael.

Morada: In general, a dwelling; specifically, a meeting house for members of the Penitente Brotherhood.

Nacimiento: Birth.

Nepomucemo: of Nepomuk, a town in the present-day Czech Republic. St. John of Nepomuk, 1345–1393, was drowned in the Vltava River by order of King Wenceslaus IV of Bohemia for refusing to divulge the contents of the queen's confession.

Niño: Child. Santo Niño de Atocha, Hispanic Catholic image of the Christ Child.

Nuestra Señora (de): Our Lady (of). The Virgin Mary: Usually followed by los Dolores (Sorrows), or other aspects of her life or community circumstances; or by a place name, such as Guadalupe in Mexico, where apparitions of the Virgin Mary were reported.

Parroquia: Parish church.

Pastura: Pasture or shepherdess. La Divina Pastura (the Divine Shepherdess, the Virgin Mary) is a wooden statue in Siparia, Trinidad reflecting its interfaith tradition. The origin of the statue is unknown.

Patricio: Patrick. Saint Patrick of Ireland, 5th century missionary, never actually canonized.

Pedro: Peter. Saint Peter, approximately 1–66 AD, apostle and first Pope.

Porciúncula: Porziuncola, a place near Assisi with a small chapel that Saint Francis rebuilt in the 13th century on his interpretation of God's order; of great importance to Franciscans. The full name of the chapel was Our Lady Queen of the Angels, hence the name of the church in Pecos National Historical Park and of the City of Los Angeles.

Promesa: Promise or vow. An offer to perform some action or sacrifice in return or gratitude for the grant of a prayer request.

Pueblo: Village or settlement. In New Mexico usually applied to a distinct cultural or tribal group and its village.

Purísima: Most pure.

Rafael: Raphael. Archangel Raphael, first mentioned 3rd century BCE.

Refugio: Refuge. Our Lady of Refuge is a name for the Virgin Mary.

Remedio: Remedy or cure. Nuestra Señora de los Remedios is a name for the Virgin Mary.

Reredos: An altar screen, usually of wood or stone, containing religious images.

Rey: King.

Rio: River.

Rita: Rita. Saint Rita of Cascia, 1381–1457.

Rito: Small river or creek. Also a religious rite, e.g., baptism.

Rosa: Rose. Saint Rose of Lima, Peruvian saint, 1586–1617.

Rosalia: Rosalia, Saint Rosalia of Palermo, Sicily, 1130–1166. Also patron saint of three Venezuelan towns and often invoked in times of epidemics, especially but not only plague.

Rosario: Rosary. Nuestra Señora del Rosario or Our Lady of the Rosary is a term for the Virgin Mary.

Sagrada: Sacred, holy.

Sagrada Familia: Holy Family.

San, Santa, Santo: Saint (in a name, e.g., San Ignacio, Santa Ana).

Sangre: Blood.

Santa, Santo: Holy, also a saint or an image of a saint.

Santera or santero: A maker of carved or painted images of saints, or, more broadly, a church artist.

Santiago: Saint James, through a contraction of Santo Iago to Sant'Iago. Saint James the Apostle.

Santísima: Most holy.

Señor: Lord.

Señora: Lady.

Teresa: Teresa. Saint Teresa of Avila, Spanish noblewoman, 1515–1582. But see Teresita.

Teresita: Thérèse, the French Saint Thérèse of Lisieux, 1873–1897. In Spanish, Santa Teresita (or Teresa) del Niño Jesus.

Tomás: Thomas. Saint Thomas the Apostle, Jewish–Christian apostle and saint, died AD 72; or Thomas Aquinas, 1225–1274; Italian friar, priest, philosopher, and jurist.

Toribio: Turibius. Turibius of Mogrovejo, Saint Turibius, Spanish–Peruvian Archbishop of Lima, 1538–1606.

Trucha: Trout.

Vicente de Paula: Vincent de Paul. Saint Vincent de Paul, French saint, 1581–1660.

Viga: A beam in the ceiling of an adobe building, often supported by corbels. Exposed ends of vigas projecting beyond the exterior walls are typical of Pueblo and Spanish colonial architecture, and are in some famous adobe churches in New Mexico.

Virgen: Virgin.

Ysidro: Isidore. See Isidro.

Index to Churches by Location

www.ingramcontent.com/pod-product-compliance
Lightning Source LLC
LaVergne TN
LVHW072329100826
845147LV00005B/662
* 9 7 8 1 6 3 2 9 3 7 4 1 4 *